# DINOSAURS
## AND PREHISTORIC LIFE

# DINOSAURS
## AND PREHISTORIC LIFE

HAZEL RICHARDSON

Consultant
DR DAVID NORMAN

**A Dorling Kindersley Book**

LONDON, NEW YORK, MUNICH,
MELBOURNE, and DELHI

**Project Editor** Cathy Meeus
**Art Editor** Lee Riches
**Designers** Tracy Miles, Rebecca Milner
**Picture Researcher** Mariana Sonnenberg
**DTP Designer** Rajen Shah
**Production Controller** Melanie Dowland
**Senior Editor** Angeles Gavira
**Senior Art Editor** Ina Stradins
**Managing Editor** Liz Wheeler
**Managing Art Editor** Phil Ormerod

**Consultant** Dr David Norman

**2/3D Digital illustrations** Jon Hughes
**Additional 3D content** Russell Gooday

First published in Great Britain in
2003 by Dorling Kindersley Limited,
80 Strand, London WC2R ORL
Copyright © 2003
Dorling Kindersley Limited
A Penguin Company

ISBN 0-7513-3734-X

Reproduced by Media Development
Printing, Great Britain
Printed and bound by
TBB, Slovakia

see our complete catalogue at
www.dk.com

# CONTENTS

# HOW THIS BOOK WORKS

This book opens with an introductory section that describes the evolution of early animals, followed by a summary of the environment on Earth during its early history. The main part of the book contains profiles of the major prehistoric animals from the Mesozoic and Cenozoic Eras.

• *a map and description of the positions of the continents during each time period*

*introduction to prehistoric life in each habitat for*
• *each time period*

△ **THE TIME PERIODS**
Each geological period is introduced in a double-page feature, detailing the climatic conditions and, where relevant, plant life and prevalent animal forms. A timeline at the base of the pages indicates the chronological position of the period.

*species name* •

*syllable-by-syllable* • *pronunciation guide*

*artist's reconstruction gives an impression of* • *the animal's appearance. Where fossil evidence is lacking, the interpretation is based on what is known about similar animals*

*the name of the palaeontologist who* • *first described the species, and the year in which the findings were published*

*habitat in which the animal lived* •

*approximate* • *length (head to tail) or height*

*approximate* • *weight*

*type of* • *food on which the animal lived*

*red dots* • *indicate the location of principal fossil finds*

## ▽ ANIMAL PROFILES

Arranged by time period, habitat (land, water, or air), and by group, each major animal is described in detail. The text includes information about the animal's physical features, diet, and lifestyle. Coloured bands summarize key information about classification, dates, dimensions, and diet. Each animal is illustrated by an artist's reconstruction and/or fossil remains. Key features are annotated. In each case a map identifies the approximate location of main fossil finds of that creature.

## COLOUR KEY

## COLOUR KEY

The bands at the top of each entry are colour-coded to identify the time period to which it belongs. The bands at the base of each entry are coloured according to the habitat in which the animal lived.

### TIME-PERIOD COLOURS

| | | | |
|---|---|---|---|
| ☐ | Precambrian | ☐ | Cretaceous |
| ☐ | Cambrian | ☐ | Early Tertiary |
| ☐ | Ordovician | ☐ | Late Tertiary |
| ☐ | Silurian | ☐ | Quaternary |
| ☐ | Devonian | | |
| ☐ | Carboniferous | **HABITAT COLOURS** | |
| ☐ | Permian | ☐ | Land |
| ☐ | Triassic | ☐ | Water |
| ☐ | Jurassic | ☐ | Air |

*scientific name of main group*

*scientific name of family*

*time when the animal existed in millions of years ago (mya) or years ago (ya)*

ON THE LAND • 61

| Group Theropoda | Family Ceratosauridae | Time 150–144mya |
|---|---|---|

### CERATOSAURUS
KER-AT-OH-SAW-RUS

*Ceratosaurus* ("horned lizard") was named for the short horn above its nose. Another striking feature was the line of bony plates than ran down its back – so far, it is the only theropod known to have had them. It had strong, yet short, arms, with four fingers on each hand. Three of the fingers were clawed. It had a deep, broad tail, and feet with three large toes and a reduced back toe. Its teeth were long and blade-like. Although it superficially resembled a carnosaur such as *Allosaurus*, it was more primitive, and its tail was flexible rather than stiffened with bony ligaments as was the case with the carnosaurs.
 • **DESCRIBED BY** Othniel C. Marsh; 1884.
 • **HABITAT** Forested plains.

light skull

body balanced at hips

saurischian hip structure

three long, forward-facing, clawed toes

flattened snout horn

bony plates running along back

blade-like teeth

long, flexible tail

long, powerful hind legs

long foot

reduced back toe

| Length 4.5–6m (15–20ft) | Weight 1 tonne (1 ton) | Diet Herbivorous di... |
|---|---|---|

### ▽ FEATURE SPREAD
Animals of special interest are featured in a double-page entry. These show the animal in the type of landscape in which it is believed to have lived. Additional photographs and information boxes expand on the standard information for each featured animal.

78 • JURASSIC PERIOD

ON THE LAND • 79

### BRACHIOSAURUS
BRACK-EE-OH-SAW-RUS

*Brachiosaurus* ("arm lizard") is known from all parts of the skeleton except for the important nerve arches of the vertebrae at the base of the neck. It was one of the tallest and largest sauropods, and the one in which the lengthening of the forelimbs relative to the hindlimbs reached its extreme. Together with its long neck, ending in a small head, *Brachiosaurus'* giraffe-like stance gave it a great height up to 13m (50ft). The tail was relatively short and thick. Like other members of its family, *Brachiosaurus* had chisel-like teeth – 26 on each jaw – towards the front of the mouth. The nostrils were large and were situated on a bulge on the top of the head. The legs were pillar-like, and the feet all had five toes with fleshy pads behind. The first toe of each foot from a claw, as did the first three toes of the hind feet. Like other sauropods, it probably travelled in herds. *Brachiosaurus* was adapted for feeding off vegetation from the tops of trees. The length of its neck means that it would have had to have an immensely large, powerful heart, and very high blood pressure to pump blood up to its head. *Brachiosaurus* is thought to have laid its eggs while walking, leaving the young to fend for themselves.
 • **DESCRIBED BY** Elmer S. Riggs; 1903.
 • **HABITAT** Plains.

nostrils on bulge on top of head

chisel-like teeth at front of mouth

long and neck up to 13m (50ft) long vertebrae

body sloping downwards from shoulder to hip

relatively thin, rather thin tail

#### MASSIVE BONES
The femur (thigh bone) of *Brachiosaurus* was over 2.1m (6ft) long and massively thick to support the dinosaur's weight. One of the first bones discovered by Elmer S. Riggs, in 1900, was the humerus (upper arm bone). It was over 2.1m (7ft) long, which was so much greater than that of any known humerus, that Riggs thought it was a crushed femur of an *Apatosaurus* (p.76).

bulb-like head of femur

| Length 26m (85ft) | Weight 50 tonnes (49¼ tons) | Diet Plants |
|---|---|---|

• *the length or height of each animal is indicated in comparison to human dimensions*

20cm (8in)

1.8m (6ft)

# CLASSIFICATION OF LIFE

An accurate understanding of living things and how they have evolved relies on their being classified into groups according to their similarity. Animals are classified in groups of decreasing diversity. The diagram outlines the evolution of the major groups of vertebrates through time, from the primitive jawless fish to mammals. This is based on an analysis of shared features between species and their ancestors.

## THE CLADISTIC SYSTEM

Cladistic analysis shows the closeness of a relationship between a species and its most recent ancestor by a branching diagram called a cladogram. This is constructed by assessing characteristics that are shared between species and the order in which these arise.

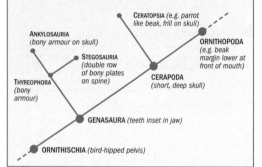

CERATOPSIA *(e.g. parrot like beak, frill on skull)*

ANKYLOSAURIA *(bony armour on skull)*

ORNITHOPODA *(e.g. beak margin lower at front of mouth)*

STEGOSAURIA *(double row of bony plates on spine)*

THYREOPHORA *(bony armour)*

CERAPODA *(short, deep skull)*

GENASAURA *(teeth inset in jaw)*

ORNITHISCHIA *(bird-hipped pelvis)*

## THE LINNAEAN SYSTEM

Devised by Karl von Linné (Carolus Linnaeus), this system subdivides all living things into ever more specific groups down to species level. Many palaeontologists prefer to use cladistic analysis to describe the relationships between species, but the Linnaean system of Latin species names remains standard throughout the scientific community. The Linnaean classification of *Tyrannosaurus rex* is shown below.

| KINGDOM : Animalia |
| --- |
| PHYLUM : Chordata |
| CLASS : Reptilia |
| ORDER : Saurischia |
| FAMILY : Tyrannosauridae |
| GENUS : Tyrannosaurus |
| SPECIES : Tyrannosaurus rex |

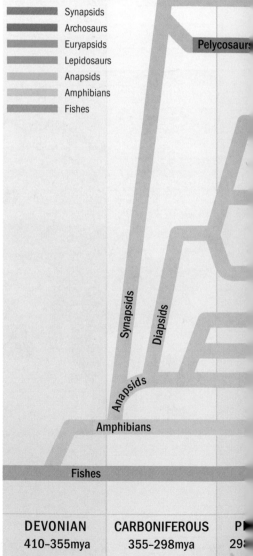

### KEY TO FOSSIL EVIDENCE

- Synapsids
- Archosaurs
- Euryapsids
- Lepidosaurs
- Anapsids
- Amphibians
- Fishes

Pelycosaurs

Synapsids

Diapsids

Anapsids

Amphibians

Fishes

| DEVONIAN | CARBONIFEROUS | P |
| --- | --- | --- |
| 410–355mya | 355–298mya | 29: |

Mammals

See pp.14–15

Cynodonts

Dicynodonts

Crocodilians

Archosaurs

Dinosaurs

See pp.12–13

Aves (birds)

See pp.14–15

Euryapsids

Mosasaurs

Lepidosaurs

Lizards

Snakes

Procolophonids

Choristoderes

Pareiasaurs

Turtles and tortoises

| RMIAN | TRIASSIC | JURASSIC | CRETACEOUS | TERTIARY |
|---|---|---|---|---|
| -250mya | 250–208mya | 208–144mya | 144–65mya | 65–1.75mya |

# WHAT WERE DINOSAURS?

Dinosaurs dominated the Earth's ecosystems for 165 million years. Although they evolved from a group of reptiles called the archosaurs, they possessed certain un-reptilian features, as did other non-dinosaur groups such as the pterosaurs. Dinosaurs are defined as a group that shares certain characteristics. These include: upright limb posture (see facing page), three or fewer phalanges in the fifth finger of the hand, an elongate deltopectoral crest on the humerus, three or more sacral vertebrae, a ball-like head on the femur, and a fully-open acetabulum (hip-socket in the pelvis).

cervical ribs

thoracic ribs

coracoid

deltopectoral crest

sternum

humerus

radius

ulna

metacarpals
(hand bones)

phalanges
(finger
bones)

dorsal (back)
vertebrae

scapula (shoulder
blade)

sacral
vertebrae

femur
(thigh
bone)

pelvis

tibia (shin
bone)

ischium

fibula

metatarsals
(foot bones)

## DINOSAUR SKELETON
In most cases, all we know of dinosaurs is their bones and/or teeth. Dinosaurs are tetrapod (four-limbed) vertebrates, as are reptiles, mammals, and birds, and so they share the same basic body structure as these other groups. Bones such as the metacarpals (hand bones) are given the same Latin name as those of other vertebrates. The dinosaur shown is *Muttaburrasaurus*, an ornithischian.

## UPRIGHT POSTURE

All living reptiles have a sprawling gait, with their knees and elbows held out at an angle from their bodies. One of the factors that led to the success of dinosaurs was their upright stance. This provides great advantages over the normal reptilian posture: it allows for longer strides, and therefore faster movement. Early meat-eating archosaurs and dinosaurs were often fast and agile hunters. The upright posture of the dinosaurs also allowed the evolution of bipedal (two-legged) walking.

UPRIGHT DINOSAUR STANCE

TYPICAL SPRAWLING
LIZARD STANCE

## WARM-BLOODED?

The traditional view of sluggish, cold-blooded dinosaurs has largely given way to the theory that they were warm-blooded. Some were feathered, many were fast runners, and some lived in cold climates that would have been unsuitable for cold-blooded reptiles.

*close similarities to warm-blooded birds, • including feathers*

• *moderately large brain would need warm-blooded metabolism*

VELOCIRAPTOR

## DINOSAUR HIPS

In 1887, the English anatomist Harry Seeley recognized that there were two different types of dinosaur pelvis. Some dinosaurs had a typical lizard-like pelvic structure: Seeley called these saurischian ("lizard-hipped"). Another group had a pelvis that looked like that of modern birds. He called these ornithischian ("bird-hipped"). It is not clear whether the two groups evolved independently or from a common saurischian ancestor.

*caudal (tail) • vertebrae*

*tarsus (ankle) •*

• *phalanges (toe bones)*

### SAURISCHIAN PELVIS

The pelvis is made up of the ilium, pubis, and ischium. In most saurischians, the ischium points backwards and the pubis points forwards.

*ilium*

*acetabulum •*

*ischium •*

*pubis*

### ORNITHISCHIAN PELVIS

In ornithischian dinosaurs, and some rare saurischian groups, the pubis lies against the ischium.

*ilium •*

*acetabulum •*

*pubis*

• *ischium*

# EVOLUTION OF THE DINOSAURS

The dinosaurs and their closest relatives were the dominant animals throughout the Mesozoic Era. The first step in the evolution of the dinosaurs occurred in the Permian Period. A new line of reptiles evolved, called the archosaurs ("ruling reptiles"). Some of these developed the ability to walk upright in two feet. The dinosaurs, crocodiles, and the pterosaurs all evolved from these early archosaurs during the Triassic Period. There are two main groups of dinosaurs: the saurischian ("lizard-hipped") group and the ornithischian ("bird-hipped") dinosaurs. Birds are believed to have evolved from the theropod group of saurischian dinosaurs towards the end of the Jurassic Period. Together with the crocodiles, they are the only surviving archosaurs.

## ARCHOSAURS

The first true archosaurs appeared late in the Permian. Many had rows of bony armour along the back. Some groups took to a marine way of life, and in the Triassic the first true crocodiles appeared. A wide variety of land-based archosaurs evolved, including lightly built bipedal runners, such as *Lagosuchus* (see p.42). It seems probable that the first dinosaurs evolved from these small archosaurs. The origins of the pterosaur group of flying archosaurs are still debated. They share many characteristics with early dinosaurs and some palaeontologists believe they evolved from a *Lagosuchus*-type archosaur. Others feel that pterosaurs evolved from an earlier diapsid reptile.

## SAURISCHIANS

The theropods, which were the first saurischians to appear, were bipedal. The two main groups were the ceratosaurs and tetanurans. The more-primitive ceratosaurs had many of the bones in their hips and feet fused. The tetanurans had a stiff tail and three fingers on each hand and included large, heavily built predators, such as the carnosaurs and the tyrannosaurs, as well as more lightly built animals with small heads and long arms, such as the oviraptorids. Advanced theropods, such as dromaeosaurs, had many bird-like features and it is likely that birds evolved from this group of dinosaurs. Among the saurischians were also the sauropodomorphs, a group of often enormous, quadrupedal herbivorous dinosaurs that included the prosauropods and sauropods.

**KEY TO FOSSIL EVIDENCE**

- Theropods
- Sauropodomorphs
- Ornithischians
- Non-dinosaur archosaurs

Tetanurans

Theropods

Sauropod

Sauropod

Saurischians

Thyre

Ornithischians

Cerapod

Dinosaurs

Thecodonts

Archosaurs

**PERMIAN**
298–250mya

**TRIASSIC**
250–208mya

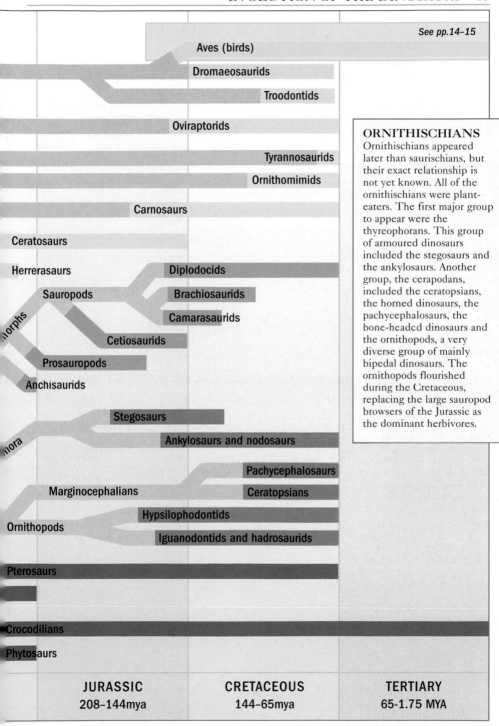

See pp.14–15

Aves (birds)

Dromaeosaurids

Troodontids

Oviraptorids

Tyrannosaurids

Ornithomimids

Carnosaurs

Ceratosaurs

Herrerasaurs

Diplodocids

Sauropods

Brachiosaurids

Camarasaurids

Cetiosaurids

Prosauropods

Anchisaurids

Stegosaurs

Ankylosaurs and nodosaurs

Pachycephalosaurs

Marginocephalians

Ceratopsians

Hypsilophodontids

Ornithopods

Iguanodontids and hadrosaurids

Pterosaurs

Crocodilians

Phytosaurs

**ORNITHISCHIANS**
Ornithischians appeared later than saurischians, but their exact relationship is not yet known. All of the ornithischians were plant-eaters. The first major group to appear were the thyreophorans. This group of armoured dinosaurs included the stegosaurs and the ankylosaurs. Another group, the cerapodans, included the ceratopsians, the horned dinosaurs, the pachycephalosaurs, the bone-headed dinosaurs and the ornithopods, a very diverse group of mainly bipedal dinosaurs. The ornithopods flourished during the Cretaceous, replacing the large sauropod browsers of the Jurassic as the dominant herbivores.

| JURASSIC | CRETACEOUS | TERTIARY |
|----------|------------|----------|
| 208–144mya | 144–65mya | 65-1.75 MYA |

# MAMMAL AND BIRD EVOLUTION

Modern theories of the evolution of mammals hold that the advanced group of synapsids called cynodonts were the direct ancestors of modern mammals. The origin and evolution of birds is still a matter of debate among palaeontologists. *Archaeopteryx* is widely regarded as the first true bird, and provides a link between theropod dinosaurs and modern birds. However, the fossil record of the ancestors of birds between *Archaeopteryx* and modern bird species is patchy and inconclusive.

**KEY TO FOSSIL EVIDENCE (Birds)**

- Ratites
- Euornithes
- Ichthyornithiforms
- Hesperornithiforms
- Enantiornithes
- Primitive birds

**KEY TO FOSSIL EVIDENCE (Mammals)**

- Placentals
- Marsupials
- Primitive mammals
- Monotremes
- Morganucodontoids

## MAMMALS

The synapsids were a group of reptiles that dominated the land throughout the Permian and through much of the Triassic. These had a pair of openings in the skull behind each eye socket, giving them a more powerful bite. This group also evolved different types of teeth: molars, canines, and incisors. The earliest synapsids were the pelycosaurs (see p.8). These were followed by the dicynodonts. True mammals probably evolved from a later group of advanced synapsids, the cynodonts. After the mass extinction event at the end of the Cretaceous, primitive mammal groups underwent a massive evolutionary spurt and diversified into many forms including marsupials and placental mammals. By the Tertiary, most modern mammal groups were well established.

## BIRDS

Although the first birds probably arose in the Jurassic, up until the Cretaceous there is only a sparse record of birds. It seems that their evolution first provided them with shorter tails, then further feather and skeletal adaptations. By the time of the appearance of the Carinates, birds were powerful fliers. Teeth were only lost from the jaws in modern birds (the Euornithes).

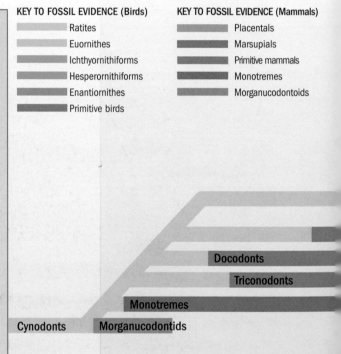

Docodonts

Triconodonts

Monotremes

Cynodonts

Morganucodontids

Archaeopteryx

Ornithothoraces

Aves

Theropods

| TRIASSIC | JURASSIC |
|---|---|
| 250–208mya | 208–144mya |

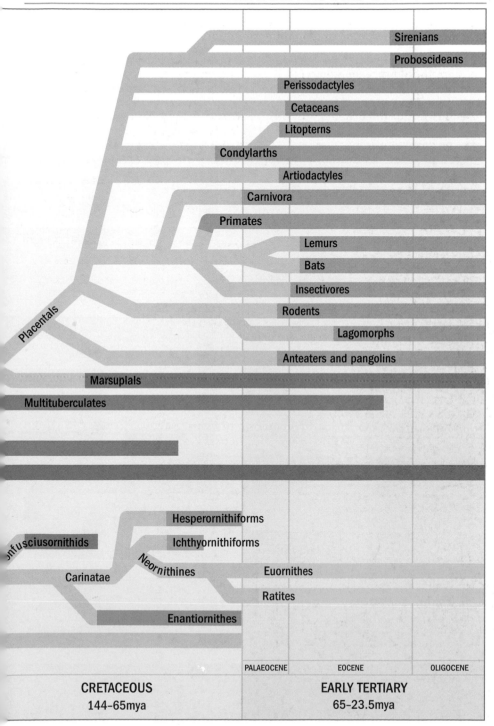

Sirenians
Proboscideans
Perissodactyles
Cetaceans
Litopterns
Condylarths
Artiodactyles
Carnivora
Primates
Lemurs
Bats
Insectivores
Rodents
Lagomorphs
Anteaters and pangolins
Placentals
Marsupials
Multituberculates

Hesperornithiforms
Ichthyornithiforms
nfusciusornithids
Neornithines
Carinatae
Euornithes
Ratites
Enantiornithes

PALAEOCENE | EOCENE | OLIGOCENE

CRETACEOUS
144–65mya

EARLY TERTIARY
65–23.5mya

# GEOLOGICAL TIME

Geologists subdivide the history of the Earth into very long time intervals called eons. Eons are, in turn, subdivided into eras, eras into periods, and periods into epochs.

The oldest rocks that have survived to be excavated were formed about four billion years ago, in the Archean Eon. The earliest fossils come from rocks of about this age.

## ROCKS OF AGES

Where rock strata have remained undisturbed, a vertical section through the layers can reveal the rock types laid down during each time period. From these, it is possible to identify the environment (such as desert) and sometimes the age of fossils embedded in that rock, as shown below for rock strata at the Grand Canyon, USA.

| ROCK | ENVIRONMENT | PERIOD |
|---|---|---|
| Shale, siltstone, mudstone | Tidal flat | Triassic |
| Limestone | Marine | Permian |
| Sandstone | Desert | |
| Shale | Savanna | |
| Mixed strata – shales, sandstones, limestones | Flood plain | Permian and Late Carboniferous |
| Limestone | Marine | Early Carboniferous |
| Limestone | Marine | Devonian |
| Limestone | | Cambrian |
| Shale | Marine | |
| Sandstone | Marine | |
| Complex mixed strata | Marine and volcanic | Precambrian |

| ERA | Age | Period |
|---|---|---|
| CENOZOIC ERA | 1.75mya–present | QUATERNARY |
| | 23.5–1.75mya | LATE TERTIARY |
| | 65–23.5mya | EARLY TERTIARY |
| MESOZOIC ERA | 144–65mya | CRETACEOUS |
| | 208–144mya | JURASSIC |
| | 250–208mya | TRIASSIC |
| PALAEOZOIC ERA | 298–250mya | PERMIAN |
| | 355–298mya | CARBONIFEROUS |
| | 410–355mya | DEVONIAN |
| | 435–410mya | SILURIAN |
| | 490–435mya | ORDOVICIAN |
| | 542–490mya | CAMBRIAN |
| | 4,600–542mya | PRECAMBRIAN |

| 4,600mya | 4,000mya | 3,000mya |
|---|---|---|

**GRAND CANYON**
The Grand Canyon in Arizona, USA, provides the world's most impressive display of sedimentary deposition of rocks. It is over 2,000m (6,000ft) deep, and shows a clear progression over 300 million years. Layers include sandy limestone, petrified sand dunes, and shale.

MACRAUCHENIA

*The ice ages of the Quaternary Period led to the evolution of many mammals adapted to cold climates, such as mammoths. Modern humans evolved.*

*In the Late Tertiary, large expanses of grassland spread, inhabited by grazing mammals and predatory giant birds. The first humans evolved from primate ancestors.*

TITANIS

AMBULOCETUS

*After the end-Cretaceous mass extinctions, mammals evolved into large forms. Some took to a marine way of life. Giant flightless birds evolved.*

*The Cretaceous was a time of flowering plants, browsing duck-billed dinosaurs, immense tyrannosaurid predators, armoured ankylosaurs, and horned ceratopsians.*

ALPHADON

BAROSAURUS

*In Jurassic times, the land was dominated by huge sauropods and large predators. A wide variety of pterosaurs evolved. Mammals remained small.*

*The Triassic marked the dawning of the age of dinosaurs. Advanced synapsids died out after giving rise to mammals.*

HERRERASAURUS

DIMETRODON

*Synapsids became the dominant land animals during the Permian. The period ended with the largest mass extinction event ever.*

*Tropical forests flourished and oxygen levels were very high during this period. The first four-limbed animals and, later, the first reptiles moved onto the land.*

GRAEOPHONUS

*The Devonian Period was a time of rapid evolution. Ammonoids and bony fish evolved and diversified. Trees appeared on land, as did insects.*

EASTMANOSTEUS

*Invertebrate species recovered rapidly during the Silurian, and the first jawed fish appeared. Primitive lycopods and myriapods became the first true land organisms.*

SAGENOCRINITES

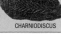
ESTONIOCERAS

*Ordovician seas teemed with primitive fish, trilobites, corals, and shellfish. Plants made their first approaches onto land. The period ended with mass extinctions.*

*The first animals with skeletons evolved during the Cambrian "explosion of life". The oceans teemed with trilobites, brachiopods, and the first jawless fish.*

XYSTRIDURA

CHARNIODISCUS

*During the Precambrian, life arose in the oceans – first as single-celled bacteria and algae, then evolving into soft-bodied, multicellular animals, such as jellyfish and worms.*

| 2,000mya | 1,000mya | 500mya | 250mya | 0 |

# FOSSIL EVIDENCE

Evidence of prehistoric life comes from remains (such as bones) that over time have become mineralized to form fossils. Most animal fossils are of creatures that died in or near water. After death, if the hard remains, such as teeth and bones, quickly become covered in mud or sand, dissolved minerals in water are able to seep into the bone pores, initiating a process called permineralization. This reinforces the bones and makes them harder. Sometimes minerals replace the bone completely, petrifying it, or minerals dissolve the bone away, leaving a bone-shaped hollow called a mould.

dinosaurs congregate near water source

compressed layers of sand and mud form rock strata

dinosaur dies and decomposes in riverbed

river sediments cover skeleton

## DISCOVERY AND EXCAVATION

Only certain rock types are rich in dinosaur fossils. These include sedimentary sandstones, shales, and mudstones formed in deserts, swamps, and lakes. Most fossil discoveries come from areas where severe erosion exposes deep layers of rock, such as cliffs and mountain slopes, or from places such as quarries and coalmines. Excavating dinosaurs from hard rock may necessitate the use of power tools or explosives. Fossils in desert areas can sometimes be exposed by carefully brushing away the sand covering them.

**EXCAVATION**
Palaeontologists dig around bones to estimate the fossil's state of preservation and size. Delicate scraping and chiselling is needed to reveal delicate structures without causing damage.

skeleton becomes mineralized, enabling it to withstand weight of rock forming overhead

## TRACE FOSSILS

Besides fossil remains such as bones, skin impressions, and teeth, dinosaurs left other clues to their existence and lifestyle. Trace fossils include fossil footprint trackways made in mud that dried out in the sun (below right). Coprolites (fossilized droppings) give further clues about a dinosaur's anatomy and lifestyle. Piles of gizzard stones (stones that were swallowed to aid digestion) are also often found.

**FOSSIL OF THE FUTURE?**
Dinosaur fossils found in the Sahara Desert were formed when the area was a swamp. This recent camel skeleton may become fossilized if it is buried by the sand.

*remains of more recent animals and plants form a separate – "younger"*
● *fossil layer*

**TRACKS**
Fossilized dinosaur tracks, also called ichnites, can provide information of foot structure, speed, and in what position the tail was held. Importantly, they can also show whether the animal walked on two or four feet. The tracks pictured left are those of a theropod dinosaur.

*excavation or natural erosion of rocks reveals fossil-*
● *bearing strata*

**THE FOSSILIZATION PROCESS**
Fossilization depends on the rapid covering of remains by sediments that exclude air and water and thereby arrest the normal processes of decay. In time, minerals from the covering sediments permeate the bone or other tissues, replacing the original material. The soft tissues usually decompose before the process of fossilization begins, so soft-bodied animals, such as jellyfish and worms, are generally poorly preserved.

# PRECAMBRIAN TIME

UP TO 542 MILLION YEARS AGO

Current estimates put the age of the Earth at 4,600 million years. The years from that date up until about 542 million years ago (mya) are grouped in one large division of geological time – the Precambrian. This was the time when life first evolved, although evidence of living creatures is sparse. During the first million years of its existence, the world was hot, molten, and totally inhospitable to life. As the earth cooled, volcanic gases and water vapour formed a crude atmosphere, and the oceans began to form. Before about 3,000mya, most of the Earth's surface was volcanic rock, with craters and many unstable regions of volcanic activity. Stable continental areas then began to form. Fossil evidence of life is first seen in rocks dated at 3,800 million years old. The earliest life forms on Earth were simple cells and bacteria. More complex cells and algae first evolved about 1,000mya. Multicelled plants and animals did not appear until near the end of the Precambrian – about 550mya.

## VENDIAN LIFE

*impression of early jellyfish burrow or track of simple worm*

Extraordinary fossils found in in Precambrian rocks of the Vendian Period date from 600mya, and are thought to be the remains of the earliest multicellular animals. The *Mawsonites* fossil (above) has been interpreted as a jellyfish or traces of a primitive worm.

4,600mya      4,000mya      3,000mya

## PRECAMBRIAN LANDMASSES

Landmasses began to form about 3,000mya. About 900mya they joined to form the first supercontinent, Rodinia. By 750mya, Rodinia was sitting across the Equator, but it then started to move southwards. This triggered the Verangian Ice Age. Between 750 and 650mya, Rodinia split into two halves (see map), but by the end of the Precambrian Rodinia again formed a single continent.

## PRECAMBRIAN LIFE

The first living cells were microscopic organisms possibly living in hot springs. By about 3,500mya, photosynthesizing algae may have formed layered structures called stromatolites. As oxygen built up in the atmosphere, multicellular animals evolved.

### STROMATOLITES

These layered silica or limestone structures were created by colony-forming algae and provide evidence of early life. *Collenia* (left) was a type of Precambrian stromatolite.

### FIRST ANIMALS

Late in the Precambrian, the first true animals and plants appeared. *Spriggina* (above) was a strange, long, tapering animal, with V-shaped segments running along the length of its body.

### FILTER FEEDER

The feather-shaped fossil of *Charniodiscus* is thought to represent an early filter-feeding animal that lived on the sea floor late in the Precambrian.

| 2,000mya | 1,000mya | 500mya | 250mya | 0 |

# CAMBRIAN PERIOD

542–490 MILLION YEARS AGO

The beginning of the Cambrian Period marks the start of the Phanerozoic Era, known as the "Era of Abundant Life". The Cambrian is remarkable for the amazing increase in the number of marine animals and plants. However, the land remained barren. The evolutionary spurt was probably helped by the relatively warm climate. Rapid continental movements led to high sea levels and large expanses of shallow-water environments covered large parts of the continents. These shallow seas were warm worldwide as there were no ice caps at either pole.

## BURGESS SHALE

A huge variety of fossil animals, called the Burgess Shale fauna, have been found in shale rocks of the Cambrian Period in British Columbia, Canada. Over 120 species of invertebrates have been discovered there. Chordates (creatures with a primitive backbone called a notochord), such as *Pikaia* (right), are also preserved in the Burgess Shale.

notochord
(primitive
backbone)

4,600mya          4,000mya                    3,000mya

## CAMBRIAN LANDMASSES

Continental drift was remarkably rapid during the Cambrian. The Rodinia supercontinent broke up, and the continents moved apart (see map). This caused a rise in sea levels. By 500mya, the continents of Laurentia, Baltica, and Siberia were lined up along the Equator, with the supercontinent Gondwana (present-day South America, Africa, Antarctica, Australia, and Asia) extending into temperate regions.

## CAMBRIAN LIFE

Almost all of the present-day major groupings of animals started to appear during this 50 million-year period, including worms, crabs, shellfish, and sponges. Many of the new animals had a hard external skeleton. This provided protection within which multicellular organisms could grow.

### TRILOBITES

This group of early animals were remarkable for being the first organisms with eyes – compound eyes rather like those of insects. *Xystridura* (left), like other trilobites, lived on the sea bed, and had a skeleton composed of a head shield, a jointed thorax, and a tail shield.

*jointed bony thorax with many legs*

*many small protective plates*

### WIWAXIA

Many mollusc- and worm-like animals evolved. *Wiwaxia* (right), a mollusc-like creature covered with hard spines, lived on the ocean floor.

| 2,000mya | | 1,000mya | | 500mya | 250mya | 0 |

# ORDOVICIAN PERIOD

490–435 MILLION YEARS AGO

The Ordovician Period saw the first movement of life from the oceans onto the land. Before about 450mya, the land was barren apart from mats of algae close to shores. After this time, early forms of liverwort-type plants evolved, possibly from larger algae. They quickly colonized boggy regions and areas around lakes and ponds. In the oceans, the earliest jawless fish (agnathans) appeared, which were mainly tear-drop-shaped animals covered in bony plates. An extreme Ice Age occurred at the end of the period. Fluctuations in the climate and sea levels caused by the advance and retreat of glaciers may have led to a second mass extinction. Warm-water coral reefs died out, and three-quarters of all marine species became extinct within less than a million years.

**BRACHIOPODS**
Mainly living attached to reefs, these were the most abundant two-shelled organisms in the oceans. *Strophomena* (left) was a medium-sized brachiopod.

4,600mya     4,000mya     3,000mya

## ORDOVICIAN LANDMASSES

At the beginning of the Ordovician Period, the supercontinent Gondwana still lay in the southern hemisphere. The other continents were spread out along the Equator and were gradually pushed apart by the expansion of the Iapetus Ocean (see map). Later in the Ordovician Period, the movement of Gondwana towards the South Pole triggered another ice age. By 440mya, present-day North Africa lay over the South Pole.

SIBERIA

LAURENTIA

IAPETUS OCEAN

BALTICA

GONDWANA

GONDWANA

## ORDOVICIAN LIFE

The warm equatorial seas that existed for much of the Ordovician were ideal for the evolution of marine life. Coral reefs appeared, and soon spread widely. The oceans were also filled with jellyfish, sea anemones, and other colony-forming organisms. A variety of shelled animals, such as brachiopods, lived on sea beds around the reefs.

• *fanlike colonies held in branching, tube-like structures*

*segmented body* •

**GRAPTOLITES**
Graptolites, such as *Rhabdinopora* (above), were unusual colony-forming organisms that floated through the water feeding through minute tentacles.

**NAUTILOIDS**
Primitive shelled cephalopods (a group that includes modern cuttlefish) called Nautiloids were abundant. Many, such as *Estonioceras* (left), were coiled. They moved by squirting water out of a tube in their body cavity.

**TRILOBITES**
The new coral reefs were an ideal habitat for Trilobites. *Sphaerexochus* (above) was a typical Ordovician trilobite, with a body of 11 segments.

| 2,000mya | 1,000mya | 500mya | 250mya | 0 |

# SILURIAN PERIOD

435–410 MILLION YEARS AGO

Before the Silurian Period, the land had been largely barren apart from some mossy growth and liverworts close to water. The landscape was transformed by the appearance of the first true land plants. These were primitive and simple, but had branching stems, roots, and tubes for water transport. Such plants were able to grow to larger sizes than their more primitive antecedants. As areas around water began to be covered by vegetation, soil built up, and water became trapped in the land. These conditions allowed the first advances of animal life onto the land. By the end of the Silurian, there were many land arthropods, including primitive centipedes, and spider- and scorpion-like arachnids.

## SILURIAN LIFE

After the mass extinctions at the end of the Ordovician, evolution progressed at a rapid rate. The earliest true jawed fish (acanthodians) appeared, and were followed in the Late Silurian by another major group of jawed fish, the placoderms. Many new aquatic invertebrates, such as sea urchins also appeared. Trilobites and molluscs increased in diversity.

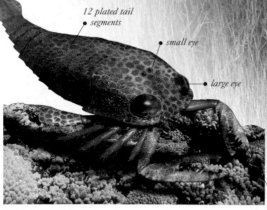

*12 plated tail segments*

*small eye*

*large eye*

*large, powerful claw*

**SEA SCORPION**
The largest Silurian marine invertebrates were the sea scorpions (eurypterids), such as *Pterygotus* (above). In some cases longer than a man, these were the dominant hunters of the early seas, and a few may have been able to crawl ashore.

## SILURIAN LANDMASSES

The end of the Ordovician Ice Age led to rising sea levels and flooding of some low-lying areas. The climate became warmer and less seasonal. The supercontinent Gondwana was still lying over the South Pole, with Laurentia sitting astride the Equator (see map). The collision of smaller landmasses formed new mountain ranges. By the end of the Silurian, all of the landmasses were grouped closely together.

*freely moving arms*

### EARLY PLANTS
The earliest plants, such as *Cooksonia* (left), had a simple branching form. They had water-conducting vessels, and reinforced stems.

*characteristic Y-shaped branching stems*

### CRINOIDS
Despite their plant-like appearance, crinoids (sea lilies) were animals. Many species populated Silurian seabeds. *Sagenocrinites* (above) was a small one, with a very compact head and many slender tentacles.

### BIRKENIA
Despite the evolution of the jawed fish, jawless fish (agnathans) were still thriving. *Birkenia* (right) was a freshwater fish that probably fed on the algae that it strained out of muddy lake- and riverbeds.

| 2,000mya | 1,000mya | 500mya | 250mya | 0 |

# DEVONIAN PERIOD
410–355 MILLION YEARS AGO

During the Devonian green plants of increasing size started to spread across the landscape. Later in the period, some plants evolved woody tissue and the first trees appeared. Towards the end of the Devonian, the climate became much warmer. Droughts were common and alternated with periods of heavy rain. Sea-levels fell worldwide, and large deserts formed. A wide variety of fish evolved – the Devonian is often called "the Age of Fish". Swampy deltas and river estuaries provided an important habitat for the emergence of animal life onto land.

### LIFE ON LAND
About 370mya, the first four-legged amphibians, such as *Acanthostega* (right), ventured out of the water onto the land. They evolved from one of the groups of lobe-finned fish, whose living relatives are lungfish. The paired fleshy fins of these fish could have evolved into limbs.

*sharp teeth suggest a diet of fish*

4,600mya      4,000mya                        3,000mya

## DEVONIAN LANDMASSES

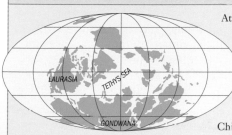

LAURASIA
TETHYS SEA
GONDWANA

At the start of the Devonian the northern landmasses formed one large supercontinent called Laurasia, separated from Gondwana by the Tethys Sea (see map). Huge mountain ranges formed in the future eastern North America and western Europe. By the mid Devonian, Gondwana and most of Laurasia had moved south of the Equator. The lands that would become China and Siberia were north of the Equator.

## DEVONIAN LIFE

The most important evolutionary step during the Devonian was the development of four-limbed land animals. Arthropods also moved onto the land and the first insects appeared. The oceans teemed with armoured jawless fish and the more modern jawed fish. Sharks and ammonoids (a group of molluscs) were common.

*body armour*

### PLACODERMS

Abundant in Devonian seas, placoderms were jawed fish. Towards the end of the Devonian some of these creatures reached 10m (33ft) in length. *Eastmanosteus* (above), although less than 2m (6½ft) long, was a fearsome hunter.

*pointed fins*

### LUNGFISH

Lungfish, such as *Dipterus* (above) have primitive lungs as well as gills, and survive during seasons of drought by breathing air in watertight burrows in the mud.

*dorsal fin*

### EARLY SHARKS

The seas of the Late Devonian teemed with squid, small fish, and crustaceans, which were ideal prey for early sharks such as *Cladoselache* (right). This shark did not have scales on its body.

*numerous sharp teeth*

| 2,000mya | 1,000mya | 500mya | 250mya | 0 |

# CARBONIFEROUS PERIOD

355–298 MILLION YEARS AGO

The Carboniferous Period opened with tropical conditions over much of the Earth. There were large coastal seas and vast swamps covering the coastal plains. Insects and amphibians found the swamps an ideal environment. Early amphibians looked rather like salamanders, but they soon evolved into many forms, including giant ones. In the warm, moist climate, huge forests of giant tree ferns flourished, producing an oxygen-rich environment. There were also giant horsetails, clubmosses, and seed-bearing plants. Large amounts of decaying vegetation led to the build up of thick layers of peat, which would later become coal deposits.

## CARBONIFEROUS LIFE

There were many types of amphibian tetrapods, ranging from newt-like animals to those the size of crocodiles. By the late Carboniferous, the first reptiles appeared, with the evolution of a shelled egg. The early reptiles were small, but they spread rapidly on land, moving into drier, upland areas.

*diamond-shaped leaf bosses*

**TREES**
Huge forests of woody trees, such as *Lepidodendron* (a specimen of fossilized bark is shown left), spread worldwide. This giant clubmoss had a column-like trunk with skeletal, spreading branches and could grow to heights of 35m (115ft), with a trunk diameter of over 2m (6½ft).

*small, slim, yet sturdy body*

**FIRST REPTILE?**
When first discovered, *Westlothiana lizziae* (right) was hailed as the first real reptile. It is now regarded as reptile-like rather than a true reptile. *Westlothiana* has features that indicate an evolutionary position between primitive tetrapods and true reptiles.

**INSECTS AND ARTHROPODS**
Already populous by the Carboniferous, insects and arthropods continued to diversify. *Graephonus* (above) was a whip scorpion, with six legs and a pair of pincers.

## CARBONIFEROUS LANDMASSES

At the beginning of the Carboniferous, most of the Earth's landmasses were arranged in two great supercontinents: Laurasia in the north and Gondwana in the south (see map). Later in the Carboniferous they moved closer together. Gondwana started to move over the South Pole again. The advance and retreat of the ensuing icesheets led to at least two ice ages in the last half of the Carboniferous.

### LIFE IN A SWAMP

The spread of the forests raised oxygen levels around the world, and this factor, combined with the increasingly humid conditions, may have allowed the evolution of very large amphibians and insects. Crocodile-like amphibians, such as *Eryops*, hunted at the bottom of the swamps. The largest Carboniferous dragonflies had wingspans of up to 2m (6½ft), and some early scorpions were more than 60cm (2ft) long.

*early reptiles, such as* Hylonomus *migrated to drier areas*

*the dragonfly* Meganeura, *one of the largest flying insects*

Eryops, *a large, amphibian aquatic hunter*

2,000mya    1,000mya    500mya    250mya    0

# PERMIAN PERIOD

298–250 MILLION YEARS AGO

The Permian was a time of dramatic climatic changes. At the start of the Permian, Gondwana was still in the grip of an ice age. It gradually warmed over the next few million years, as it moved northwards. Large parts of Laurasia became very hot and dry, and massive expanses of desert formed. This had a damaging effect on amphibian populations: they were confined to the fewer damp areas and many species became extinct. This provided the opportunity for reptiles to spread more widely and diversify. Continental upheavals and further extreme climate changes at the end of the Permian led to the largest mass extinction event ever. More than half of all animal families became extinct.

## PERMIAN LIFE

Reptiles continued to spread rapidly. Among the dominant land animals of the time were the synapsids (mammal-like reptiles). By the mid Permian, these had diversified into the therapsids. Later in the period, a mammal-like group of therapsids called the cynodonts ("dog teeth") evolved.

• *bony spike*

### PAREIASAURS

These were large, primitive, herbivorous reptiles. *Elginia* (a fossil skull is shown left) was one of the smaller pareiasaurs and one of the last of the group.

*broad vertebrae at*
• *base of spine*

• *ribs enclosing rounded body*

### EARLY ANAPSID

*Procolophodon* (right) was a small, primitive member of the anapsid group of reptiles. It may have eaten insects. Later members of its family were larger, and had teeth designed for eating plants.

| 4,600mya | 4,000mya | 3,000mya |

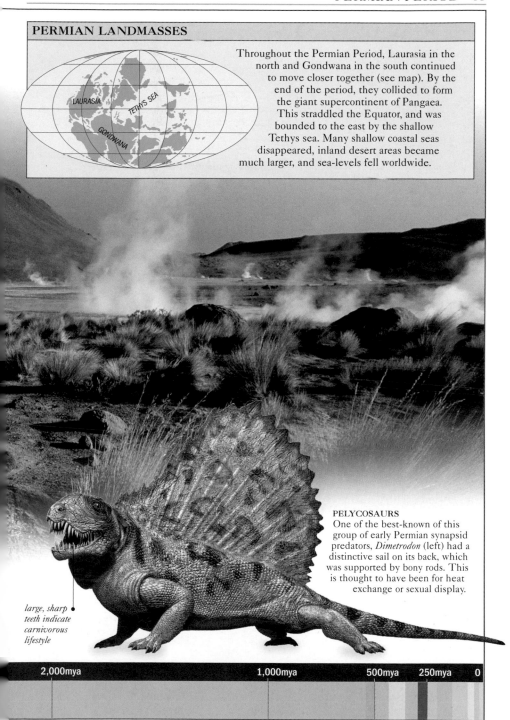

## PERMIAN LANDMASSES

Throughout the Permian Period, Laurasia in the north and Gondwana in the south continued to move closer together (see map). By the end of the period, they collided to form the giant supercontinent of Pangaea. This straddled the Equator, and was bounded to the east by the shallow Tethys sea. Many shallow coastal seas disappeared, inland desert areas became much larger, and sea-levels fell worldwide.

LAURASIA

TETHYS SEA

GONDWANA

### PELYCOSAURS
One of the best-known of this group of early Permian synapsid predators, *Dimetrodon* (left) had a distinctive sail on its back, which was supported by bony rods. This is thought to have been for heat exchange or sexual display.

*large, sharp teeth indicate carnivorous lifestyle*

2,000mya          1,000mya          500mya     250mya      0

# MESOZOIC ERA
## AGE OF THE DINOSAURS

The Mesozoic Era lasted nearly 180 million years, and comprised three periods: the Triassic, Jurassic, and the Cretaceous. During the Triassic, the world's climate grew steadily hotter and drier, and the first dinosaurs and mammals appeared.

During the Jurassic, lush forests spread over much of the world and dinosaurs and pterosaurs (flying reptiles) flourished. This was the time of the largest land animals ever to have existed – the giant sauropods. The first birds appeared and new groups of mammals evolved.

The climate grew cooler again in the Cretaceous, and the first flowering plants appeared late in the period. Placental mammals evolved and birds diversified. At the end of the Mesozoic, the end-Cretaceous mass extinction event saw the disappearance of the dinosaurs.

# TRIASSIC PERIOD

250–208 MILLION YEARS AGO

After the mass extinctions at the end of the Permian, the oceans and land were left startlingly empty of life. It took about 10 million years for the Earth's ecosystems to recover. During the Triassic, the surviving reptile groups spread widely and the first true dinosaurs appeared. A large area of the world's landmasses lay in the equatorial belt, and interior regions were subject to alternating seasons of heavy monsoonal rains and drought. The climate was generally warm, and there were no polar ice caps. These conditions favoured certain types of plants, such as seed ferns and conifers, which could cope with arid conditions, and horsetails in damper areas. The climate grew even drier at the end of the Triassic.

## TRIASSIC LIFE

Most of the synapsids, which had dominated the land in Permian times, did not survive into the Triassic. The surviving groups radiated again, but lost a number of their ecological niches to new reptile groups – the archosaurs ("ruling reptiles") and the rhynchosaurs (a short-lived group of diapsid reptiles). Several lines of aquatic reptiles also evolved. These were the nothosaurs, placodonts, and ichthyosaurs. The Late Triassic saw the arrival of the dinosaurs, crocodilians, pterosaurs, turtles, and primitive mammals.

*saurischian ("lizard-hipped") pelvic structure* •

## CYNODONTS

The cynodonts (dog-like mammal ancestors) were a group that survived into the Triassic. *Cynognathus* (above) was a large Triassic carnivorous cynodont.

## FIRST DINOSAURS

The earliest dinosaurs evolved about 230mya. *Herrerasaurus* (right) and *Eoraptor*, both found in Argentina, are thought to be among the earliest dinosaurs. Both of them were agile bipedal hunters.

• *long toe bones*

| 4,600mya | 4,000mya | 3,000mya |

## TRIASSIC LANDMASSES

The supercontinent Pangaea reached its maximum state of fusion in the mid Triassic about 230mya. Parts of present-day Asia may have formed islands, but most of the landmasses of the Earth were in contact. Pangaea straddled the Equator, reaching from pole to pole. The temperature gradient between the Equator and the poles was far less extreme than it is in modern times, and there were no polar ice caps.

TETHYS SEA

PANGAEA

### FLYING REPTILES

The earliest known flying reptiles are pterosaurs, found in Late Triassic deposits. They were accomplished flyers with wings made of skin attached to an elongated fourth finger. *Peteinosaurus* (above) was a rhamphorynchoid pterosaur (a primitive form) with a short neck, and a long bony tail.

## TRIASSIC VEGETATION

Many plants of the Palaeozoic Era relied on high rainfall and damp conditions. *Dicroidium* (right) was a seed fern the size of a small tree. It thrived in swampy areas of the Triassic southern hemisphere. In many areas, however, such tropical vegetation was gradually replaced by plants, such as cycads, ginkgos, and evergreen trees, which were better suited to the prevailing arid conditions.

• *opposing pairs of leaflets*

•*"Y"-forked leaf*

# ON THE LAND

A s the first period in the Mesozoic Era, the Triassic was the start of what is popularly called "The Age of Reptiles". Several groups of mammal-like reptiles (synapsids) survived the end-Permian extinction event. One of these groups, the herbivorous dicynodonts, radiated worldwide, reaching large sizes towards the end of the Triassic before dying out. The cynodonts, a group of advanced synapsids, were also important. Some of them, such as *Thrinaxodon*, were very successful predators, and are thought to have been "warm-blooded" and covered with fur. The first true mammals evolved at the end of the Triassic. These were tiny, shrew-like animals, and were probably nocturnal.

The first archosaurs ("ruling reptiles") appeared in the Early Triassic. They branched into two main groups – one led to the crocodilians, and the other to dinosaurs. The Late Triassic saw the appearance of the first true dinosaurs, which evolved from bipedal archosaurs, such as *Lagosuchus*.

The early dinosaurs were bipedal, small carnivorous theropods, such as *Eoraptor*. However, by the end of the Triassic Period, the quadrupedal prosauropods had evolved. They were all small, lightly built animals, with long necks and tails. Their blunt, rounded teeth suggest a mixed diet of plants and animals.

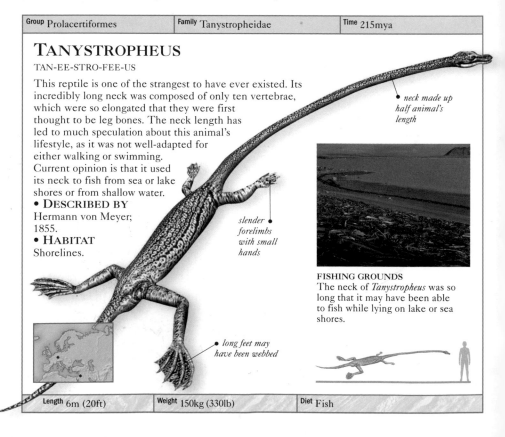

| Group Prolacertiformes | Family Tanystropheidae | Time 215mya |
| --- | --- | --- |

## TANYSTROPHEUS

TAN-EE-STRO-FEE-US

This reptile is one of the strangest to have ever existed. Its incredibly long neck was composed of only ten vertebrae, which were so elongated that they were first thought to be leg bones. The neck length has led to much speculation about this animal's lifestyle, as it was not well-adapted for either walking or swimming. Current opinion is that it used its neck to fish from sea or lake shores or from shallow water.

• **DESCRIBED BY** Hermann von Meyer; 1855.
• **HABITAT** Shorelines.

*neck made up half animal's length*

*slender forelimbs with small hands*

*long feet may have been webbed*

**FISHING GROUNDS**
The neck of *Tanystropheus* was so long that it may have been able to fish while lying on lake or sea shores.

| Length 6m (20ft) | Weight 150kg (330lb) | Diet Fish |
| --- | --- | --- |

| Group Rhynchosauria | Family Rhynchosauridae | Time 230mya |
|---|---|---|

# SCAPHONYX

SCA-FON-IKS

*Scaphonyx* ("canoe-claw") was an early rhynchosaur. Like other members of the group, it was a heavy-bodied, four-legged plant eater. Its body was pig-shaped and its head was large and deep. At the front of the mouth was a curved beak, and the mouth also bore two short tusks.
- **DESCRIBED BY** Sir Arthur Smith Woodward; 1908.
- **HABITAT** Woodland.

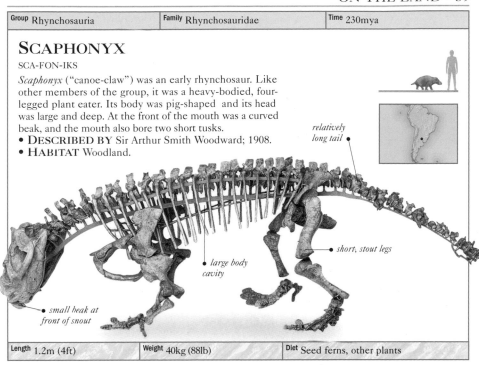

*relatively long tail*

*small beak at front of snout*

*large body cavity*

*short, stout legs*

| Length 1.2m (4ft) | Weight 40kg (88lb) | Diet Seed ferns, other plants |
|---|---|---|

| Group Rhynchosauria | Family Rhynchosauridae | Time 230– 210mya |
|---|---|---|

# HYPERODAPEDON

HI-PER-OH-DA-PEE-DON

This rhynchosaur was abundant in the Mid Triassic. It had a squat, short, barrel-shaped body, with a large head and moderately long tail. Its mouth ended in a beak, used to nip off vegetation, and its teeth were designed for efficient chopping of tough plant material. A groove ran through the middle of row of teeth on the upper jaw, and a single row of teeth on the lower jaw fitted into it when the mouth was closed.
- **DESCRIBED BY** Thomas H. Huxley; 1859.
- **HABITAT** Woodland.

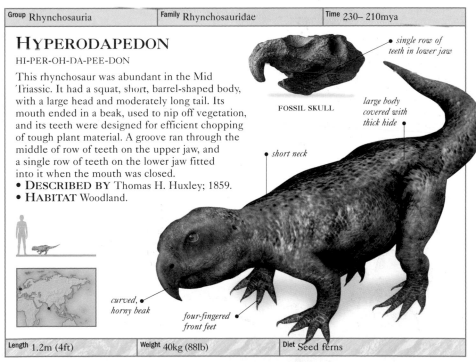

*single row of teeth in lower jaw*

*large body covered with thick hide*

FOSSIL SKULL

*short neck*

*curved, horny beak*

*four-fingered front feet*

| Length 1.2m (4ft) | Weight 40kg (88lb) | Diet Seed ferns |
|---|---|---|

| Group Archosauria | Family Proterosuchidae | Time 250mya |
|---|---|---|

# CHASMATOSAURUS

KAZ-MAT-OH-SAW-RUS

Formerly known as *Proterosuchus*, *Chasmatosaurus* was one of the earliest known archosaurs. It had a large, heavy body, and its legs were angled out from the body, resulting in a sprawling, lizard-like gait. It probably lived a lifestyle similar to that of crocodiles, spending most of its time hunting in rivers. Its teeth were sharp and curved backwards, and there were also primitive teeth on the palate. Some reconstructions show this animal with a pointed snout.

• **DESCRIBED BY** Thomas H. Huxley; 1865.
• **HABITAT** Riverbanks.

*large head with long snout*

*long, heavy tail*

*sprawling, stout limbs*

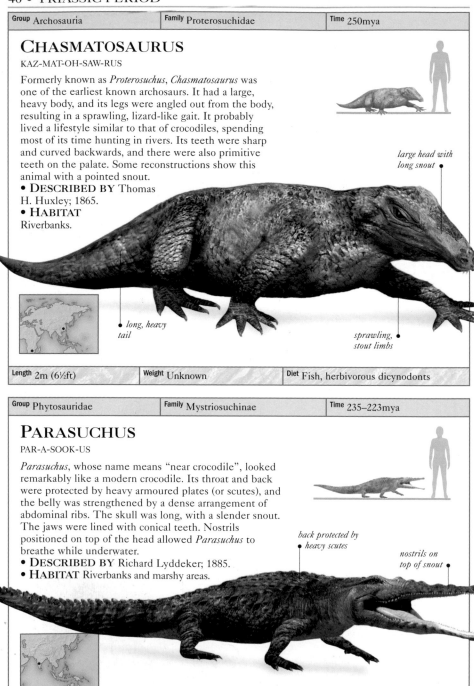

| Length 2m (6½ft) | Weight Unknown | Diet Fish, herbivorous dicynodonts |
|---|---|---|

| Group Phytosauridae | Family Mystriosuchinae | Time 235–223mya |
|---|---|---|

# PARASUCHUS

PAR-A-SOOK-US

*Parasuchus*, whose name means "near crocodile", looked remarkably like a modern crocodile. Its throat and back were protected by heavy armoured plates (or scutes), and the belly was strengthened by a dense arrangement of abdominal ribs. The skull was long, with a slender snout. The jaws were lined with conical teeth. Nostrils positioned on top of the head allowed *Parasuchus* to breathe while underwater.

• **DESCRIBED BY** Richard Lyddeker; 1885.
• **HABITAT** Riverbanks and marshy areas.

*back protected by heavy scutes*

*nostrils on top of snout*

| Length 2.5m (8¼ft) | Weight Unknown | Diet Fish |
|---|---|---|

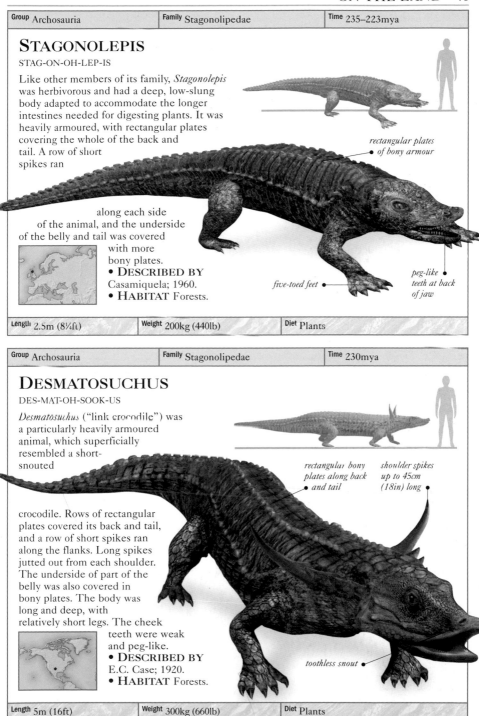

| Group Archosauria | Family Stagonolipedae | Time 235–223mya |

# STAGONOLEPIS

STAG-ON-OH-LEP-IS

Like other members of its family, *Stagonolepis* was herbivorous and had a deep, low-slung body adapted to accommodate the longer intestines needed for digesting plants. It was heavily armoured, with rectangular plates covering the whole of the back and tail. A row of short spikes ran along each side of the animal, and the underside of the belly and tail was covered with more bony plates.
• **DESCRIBED BY** Casamiquela; 1960.
• **HABITAT** Forests.

*rectangular plates of bony armour*

*five-toed feet*

*peg-like teeth at back of jaw*

| Length 2.5m (8¼ft) | Weight 200kg (440lb) | Diet Plants |

| Group Archosauria | Family Stagonolipedae | Time 230mya |

# DESMATOSUCHUS

DES-MAT-OH-SOOK-US

*Desmatosuchus* ("link crocodile") was a particularly heavily armoured animal, which superficially resembled a short-snouted crocodile. Rows of rectangular plates covered its back and tail, and a row of short spikes ran along the flanks. Long spikes jutted out from each shoulder. The underside of part of the belly was also covered in bony plates. The body was long and deep, with relatively short legs. The cheek teeth were weak and peg-like.
• **DESCRIBED BY** E.C. Case; 1920.
• **HABITAT** Forests.

*rectangular bony plates along back and tail*

*shoulder spikes up to 45cm (18in) long*

*toothless snout*

| Length 5m (16ft) | Weight 300kg (660lb) | Diet Plants |

| Group Archosauria | Family Ornithosuchidae | Time 235mya |
| --- | --- | --- |

# EUPARKERIA

EWE-PARK-ER-EE-A

*Euparkeria* was an early archosaur, and was unusual among its contemporaries in that the relative length of its hind legs to its forelegs was greater than that of contemporary reptiles. It probably spent most of its time on all fours, but was capable of rising onto its hind legs to run. Its tail made up about half its body weight, and was held outstretched as it ran for balance. The body was small and slim, with thin bony plates covering the middle of the back and

tail. The head was large but light, and the many teeth were sharp, serrated, and curved backwards, indicating a carnivorous way of life.
• **DESCRIBED BY** E. D. Cope; 1869.
• **HABITAT** Woodland.

*ridge of light bony plates running along back*

*lightly built head despite large size*

*four-fingered hands*

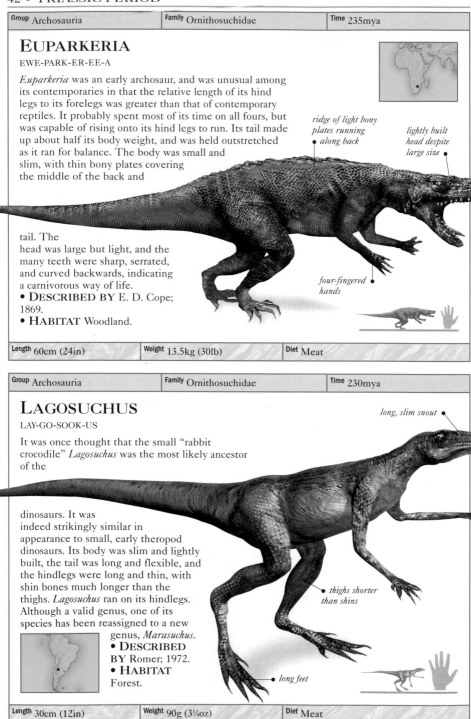

| Length 60cm (24in) | Weight 13.5kg (30lb) | Diet Meat |
| --- | --- | --- |

| Group Archosauria | Family Ornithosuchidae | Time 230mya |
| --- | --- | --- |

# LAGOSUCHUS

LAY-GO-SOOK-US

It was once thought that the small "rabbit crocodile" *Lagosuchus* was the most likely ancestor of the

dinosaurs. It was indeed strikingly similar in appearance to small, early theropod dinosaurs. Its body was slim and lightly built, the tail was long and flexible, and the hindlegs were long and thin, with shin bones much longer than the thighs. *Lagosuchus* ran on its hindlegs. Although a valid genus, one of its species has been reassigned to a new genus, *Marasuchus*.
• **DESCRIBED BY** Romer; 1972.
• **HABITAT** Forest.

*long, slim snout*

*thighs shorter than shins*

*long feet*

| Length 30cm (12in) | Weight 90g (3¼oz) | Diet Meat |
| --- | --- | --- |

| Group Theropoda | Family Herrerasauridae | Time 228mya |
|---|---|---|

# HERRERASAURUS

HERR-RAY-RAH-SAW-RUS

Analysis of a complete skeleton of *Herrerasaurus* ("Herrera's lizard") discovered in the 1990s, confirmed that it was one of the most primitive dinosaurs. However, palaeontologists are still disputing whether it can be classified as a theropod. *Herrerasaurus* was an agile hunter, probably able to prey on slower creatures such as *Scaphonyx* (p.39). It had powerful hindlimbs, and a long tail used for balance. It probably ran with its back nearly horizontal to balance the body at the hips. The jaws were lined with sharp, long teeth that were curved backwards.

• **DESCRIBED BY** Osvaldo A. Reig; 1963.
• **HABITAT** Woodland.

small ridge running down snout

long, sharp teeth

probably scaly skin

claws on three fingers

tail held outstretched for balance

sturdy thighs

four-toed feet

long, flexible tail

skull lightened by holes

ridge running down front edge of humerus

strong, grasping arms and hands

SKELETAL RECONSTRUCTION

| Length 3.1m (10ft) | Weight 210kg (460lb) | Diet Meat |
|---|---|---|

| Group Theropoda | Family Uncertain | Time 228mya |
|---|---|---|

# EORAPTOR

EE-OH-RAP-TOR

The recently-discovered *Eoraptor* ("dawn raptor") is now regarded as one of the earliest dinosaurs. It was a very small, lightly-built, bipedal carnivore with hollow bones. The head was long and slim, with many small, sharp teeth. The arms were far shorter than the legs, and had five-fingered hands, although two of the fingers were reduced. *Eoraptor* appears to lack the specialized features of any of the major groups of dinosaurs, and for this reason is consistent with what would be expected for the earliest dinosaur ancestors.

• **DESCRIBED BY** Paul Sereno, Forster, Rogers, and Monetta; 1993.

• **HABITAT** Forests.

long, slim legs •

• five-fingered hands

| Length 1m (39in) | Weight Unknown | Diet Meat |
|---|---|---|

| Group Theropoda | Family Uncertain | Time 231–225 mya |
|---|---|---|

# STAURIKOSAURUS

STORE-EE-KOH-SAW-RUS

*Staurikosaurus* ("Southern Cross lizard") was a primitive, bipedal dinosaur. It had the typical theropod body shape – long, slim tail, long, powerful hind legs, and short arms.

slim, lightweight body balanced at • hip level

long, thin head •

The back was held horizontally, with the tail used for balance. The lower jaw had a joint that allowed the tooth-bearing part to move independently of the back part of the jaw.

• **DESCRIBED BY** Edwin Colbert; 1970.

• **HABITAT** Forests and scrub.

five-fingered • hands

• long, slim hind legs with long feet

| Length 2m (6½ft) | Weight 20–40kg (44–88lbs) | Diet Meat |
|---|---|---|

| Group Theropoda | Family Coelophysidae | Time 208–200mya |
| --- | --- | --- |

# COELOPHYSIS

SEE-LOW-FIE-SIS

*Coelophysis* ("hollow face") was a small, lightly built, early dinosaur with open skull bones (hence its name). The body was long and slim, and the head was pointed, with many small, serrated teeth. *Coelophysis* is one of the best-known dinosaurs due to the excavation of dozens of skeletons from New Mexico, USA (see right). Many of these fossils contained bones of young *Coelophysis* in their abdominal regions, suggesting that in some circumstances this dinosaur may have eaten its own young. Two types of *Coelophysis* have been described: robust and gracile. These probably represent male and female forms.
• **DESCRIBED BY** Edward Drinker Cope; 1889.
• **HABITAT** Desert plains.

**GHOST RANCH, NEW MEXICO**
Many fossil skeletons of *Coelophysis* have been found at this site.

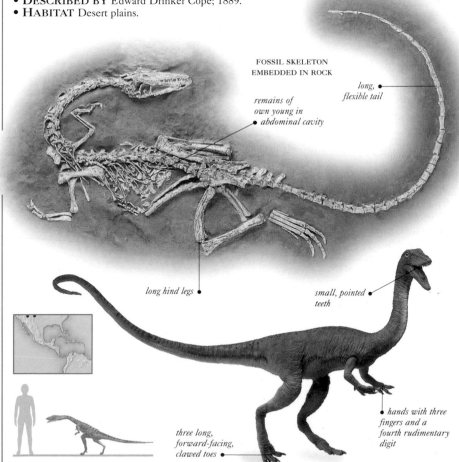

FOSSIL SKELETON
EMBEDDED IN ROCK

long,
flexible tail

remains of
own young in
abdominal cavity

long hind legs

small, pointed
teeth

hands with three
fingers and a
fourth rudimentary
digit

three long,
forward-facing,
clawed toes

| Length 2.8m (9ft) | Weight 46kg (100lb) | Diet Lizards, fish, young *Coelophysis* |
| --- | --- | --- |

| Group Prosauropoda | Family Anchisauridae | Time 220–209mya |
|---|---|---|

# EFRAASIA

EE-FRAA-ZIA

This early prosauropod, which was named after its discoverer, E. Fraas, is believed by some palaentologists to be a juvenile *Sellosaurus* (see Additional Dinosaurs). It was lightly built, with a small head, fairly long neck, bulky body, and long tail. Its legs were longer than its arms, and its five-fingered hands had a large thumb claw. It may have walked on all fours to browse, rising onto its hind legs to run.

• **DESCRIBED BY** Eberhard Fraas; 1909.
• **HABITAT** Dry upland plains.

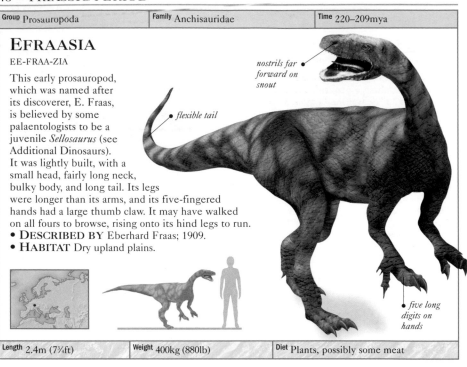

*nostrils far forward on snout*

*flexible tail*

*five long digits on hands*

| Length 2.4m (7¾ft) | Weight 400kg (880lb) | Diet Plants, possibly some meat |
|---|---|---|

| Group Prosauropoda | Family Plateosauridae | Time 219–210mya |
|---|---|---|

# PLATEOSAURUS

PLAT-EE-OH-SAW-RUS

This "flat lizard" was one of the most common dinosaurs of the Late Triassic Period. The large number of fossil finds suggest that *Plateosaurus* may have lived in herds and migrated to avoid seasonal droughts. It walked on all fours, rearing up on its hind legs to browse from high vegetation. The thumbs on its hands were partially opposable, allowing it to grasp food. Its small skull was deeper than in most other prosauropods, and its fairly short neck was thinner. *Plateosaurus* had many small, leaf-shaped teeth, and the hinge of the lower jaw was low-slung to give greater leverage. These factors indicate a diet primarily composed of plants. This dinosaur also had a very large nasal chamber, but the reason for this is as yet unknown.

*beak-like upper jaw*

*fairly short, thin, flexible neck*

*clawed fingers*

• **DESCRIBED BY** Hermann von Meyer; 1837.
• **HABITAT** Dry plains, desert.

| Length 8m (26ft) | Weight 1.5 tonnes (1½ tons) | Diet Leaves, small amounts of meat |
|---|---|---|

| Group Prosauropoda | Family Anchisauridae | Time 223–209mya |
|---|---|---|

# THECODONTOSAURUS

THEE-COH-DONT-OH-SAW-RUS

This dinosaur was the first prosauropod to be discovered, and is one of the most primitive known. Its name ("socket-toothed lizard") was given because its saw-edged teeth looked like those of a monitor lizard, but were embedded in the sockets in the jaw bones. *Thecodontosaurus* had a relatively small head and a

*fairly short neck*

*small head*

*large thumb claw*

*four-toed feet*

long tail. Mainly bipedal, it seems to have had some ability to walk on all fours.
• **DESCRIBED BY** H. Riley and S. Stutchbury; 1836.
• **HABITAT** Desert plains, dry upland areas.

| Length 2.1m (7ft) | Weight 50kg (110lb) | Diet Plants, possibly omnivorous |
|---|---|---|

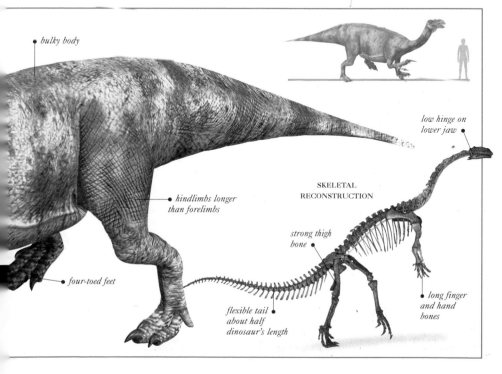

*bulky body*

*low hinge on lower jaw*

SKELETAL RECONSTRUCTION

*hindlimbs longer than forelimbs*

*strong thigh bone*

*four-toed feet*

*long finger and hand bones*

*flexible tail about half dinosaur's length*

| Group Dicynodontia | Family Lystrosauridae | Time 240mya |

# LYSTROSAURUS

LIS-TRO-SAW-RUS

*Lystrosaurus*, whose name means "shovel lizard", was a heavily built, early dicynodont with a short, stubby tail. It had two tusk-like fangs made of horn. It used to be thought of as a type of reptilian hippopotamus because of its long, downturned snout and the placement of its nasal openings high on the snout. However, new analysis suggests a terrestrial lifestyle: the skull and jaw features were adaptations to a fibrous diet, the pelvis was well-developed, and the hind limbs were semi-erect.

*long spine supported barrel-shaped body*

*short, semi-erect limbs*

*long snout with two horn fangs*

• **DESCRIBED BY** E.D. Cope; 1870.
• **HABITAT** Dry floodplains.

| Length 1m (39in) | Weight 92kg (200lbs) | Diet Plants |

---

| Group Dicynodontia | Family Kannemeyeriidae | Time 235mya |

# SINOKANNEMEYERIA

SY-NOH-KAN-EH-MEY-REE-A

This long-snouted member of the dicynodont ("two-dog teeth") group of synapsids was well adapted for a lifestyle as a terrestrial herbivore. Its head was massive, with large openings for the eyes, nostrils, and jaw muscles. These reduced the weight of the skull. A hinge between the lower jaw and the skull allowed the jaws to move backwards and forwards with a shearing action. Although the jaws were toothless, this motion would have ground up the toughest vegetation. The front of the jaw had a small horn-covered beak, and there were two small tusks growing from bulbous projections on the upper jaw. These tusks could have been used to dig up roots. *Sinokannemeyeria* had relatively short, stumpy legs, which were held in a slightly sprawling gait to the sides of its body. The limb girdles were formed into large, heavy plates of bone to support the weight of the wide, heavily built body. *Sinokannemeyeria* was probably not a fast or agile mover.
• **DESCRIBED BY** N. King; 1990.
• **HABITAT** Plains and woodland.

*large attachment points for jaw muscles*

*large eye sockets*

*turtle-like horny beak at front of mouth*

*broad toes on flat feet*

| Length 1.8m (6ft) | Weight 100kg (220lb) | Diet Tough vegetation, roots |

| Group Dicynodontia | Family Kannemeyeriidae | Time 222–215mya |
|---|---|---|

# PLACERIAS

PLAH-SEE-REE-AS

*Placerias* was a heavily built powerful animal, with the characteristic dicynodont jaw structure. Its jaw margins were toothless, except for two horny tusks near the front of the mouth. The tip of the snout ended in a beak used for uprooting plants. *Placerias* was one of the last of the dicynodont species.

• **DESCRIBED BY** C.L. Camp, S.P. Welles; 1956.
• **HABITAT** Flood plains.

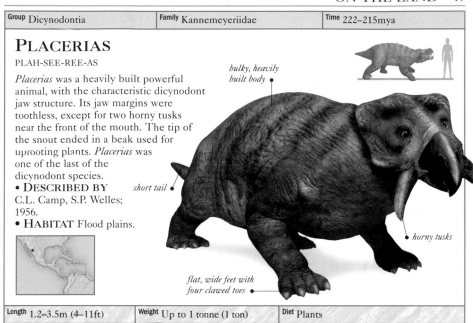

*bulky, heavily built body*

*short tail*

*horny tusks*

*flat, wide feet with four clawed toes*

| Length 1.2–3.5m (4–11ft) | Weight Up to 1 tonne (1 ton) | Diet Plants |
|---|---|---|

*capacious ribcage held large mass of intestines*

*legs held in semi-sprawling gait*

*wide, barrel-shaped body*

*short legs*

*large limb girdles*

| Group Cynodontia | Family Cynognathidae | Time 230–245mya |
|---|---|---|

# CYNOGNATHUS

SY-NOG-NAY-THUS

This wolf-sized carnivore was a ferocious Triassic predator. It was one of the largest cynodonts ("dog-toothed" synapsids), and was heavily built, with strong legs positioned directly under its body, and a tail shorter than that of most other reptiles. Its head was more than 30cm (12in) long. It is thought that it was probably warm-blooded, its skin may have been covered with hair, and that it may also have given birth to live young. *Cynognathus* ("dog jaw") had dog-like teeth, with cutting incisors, long canines, and shearing set of cheek teeth. The jaws had a wide gape and a very powerful bite.

• **DESCRIBED BY** H.G. Seeley; 1876.
• **HABITAT** Woodland.

*large eye socket*

*long canine teeth*

FOSSIL SKULL

| Length 1.5m (5ft) | Weight 40–50kg (88–110lb) | Diet Herbivorous therapsids |
|---|---|---|

| Group Cynodontia | Family Thrinaxodontidae | Time 156–145mya |
|---|---|---|

# THRINAXODON

THRIN-AXE-OH-DON

This small, solidly built carnivore had a long body, which was distinctly divided into thoracic and lumbar regions (the first time this was seen among vertebrates). The division was marked by the ribs, which were borne only on the thoracic vertebrae. This suggests that *Thrinaxodon* ("trident tooth") probably had a diaphragm, as modern mammals do. One of the foot bones had evolved into a heel, so that the foot could be levered clear of the ground for more efficient running. The teeth were set into a single bone, which made the jaws stronger.

• **DESCRIBED BY** Seeley; 1894.
• **HABITAT** Woodland.

*body may have been covered with hair*

*toes of equal length*

*teeth with three sharp cusps*

| Length 50cm (20in) | Weight Unknown | Diet Meat |
|---|---|---|

| Group Mammaliaformes | Family Morganucodontidae | Time 220–200mya |
|---|---|---|

# EOZOSTRODON

EE-OH-ZOH-STROH-DON

This shrew-like animal was one of the earliest true mammals. It probably laid eggs, but is thought to have fed its young with milk produced by mammary glands. Its four short legs had a slightly sprawling gait and ended in five-toed feet with claws. Its tail was long and possibly hairy. Its snout was long, slim, and contained true mammalian teeth (the cheek teeth comprised simple premolars and molars with multiple sharp cusps, and were replaced only once during the animal's lifetime). The large eyes suggest that *Eozostrodon* was probably a nocturnal hunter, and the sharp teeth indicate a diet predominantly of insects and small animals. This genus is probably the same as the later-named genus *Morganucodon*.

• **DESCRIBED BY** F.R. Parrington; 1941.
• **HABITAT** Forest floors.

*long, furry tail*

*small body covered with dense hair*

*large eyes*

*five clawed toes*

*short legs*

*slim pointed snout may have had whiskers*

*multi-cusped molars*

JAW BONE

| Length 10cm (4in) | Weight 150g (5oz) | Diet Insects, small animals |
|---|---|---|

# IN THE WATER

**D**uring the Mesozoic, many groups of reptiles became re-adapted to a marine or aquatic lifestyle. In the Triassic there were three main groups of marine reptiles – the placodonts, nothosaurs, and primitive ichthyosaurs.

Placodonts were the least specialized swimmers of the three, and they vanished at the end of the Triassic. Although many species evolved, they never invaded the open seas. Instead, they seem to have been restricted to the shallow, warm Tethys Sea. With the formation of coral reefs in the Triassic, many new molluscs had evolved, and the teeth and mouth of the placodonts show adaptations to a diet of shellfish and crustaceans. Some species spent equal amounts of time on land and in the water. Other groups became fully aquatic and developed turtle-like shells as protective armour.

Nothosaurs were marine animals with long, streamlined bodies. They had webbed feet and their sharp teeth were well-adapted for eating fish. They seem to have lived a lifestyle rather like modern seals – hunting at sea and coming ashore to breed. Like placodonts, nothosaurs died out at the end of the Triassic.

Ichthyosaurs were the most specialized marine reptiles. They were fish-eaters shaped rather like a modern dolphin. The Triassic forms (shastasaurs) swam in an eel-like way; later species became more fish-like. No longer able to come ashore, some species gave birth to live young at sea. Fossils have been found of female ichthyosaurs in the process of giving birth. Shastasaurs were so successful that they continued to diversify through the Jurassic and Cretaceous Periods.

| Group Placodontia | Family Henodontidae | Time 235–223mya |
|---|---|---|

## HENODUS

HEN-OH-DUS

*Henodus* ("single-tooth") was an armoured placodont shaped rather like a modern turtle. It was as wide as it was long, and its back and belly were protected by bony, many-sided plates that made up a defensive shell. This in turn was completely covered with plates of tough horn. *Henodus* was unusual among placodonts in that it was able to live in fresh water. It had a strangely square snout and no teeth in the mouth. Instead, it is thought there was a horny beak at the front of the mouth, similar to that of modern turtles. This could be used to pluck shellfish off rocks and crush them efficiently. Its short, clawed feet may have been webbed.
• **DESCRIBED BY** Friedrich von Huene; 1936.
• **HABITAT** Lagoons.

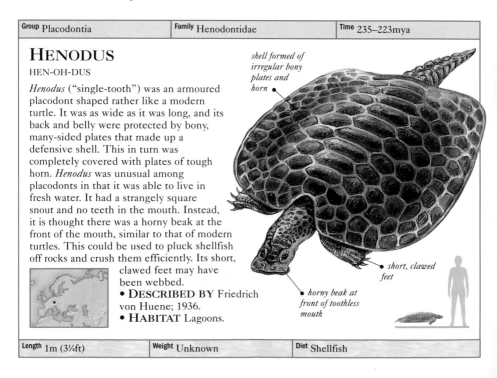

*shell formed of irregular bony plates and horn*

*short, clawed feet*

*horny beak at front of toothless mouth*

| Length 1m (3¼ft) | Weight Unknown | Diet Shellfish |
|---|---|---|

| Group Placodontia | Family Placodontidae | Time 227–205mya |
| --- | --- | --- |

# PLACODUS

PLAK-OH-DUS

This placodont shows few adaptations for an aquatic lifestyle, with a stocky body, short neck, and sprawling limbs. However, there were webs of skin between the toes and the tail was flattened from side to side. There may also have been a fin on the tail. *Placodus* ("flat tooth") had forward-pointing teeth used to pluck shellfish off rocks. Flat teeth on the palate met other teeth on the lower jaw to produce an efficient crushing action.

• **DESCRIBED BY** Georg Munster; 1830.
• **HABITAT** Seashores.

flat teeth

**LOWER JAW**  **UPPER JAW**

• *bony, raised bumps formed back armour*

• *sprawling, five-toed feet*

• *belly ribs formed protective shell*

| Length 2m (6½ft) | Weight Unknown | Diet Shellfish, crustaceans |
| --- | --- | --- |

| Group Placodontia | Family Cyamodontidae | Time 220–205mya |
| --- | --- | --- |

# PSEPHODERMA

SEF-OH-DER-MAH

This relatively well-known placodont was remarkably turtle-like in appearance. Its body was broad and flat and covered with hexagonal plates. Its limbs were paddle-shaped. *Psephoderma* ("pebble skin") had great biting power – a horny beak at the front of its mouth could pluck shellfish, which were then crushed by its teeth and jaws.

• **DESCRIBED BY** Hermann von Meyer; 1867.
• **HABITAT** Shallow seas.

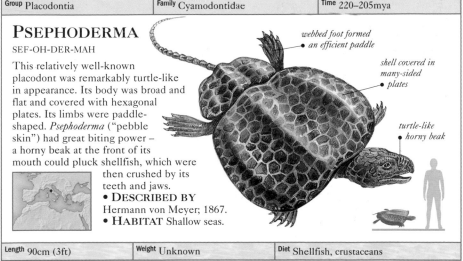

*webbed foot formed* • *an efficient paddle*

*shell covered in many-sided* • *plates*

*turtle-like* • *horny beak*

| Length 90cm (3ft) | Weight Unknown | Diet Shellfish, crustaceans |
| --- | --- | --- |

| Group Nothosauria | Family Nothosauridae | Time 250mya |
|---|---|---|

# CERESIOSAURUS

SER-EE-SEE-OH-SAW-RUS

*Ceresiosaurus* ("deadly lizard") had toes that were much longer than those of other nothosaurs due to hyperphalangy (an increased number of bones in each toe). The length of its feet, which may have been webbed, meant that efficient swimming flippers were formed. The forelegs were longer than the hind legs, suggesting that they were the ones used most for steering. *Ceresiosaurus* is thought to have swum by undulating its flexible body and tail from side to side.
- **DESCRIBED BY** Peyer; 1931.
- **HABITAT** Shallow seas.

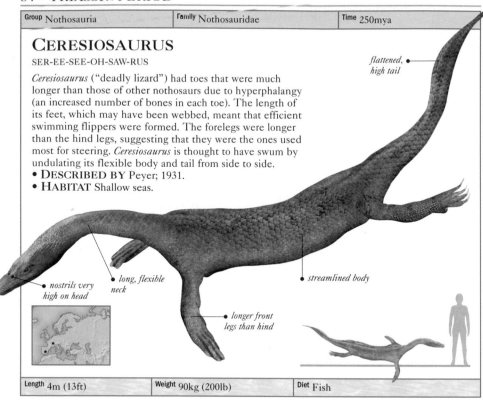

*flattened, high tail*

*streamlined body*

*nostrils very high on head*

*long, flexible neck*

*longer front legs than hind*

| Length 4m (13ft) | Weight 90kg (200lb) | Diet Fish |
|---|---|---|

| Group Nothosauria | Family Nothosauridae | Time 248–206mya |
|---|---|---|

# NOTHOSAURUS

NOH-THO-SAW-RUS

*Nothosaurus* ("false lizard") was a typical nothosaur. Its long body, neck, and tail were flexible and moderately streamlined. Some fossils have impressions of webbed skin between the five toes of the feet. The head was slim, and the jaws contained many sharp, thin teeth that interlocked when the mouth was closed. The nostrils were placed high on the head, close to the eyes.
- **DESCRIBED BY** Georg Munster; 1834.
- **HABITAT** Coastal regions.

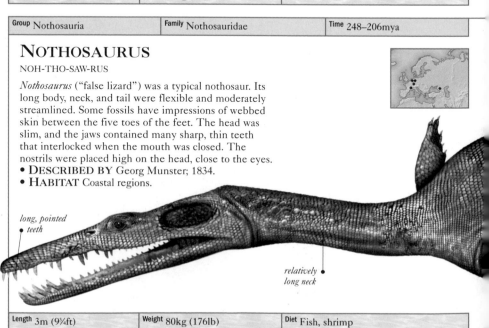

*long, pointed teeth*

*relatively long neck*

| Length 3m (9¾ft) | Weight 80kg (176lb) | Diet Fish, shrimp |
|---|---|---|

| Group Nothosauria | Family Nothosauridae | Time 234–227mya |
|---|---|---|

# LARIOSAURUS

LA-REE-OH-SAW-RUS

*Lariosaurus* was a small member of the nothosaur group of marine reptiles. It had primitive adaptations to an aquatic lifestyle. Its neck and toes were very short, and the webs of skin on its hindfeet would have been small, and therefore not much use for fast swimming. Its front feet formed paddle-like flippers. In common with other members of its group, it had flexible knee and ankle joints. *Lariosaurus* probably spent most of the time on the seashore or paddling in coastal waters.

• **DESCRIBED BY**
Curioni; 1847.
• **HABITAT**
Coastal shallows.

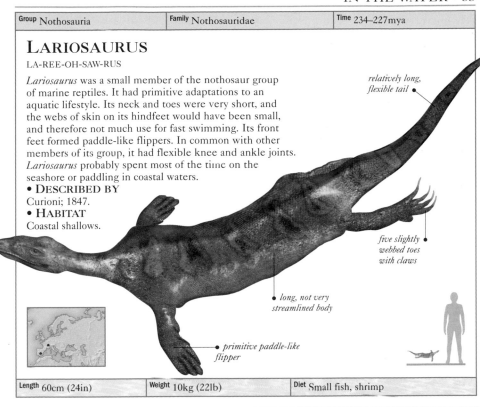

*relatively long, flexible tail*

*five slightly webbed toes with claws*

*long, not very streamlined body*

*primitive paddle-like flipper*

| Length 60cm (24in) | Weight 10kg (22lb) | Diet Small fish, shrimp |
|---|---|---|

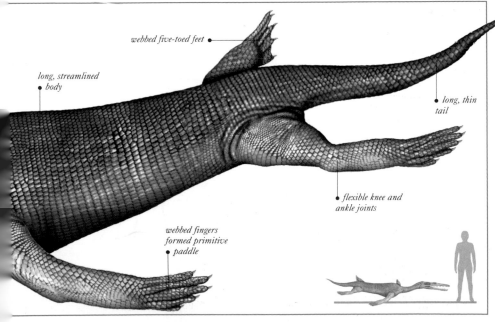

*webbed five-toed feet*

*long, streamlined body*

*long, thin tail*

*flexible knee and ankle joints*

*webbed fingers formed primitive paddle*

| Group Ichthyosauria | Family Mixosauridae | Time 225mya |
|---|---|---|

# MIXOSAURUS

MIX-OH-SAW-RUS

This "mixed reptile" is thought to have been an intermediate form between primitive ichthyosaurs and more advanced types. It had a fish-like body, typical of advanced ichthyosaurs, with a dorsal fin on its back. However, it only had a small fin on the top of its tail. Its paddles were short, with the front pair longer than the hind ones.
- **DESCRIBED BY** Baur; 1887.
- **HABITAT** Oceans.

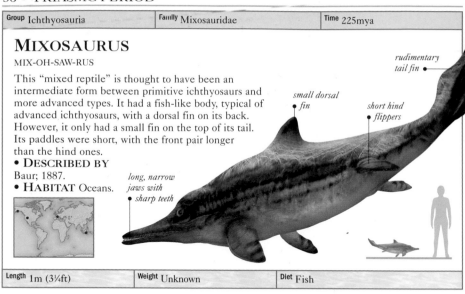

*rudimentary tail fin*

*small dorsal fin*

*short hind flippers*

*long, narrow jaws with sharp teeth*

| Length 1m (3¼ft) | Weight Unknown | Diet Fish |
|---|---|---|

| Group Ichthyosauria | Family Shastasauridae | Time 227–206mya |
|---|---|---|

# SHONISAURUS

SHON-EE-SAW-RUS

*Shonisaurus* ("Shoshone mountain reptile") is the largest ichthyosaur known. It had the typical ichthyosaur shape, with its head and neck, body, and tail making up equal thirds of its length. However, it had several features that indicate that it was an offshoot from the main ichthyosaur line. Its jaws were very long, and had teeth only at the front. Its paddles were also unusually long, and of equal length.
- **DESCRIBED BY** Charles L. Camp; 1976.
- **HABITAT** Oceans.

*tall dorsal fin*

*large eyes*

*thin, sharp, pointed teeth*

*deep, fish-like tail fin*

*elongated jaws*

*front paddles same length as hind pair*

*unusually long, thin paddles*

| Length 15m (49ft) | Weight 20.3–35.5 tonnes (20–35 tons) | Diet Fish, squid, other cephalopods |
|---|---|---|

# IN THE AIR

L ate Triassic times saw an amazing evolutionary leap – the first group of vertebrate animals took to the air. These were the pterosaurs (winged reptiles). The earliest and most primitive pterosaurs, the rhamphorhynchoids, were usually small, with a long tail stiffened by bony ligaments. Later, they gave way to a more advanced group, the pterodactyloids.

Pterosaur wings were made of extremely thin membranes of skin stretched from the incredibly long fourth finger to the thigh. Views on the flying ability, particularly of the rhamphorynchoids have changed dramatically over the years. For a long time, it was thought that pterosaurs could not actively fly – they could only glide after climbing to a high take-off point. Skeletal analysis now shows that pterosaurs were capable of flapping flight, although not as efficiently as birds. They probably had some kind of furry body covering.

| Group Rhamphorhynchoidea | Family Dimorphodontidae | Time 228–215mya |
|---|---|---|

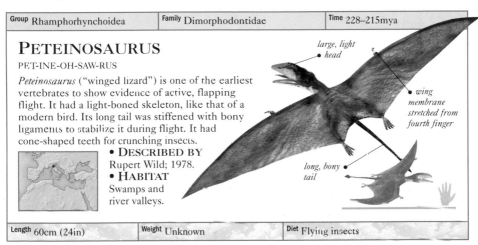

## PETEINOSAURUS

PET-INE-OH-SAW-RUS

*Peteinosaurus* ("winged lizard") is one of the earliest vertebrates to show evidence of active, flapping flight. It had a light-boned skeleton, like that of a modern bird. Its long tail was stiffened with bony ligaments to stabilize it during flight. It had cone-shaped teeth for crunching insects.

• **DESCRIBED BY** Rupert Wild; 1978.
• **HABITAT** Swamps and river valleys.

*large, light head*

*wing membrane stretched from fourth finger*

*long, bony tail*

| Length 60cm (24in) | Weight Unknown | Diet Flying insects |
|---|---|---|

| Group Rhamphorhynchoidea | Family Eudimorphodontidae | Time 210mya |
|---|---|---|

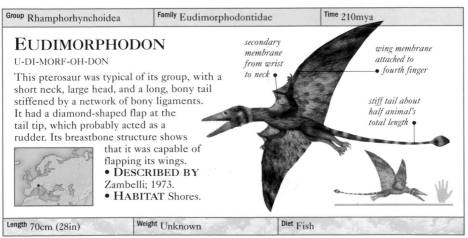

## EUDIMORPHODON

U-DI-MORF-OH-DON

This pterosaur was typical of its group, with a short neck, large head, and a long, bony tail stiffened by a network of bony ligaments. It had a diamond-shaped flap at the tail tip, which probably acted as a rudder. Its breastbone structure shows that it was capable of flapping its wings.

• **DESCRIBED BY** Zambelli; 1973.
• **HABITAT** Shores.

*secondary membrane from wrist to neck*

*wing membrane attached to fourth finger*

*stiff tail about half animal's total length*

| Length 70cm (28in) | Weight Unknown | Diet Fish |
|---|---|---|

# JURASSIC PERIOD

208–144 MILLION YEARS AGO

At the beginning of the Jurassic Period, the world was still hot and arid. Major continental movements caused climate change throughout the period: increased rainfall led to a reduction in desert areas, climates were more humid, and, as the period progressed, habitats in general became more green and luxuriant. However, lake deposits show that there were millions of cycles of dry and wet periods. Most Jurassic plants were still mainly primitive types of gymnosperms. There were also ferns, horsetails, and club mosses, and huge forests of these plants spread worldwide. Continental movements led to the creation of warm, shallow seas, which became filled with coral reefs and new forms of marine life, including large reptiles. Pterosaurs were present in large numbers, and the earliest birds appeared at the end of the period.

**JURASSIC LIFE**
Prosauropod dinosaurs still dominated Early Jurassic habitats, but as the period progressed, they were usurped by the giant sauropods, such as *Apatosaurus*. The first armoured dinosaurs – the stegosaurs – also appeared. Protective armour may have been an evolutionary response to the emergence of ever-larger carnivorous dinosaurs. The first true mammals evolved, and probably survived by remaining small and living a mainly nocturnal existence.

*relatively short tail*

**LATER PTEROSAURS**
In the Late Jurassic, new forms of pterosaurs, such as *Anurognathus* (below) appeared. Their main feature was a very short tail that gave them greater agility in the air.

**MARINE PREDATORS**
Giant pliosaurs such as *Liopleurodon* (above), filled the warm Jurassic seas, hunting large prey including other marine reptiles. They had developed an efficient "flying" action for swimming rapidly through the water.

*wing supported by greatly elongated fourth finger*

4,600mya          4,000mya                              3,000mya

## JURASSIC LANDMASSES

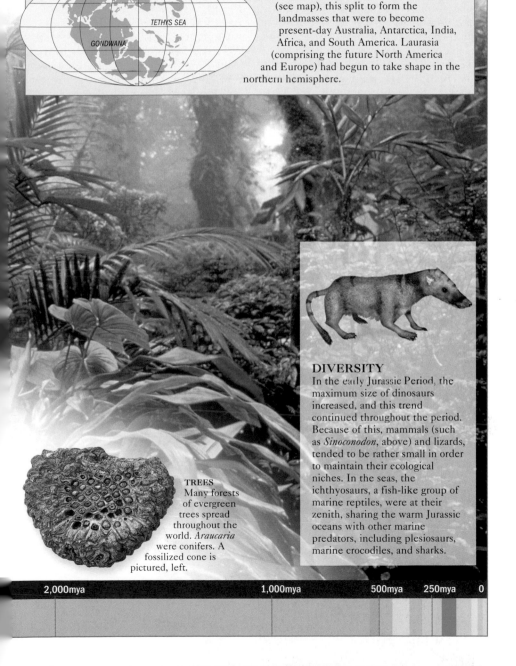

At the start of the Jurassic Period, there was once again a supercontinent called Gondwana south of the Equator. Later in the period (see map), this split to form the landmasses that were to become present-day Australia, Antarctica, India, Africa, and South America. Laurasia (comprising the future North America and Europe) had begun to take shape in the northern hemisphere.

**TREES**
Many forests of evergreen trees spread throughout the world. *Araucaria* were conifers. A fossilized cone is pictured, left.

### DIVERSITY
In the early Jurassic Period, the maximum size of dinosaurs increased, and this trend continued throughout the period. Because of this, mammals (such as *Sinoconodon*, above) and lizards, tended to be rather small in order to maintain their ecological niches. In the seas, the ichthyosaurs, a fish-like group of marine reptiles, were at their zenith, sharing the warm Jurassic oceans with other marine predators, including plesiosaurs, marine crocodiles, and sharks.

# ON THE LAND

**A** minor extinction event at the end of the Triassic Period led to many new groups of dinosaurs appearing during the Early Jurassic. The larger prosauropods were replaced by the giant sauropods – the largest land animals ever to have lived. Herds of these immense herbivores seem to have migrated long distances, probably causing massive damage to the environments they moved through. Once thought to be too heavy to live anywhere but in swamps, modern research shows that their legs were able to carry their weight on land. However, their lifestyle as high browsers has been called into question lately, as some palaeontologists have presented evidence suggesting that some could not raise their long necks much above shoulder height.

Jurassic theropod dinosaurs became a little more varied than the Triassic forms. Two main groups existed – the large carnosaurs, and the small, lightly built coelurosaurs.

The Jurassic also saw the first appearances of the armoured and plated ornithischian dinosaurs – the ankylosaurs and the stegosaurs.

Despite competition from dinosaurs, early mammals were continuing to diversify into a variety of forms, although remaining small and probably nocturnal animals.

| Group Theropoda | Family Coelophysidae | Time 201–189mya |
|---|---|---|

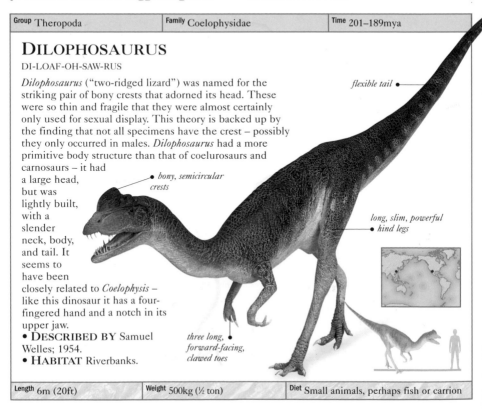

## DILOPHOSAURUS

DI-LOAF-OH-SAW-RUS

*Dilophosaurus* ("two-ridged lizard") was named for the striking pair of bony crests that adorned its head. These were so thin and fragile that they were almost certainly only used for sexual display. This theory is backed up by the finding that not all specimens have the crest – possibly they only occurred in males. *Dilophosaurus* had a more primitive body structure than that of coelurosaurs and carnosaurs – it had a large head, but was lightly built, with a slender neck, body, and tail. It seems to have been closely related to *Coelophysis* – like this dinosaur it has a four-fingered hand and a notch in its upper jaw.

*flexible tail*

*bony, semicircular crests*

*long, slim, powerful hind legs*

*three long, forward-facing, clawed toes*

• **DESCRIBED BY** Samuel Welles; 1954.
• **HABITAT** Riverbanks.

| Length 6m (20ft) | Weight 500kg (½ ton) | Diet Small animals, perhaps fish or carrion |
|---|---|---|

| Group Theropoda | Family Ceratosauridae | Time 150–144mya |
|---|---|---|

# CERATOSAURUS

KER-AT-OH-SAW-RUS

*Ceratosaurus* ("horned lizard") was named for the short horn above its nose. Another striking feature was the line of bony plates that ran down its back – so far, it is the only theropod known to have had them. It had strong, yet short, arms, with four fingers on each hand. Three of the fingers were clawed. It had a deep, broad tail, and feet with three large toes and a reduced back toe. Its teeth were long and blade-like. Although it superficially resembled a carnosaur such as *Allosaurus*, it was more primitive, and its tail was flexible rather than stiffened with bony ligaments as was the case with the carnosaurs.

• **DESCRIBED BY** Othniel C. Marsh; 1884.
• **HABITAT** Forested plains.

light skull

body balanced at hips

saurischian hip structure

three long, forward-facing, clawed toes

flattened snout horn

bony plates running along back

blade-like teeth

long, flexible tail

four-fingered hand

long, powerful hind legs

long foot

reduced back toe

| Length 4.5–6m (15–20ft) | Weight 1 tonne (1 ton) | Diet Herbivorous dinosaurs, other reptiles |
|---|---|---|

| Group Theropoda | Family Tetanurae | Time 160–155mya |
|---|---|---|

# GASOSAURUS

GAS-OH-SAW-RUS

This theropod was given its unusual name ("gas lizard") in honour of the Dashanpu gas-mining company, which was working in the quarry where the fossil remains were excavated. The single species *Gasosaurus constructus* is represented by a single specimen. Remains included a humerus, the pelvis, and a femur. Little is known about *Gasosaurus*, and its classification is still uncertain. It may be a primitive carnosaur; however, some features of the leg bones suggest that it may be an early coelurosaur instead. If so, it would be one of the oldest coelurosaurs so far discovered. *Gasosaurus* had the typical theropod body shape of a large head, long, powerful legs ending in three forward-facing clawed toes, and a long, stiff tail. It had very short arms, but they were longer than those of later carnosaurs.

• **DESCRIBED BY** Dong and Tang; 1985.

• **HABITAT** Woodland.

**RECONSTRUCTION**
This computer-enhanced reconstruction of the skeleton was based on information from other carnosaurs.

bulky body

stiffened tail

large jaws with sharp teeth

relatively long arms

heavily built hind legs

three forward-facing clawed toes

| Length 4m (13ft) | Weight 150kg (330lb) | Diet Large herbivorous dinosaurs |
|---|---|---|

| Group Theropoda | Family Allosauroidea | Time 175–163mya |
|---|---|---|

# PIATNITZKYSAURUS

PEAT-NYITS-KEE-SAW-RUS

*Piatnitzkysaurus*, whose name means "Piatnitzky lizard", seems to have been a tetanuran (stiff-tailed) theropod. Two partial skeletons have been excavated to date, and its exact classification is still under debate by palaeontologists. It had a very similar body to *Allosaurus* (p.64), but its arms were longer. Its head was large, and was carried

on a short, muscular neck. A pair of bony crests ran from between the eyes to the end of the snout. The arms were relatively small, with three clawed fingers on each hand. The body was bulky, and the tail was long and stiff.

*paired bony crests on snout*

*short, powerful arms*

- **DESCRIBED BY** José Bonaparte; 1979.
- **HABITAT** Woodland.

| Length 4.3m (14ft) | Weight 400kg (880lb) | Diet Herbivorous dinosaurs |
|---|---|---|

| Group Theropoda | Family Megalosauridae | Time 164–159mya |
|---|---|---|

# MEGALOSAURUS

MEG A LOH SAW-RUS

The first dinosaur to be scientifically named and identified, *Megalosaurus* ("great lizard") was a large, bulky, carnivorous theropod. It had a massive head carried on a short, muscular neck. Its arms and fingers were short, but strong. Fossil trackways found in southern England show how *Megalosaurus* walked with its toes pointing slightly inwards, with its tail probably swinging from side to side for balance.

- **DESCRIBED BY** William Buckland; 1824.
- **HABITAT** Forests.

*sharp, serrated teeth*

**LOWER JAW**

*three fingers with short claws*

*long, stiff tail*

*powerfully muscled hind legs*

*three-toed feet*

| Length 9m (30ft) | Weight 1–2 tonnes (1–2 tons) | Diet Large herbivorous dinosaurs |
|---|---|---|

| Group Theropoda | Family Allosauridae | Time 150–145mya |
|---|---|---|

# ALLOSAURUS

AL-OH-SAW-RUS

*Allosaurus* ("different lizard") was the most abundant, and probably the largest, predator in the late Jurassic period in the lands that were to become North America. It was typical of its family of meat-eating dinosaurs, with a massive head, short neck, and bulky body. Its tail was long and deep, with a thin, stiff end. Its three-fingered forelimbs were strong, with large claws. *Allosaurus* had distinctive bony bumps over the eyes, and a narrow ridge of bone running between them down to the tip of the snout. These features may have been used for display. Although the head was massive, it was lightened by several large openings (fenestrae) between the bones. Expandable joints between the skull bones allowed the jaws to gape open sideways to swallow large mouthfuls. Despite its large size and lack of speed, some palaeontologists believe that *Allosaurus* was agile enough to fell the giant plant-eating dinosaurs of the time.

• **DESCRIBED BY** Othniel C. Marsh, 1877.

• **HABITAT** Plains.

*distinctive ridge of bone along snout*

*teeth with serrated front and back edges*

| Length 12m (39ft) | Weight 2–3 tonnes (2–3 tons) | Diet Herbivorous dinosaurs, carrion |
|---|---|---|

*massive skull lightened by large fenestrae (openings)*

*5–10cm- (2½– 5in-) long teeth*

*large attachment points for powerful jaw muscles*

*powerful upper jaw had an axe-like action*

*blade-like teeth for slicing*

**FOSSIL SKULL**

**OTHNIEL C. MARSH**
The greatest dinosaur palaeontologist of the 19th century, Othniel C. Marsh, named *Allosaurus*.

*tail held outstretched for balance*

## FOSSIL FINDS

Many complete skeletons of Allosaurus have been excavated. Many partial skeletons have been found in the Cleveland-Lloyd Dinosaur Quarry in Utah. This site is thought to have been a place where herbivorous dinosaurs became stuck in mud and attracted predators, which also became trapped as they attacked the helpless prey.

| Group Theropoda | Family Uncertain | Time 157–156mya |
|---|---|---|

# XUANHANOSAURUS

SCHWAN-HAN-OH-SAW-RUS

This poorly understood theropod ("Xuan lizard") was named for Xuanhan County in Sichuan Province, China, where its fossils were found. At present, it is known only from vertebrae and bones from the shoulder, arm, and hand. *Xuanhanosaurus* seems to have been a *Megalosaurus*-like tetanuran theropod. It is shown here with long, powerful hind legs, clawed feet with three forward-facing toes, a large head, and a long stiff tail held outstretched for balance. The hands were short, with robust claws. The arms were very well developed and strong, despite their short length: the humerus (upper arm bone) is slightly longer than the bones of the lower arm. Its discoverer has suggested that, although it was probably mainly bipedal, it walked on all-fours for at least some of the time.
• **DESCRIBED BY** Zhiming Dong; 1984.
• **HABITAT** Forests.

*stiff tail held outstretched for balance*

| Length 6m (20ft) | Weight 250kg (550lb) | Diet Meat |
|---|---|---|

| Group Theropoda | Family Ornitholestidae | Time 156–145mya |
|---|---|---|

# ORNITHOLESTES

OR-NITH-OH-LESS-TEES

*Ornitholestes* ("bird robber") was a close relative of *Coelophysis* (see p.45). It was a slim, lightly-built dinosaur, with a small head, many conical teeth, and an S-shaped neck. A long, tapering tail contributed to greater agility when running. Its name arose because its grasping hands, light build, and long hind limbs indicated that it may have been adapted to the pursuit of Jurassic birds. Its arms were short and strong; its hands had three long, clawed fingers. An additional finger was very small. The snout bore a small, bony crest. *Ornitholestes* had many bird-like features, and its wrist structure allowed it to tuck its hands up close to its body in the same manner that a bird folds its wings.
• **DESCRIBED BY** Henry F. Osborn; 1903.
• **HABITAT** Forests.

*long, flexible neck*

*bird-like clawed feet*

*three long and one short finger on each hand*

| Length 2m (6½ft) | Weight 12kg (26lb) | Diet Meat, perhaps including birds, carrion |
|---|---|---|

skin may have
had distinctive
markings

large head

strong, well-developed
arms

three clawed fingers
on each hand

three long,
forward-facing,
clawed toes

very long, thin,
tapering tail

tail held
outstretched

small crest
on snout

body balanced
at hip

**FOSSIL-HUNTING EXPEDITION**
Leading US palaeontologist Henry F.
Osborn (1857–1935) undertook many
fossil-hunting expeditions in Mongolia
and the USA in the 1900s.

| Group Theropoda | Family Compsognathidae | Time 155–145mya |
|---|---|---|

# COMPSOGNATHUS

COMP-SOG-NAY-THUS

This theropod, whose name means "pretty jaw", was about the size of a modern chicken, making it one of the smallest known dinosaurs. Its skeletal structure shows that it must have been a fast runner – its bones were hollow, its shins were much longer than its thighs, and its long tail was held outstretched for balance. Its arms were short, probably with three fingers. Its feet were very bird-like, with three clawed toes facing forwards. *Compsognathus* was anatomically very similar to *Archaeopteryx* (p.102), with the exception of wings, and lived in similar areas. The presence of primitive feathers on a closely related genus – *Sinosauropteryx* – suggests that *Compsognathus* could also have had a downy body covering, although there is no direct evidence for this.

• **DESCRIBED BY** Johann A. Wagner; 1859.

• **HABITAT** Warm, moist areas and scrub.

relatively large eyes

slim, pointed head and snout

| Length 70cm (24in) | Weight 3kg (6½lb) | Diet Small lizards, mammals |
|---|---|---|

lightweight body
balanced at hips

tail held stiffly out
for balance

slim, short thighs

bones in stomach
region

poorly preserved
hand may have had
three fingers

## ADULT REMAINS

Only two skeletons of *Compsognathus* have
been found – an adult and a juvenile
specimen. The adult was found with a
skeleton inside. At first it was thought that
this was of a foetus, but it turned out to be
a lizard (*Bavarisaurus*).

| Group Prosauropoda | Family Anchisauridae | Time 190mya |
|---|---|---|

# ANCHISAURUS

AN-CHEE-SAW-RUS

*Anchisaurus* was an early prosauropod. It had a small head with a narrow snout, a long, flexible neck, and a slim body and tail. Although its arms were a third shorter than its legs, it spent most of its time on all fours. The thumbs had a large claw that may have been used for defence.
• **DESCRIBED BY**
Othniel C. Marsh, 1885.
• **HABITAT**
Woodland.

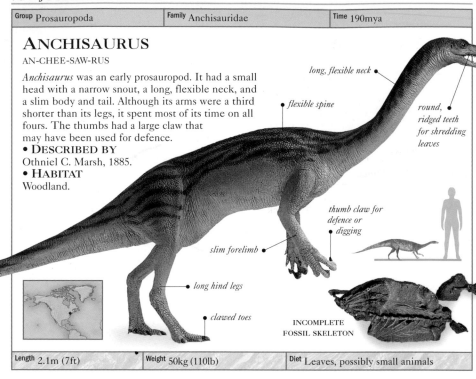

long, flexible neck

flexible spine

round, ridged teeth for shredding leaves

thumb claw for defence or digging

slim forelimb

long hind legs

clawed toes

INCOMPLETE FOSSIL SKELETON

| Length 2.1m (7ft) | Weight 50kg (110lb) | Diet Leaves, possibly small animals |
|---|---|---|

| Group Prosauropoda | Family Massospondylidae | Time 208–204mya |
|---|---|---|

# MASSOSPONDYLUS

MASS-OH-SPON-DI-LUSS

*Massospondylus* ("massive vertebrae") was named for the first remains found – a few large vertebrae. Many fossil finds have now been made, and it appears to have been the most common prosauropod in what is now southern Africa.

*Massospondylus* had a tiny head on a long, flexible neck. It probably spent most of its time on all fours, but could rear up on its hind legs to feed from trees. It had massive, five-fingered hands that could be used for holding food or for walking on. Each thumb had a large, curved claw. The front teeth were rounded, and the back ones had flat sides, indicating a tough plant diet. There may also have been a horny beak on the lower jaw. Gizzard stones have been found with some skeletons.
• **DESCRIBED BY** Richard Owen; 1854.
• **HABITAT** Scrubland and desert plains.

extremely long, flexible neck

hands with massive span

| Length 4m (13ft) | Weight 150kg (330lb) | Diet Plants, possibly small animals |
|---|---|---|

| Group Prosauropoda | Family Melanorosauridae | Time 200–195mya |

# LUFENGOSAURUS

LOO-FUNG-OH-SAW-RUS

*Lufengosaurus* ("lizard from Lufeng") was a heavy, stout-limbed prosauropod. Its small head held many widely spaced teeth that were shaped like leaves, a typical feature of prosauropod dinosaurs. Its lower jaw was hinged below the level of the upper teeth. This gave the jaw muscles greater leverage for feeding on tough plant material. Its broad feet had four long toes, and its large hands had long, clawed fingers; the thumbs bore a massive claw. *Lufengosaurus* would have moved around on all fours most of the time, sometimes rearing up and stretching out its long neck to feed on cycad or conifer trees.

• **DESCRIBED BY** Chung Chien Young; 1941.
• **HABITAT** Desert plains.

relatively large, deep head

bulky, heavy body

paired pubic bones projected back

hands with large span to support weight when walking

| Length 6m (20ft) | Weight 1–3 tonnes (1–3 tons) | Diet Cycad and conifer leaves |

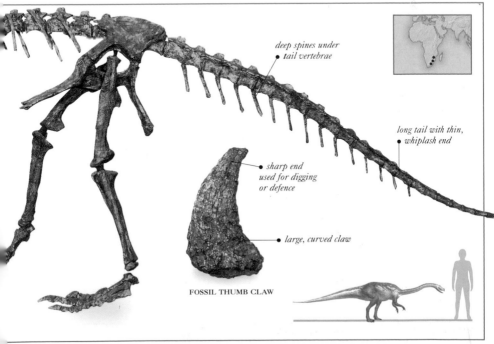

deep spines under tail vertebrae

long tail with thin, whiplash end

sharp end used for digging or defence

large, curved claw

**FOSSIL THUMB CLAW**

| Group Sauropoda | Family Vulcanodontidae | Time 208–201mya |
|---|---|---|

# VULCANODON

VUL-KAN-UH-DON

*Vulcanodon* was named after the volcanic rock in which the first skeleton was found. With the skeleton were seven teeth, which actually came from a predator that may have eaten it. One of the earliest sauropods known, *Vulcanodon* had blunt claws on its feet and an enlarged claw on each inner toe.
• **DESCRIBED BY** Raath; 1972.
• **HABITAT** Forested plains.

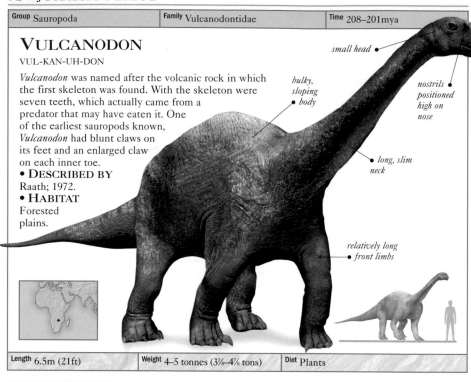

small head •

bulky, sloping • body

nostrils • positioned high on nose

long, slim • neck

relatively long • front limbs

| Length 6.5m (21ft) | Weight 4–5 tonnes (3⅞–4⅞ tons) | Diet Plants |
|---|---|---|

| Group Sauropoda | Family Cetiosauridae | Time 170–160mya |
|---|---|---|

# SHUNOSAURUS

SHOON-OH-SAW-RUS

Nearly complete skeletons of *Shunosaurus* ("Shuno lizard") have been discovered, meaning it will be only the second sauropod to be known in its entirety. The skull is long and low with small teeth. A surprising feature is the small bony club at the end of its tail, formed by enlarged vertebrae (not seen in the pictured specimen).
• **DESCRIBED BY** Dong, Zhou, and Zhang; 1983.
• **HABITAT** Plains.

long, flexible neck •

low head • with large nostrils

relatively short forelegs •

| Length 10m (33ft) | Weight 10.1 tonnes (10 tons) | Diet Plants |
|---|---|---|

| Group Sauropoda | Family Vulcanodontidae | Time 189–176mya |
|---|---|---|

# BARAPASAURUS

BA-RAP-A-SAW-RUS

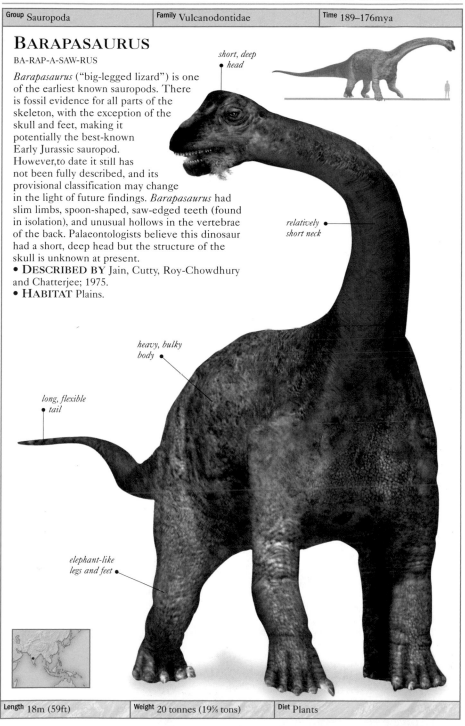

*Barapasaurus* ("big-legged lizard") is one of the earliest known sauropods. There is fossil evidence for all parts of the skeleton, with the exception of the skull and feet, making it potentially the best-known Early Jurassic sauropod. However, to date it still has not been fully described, and its provisional classification may change in the light of future findings. *Barapasaurus* had slim limbs, spoon-shaped, saw-edged teeth (found in isolation), and unusual hollows in the vertebrae of the back. Palaeontologists believe this dinosaur had a short, deep head but the structure of the skull is unknown at present.

• **DESCRIBED BY** Jain, Cutty, Roy-Chowdhury and Chatterjee; 1975.
• **HABITAT** Plains.

short, deep head

relatively short neck

heavy, bulky body

long, flexible tail

elephant-like legs and feet

| Length 18m (59ft) | Weight 20 tonnes (19¾ tons) | Diet Plants |
|---|---|---|

| Group Sauropoda | Family Diplodocidae | Time 155–145mya |
| --- | --- | --- |

# BAROSAURUS

BA-ROH-SAW-RUS

*Barosaurus* ("heavy lizard") had all the typical features of its family – a long neck and tail, a bulky body, tiny head, and relatively short legs for its size. Its limbs are indistinguishable from those of *Diplodocus* (see p.76), but its neck was much longer. Its 15 cervical vertebrae were greatly elongated – a third longer than in *Diplodocus*.

*powerful tail with whiplash end*

*Barosaurus* probably roamed in herds and relied on its huge size for defence against the large predators of the time. However, its tail had a thin whiplash end and would have imparted considerable force if swung against an attacking dinosaur.

• **DESCRIBED BY** Othniel C. Marsh; 1890.
• **HABITAT** Floodplains.

*elephant-like limbs*

| Length 23–27m (75–89ft) | Weight 20 tons (19¾ tonnes) | Diet Plants |
| --- | --- | --- |

| Group Sauropoda | Family Cetiosauridae | Time 170–160mya |
| --- | --- | --- |

# CETIOSAURUS

SEE-TEE-OH-SAW-RUS

This dinosaur, whose name means "whale lizard", was discovered early in the 18th century. Its huge bones were thought to belong to some type of immense whale – hence its name. It was a large, heavy sauropod with a shorter neck and tail than other sauropods. It was also different in that its vertebrae were solid, without hollow spaces to lighten them. Its head was blunt, and contained spoon-shaped teeth. *Cetiosaurus* is thought to have roamed in large herds, at an estimated walking speed of 10mph (15kph).

• **DESCRIBED BY** Richard Owen; 1842.
• **HABITAT** Plains.

*solid centrum of vertebra*

**FOSSIL VERTEBRA**

*tail held outstretched in life*

*1.5m- (5ft-) long shoulder blade (mounted too vertically in this reconstruction)*

| Length 18m (59ft) | Weight 9 tonnes (8⅞ tons) | Diet Plants |
| --- | --- | --- |

neck probably not raised much over shoulder height

elongated vertebra of the back

front legs shorter than hind legs

VERTEBRA

single-clawed front feet

**DINOSAUR HUNTING**
The camp at Carnegie Quarry, USA, where three *Barosaurus* skeletons were found in 1922.

| Group Sauropoda | Family Omeisauridae | Time 155–145mya |
|---|---|---|

# MAMENCHISAURUS

MAH-MEN-CHI-SAW-RUS

tiny head

This dinosaur, whose name means "Mamenxi lizard", had one of the longest necks of any dinosaur. It made up more than half of the animal's total length, and contained 19 vertebrae – more than any other dinosaur. The neck vertebrae were over twice the length of those in its back, and were overlapped by long, thin, bony struts. It is thought that this restricted movement to the joint between the head and the uppermost neck bone, with the dinosaur holding its neck not much higher than shoulder height. It could then swing it widely from the shoulders to browse on low vegetation.

- **DESCRIBED BY**
Chung Chien Young; 1954.
- **HABITAT**
Deltas and forested areas.

**FOSSIL REMAINS**
Remains of *Mamenchisaurus* have been excavated from sites in China.

enormously elongated neck

back sloping from shoulders

| Length 22m (72ft) | Weight 20 tonnes (19⅔ tons) | Diet Leaves and shoots |
|---|---|---|

| Group Sauropoda | Family Diplodocidae | Time 155–145mya |
|---|---|---|

# DIPLODOCUS

DIP-LOD-OH-KUS

*Diplodocus* was one of the longest dinosaurs. Some palaeontologists think that *Seismosaurus* was actually an aged *Diplodocus*, in which case, it would be the longest yet discovered. It was lightly built, with slim limbs and a tapered tail with a whiplash end. Its name meaning "double beam", comes from the chevron bones under its tail vertebrae.

• **DESCRIBED BY** Othniel C. Marsh; 1878.
• **HABITAT** Plains.

peg-like teeth
at front of jaws

| Length 27m (87ft) | Weight 12.2 tonnes (12 tons) | Diet Leaves |
|---|---|---|

| Group Sauropoda | Family Diplodocidae | Time 154–145mya |
|---|---|---|

# APATOSAURUS

A-PAT-OH-SAW-RUS

One species of *Apatosaurus*, *A. excelsus*, was the dinosaur originally called *Brontosaurus*. This sauropod was shorter, yet heavier and bulkier than its close relatives. It had a tiny head at the end of a long neck made up of 15 vertebrae. Its back vertebrae were hollow, and its long tail had a whip-like end. Its thick hindlegs were longer than the front ones, perhaps to allow the dinosaur to rear up when feeding. Whether *Apatosaurus* could actually do this is disputed by some palaeontologists.

• **DESCRIBED BY** Othniel C. Marsh; 1877.
• **HABITAT** Wooded plains.

neck with limited mobility

tail comprising over half the total length

relatively short front legs

| Length 21m (70ft) | Weight 35 tonnes (34½ tons) | Diet Leaves |
|---|---|---|

| Group Sauropoda | Family Diplodocidae | Time 155–144mya |
|---|---|---|

# SEISMOSAURUS

SIZE-MOH-SAW-RUS

*Seismosaurus* was aptly named "earth-shaking lizard". From the one specimen found to date, it appears to have been one of the largest animals that ever lived. A few palaeontologists have suggested that *Seismosaurus* may actually be an aged *Diplodocus*. Despite its size, it was lightly built, with relatively short legs. Its neck was incredibly long and very high blood pressure would have been needed to pump blood to the head. The neck probably could not be raised very high. This would mean that *Seismosaurus* was probably a low browser.
• **DESCRIBED BY** David Gillette; 1991.
• **HABITAT** Forested plains.

shredding teeth

*extremely long neck*

*body sloped downwards to hips*

| Length 36m (120ft) | Weight 98.5 tonnes (100 tons) | Diet Leaves |
|---|---|---|

| Group Sauropoda | Family Camarasauridae | Time 150–140mya |
|---|---|---|

# CAMARASAURUS

CAM-A-RAH-SAW-RUS

*Camarasaurus* ("chambered lizard") was the commonest sauropod in North America. It appears to have roamed in large herds. This dinosaur had a relatively large, box-shaped head and short neck and tail. The vertebrae probably contained air spaces to lighten the backbone. The front legs of *Camarasaurus* were relatively long. Its forefeet had one single claw, and the hindfeet three.
• **DESCRIBED BY** Edward Drinker Cope; 1877.
• **HABITAT** Plains.

nasal chambers high on snout

**FOSSIL SKULL**

*short head*

*massive, heavy body*

*single claw on front feet*

| Length 23m (75ft) | Weight 20.3 tonnes (20 tons) | Diet Tough vegetation |
|---|---|---|

| Group Sauropoda | Family Brachiosauridae | Time 150–145mya |
|---|---|---|

# BRACHIOSAURUS
BRACK-EE-OH-SAW-RUS

*Brachiosaurus* ("arm lizard") is known from all parts of the skeleton except for the important neural arches of the vertebrae at the base of the neck. It was one of the tallest and largest sauropods, and the one in which the lengthening of the forelimbs relative to the hindlimbs reached its extreme. Together with its long neck, ending in a small head, *Brachiosaurus'* giraffe-like stance gave it a great height: up to 16m (50ft). The tail was relatively short and thick. Like other members of its family, *Brachiosaurus* had chisel-like teeth – 26 on each jaw – towards the front of the mouth. The nostrils were large and were situated on a bulge on the top of the head. The legs were pillar-like, and the feet all had five toes with fleshy pads behind. The first toe of each front foot bore a claw, as did the first three toes of the hind feet. Like other sauropods, it probably travelled in herds. *Brachiosaurus* was adapted for feeding off vegetation from the tops of trees. The length of its neck means that it would have had to have an extremely large, powerful heart, and very high blood pressure to pump blood up to its head. *Brachiosaurus* is thought to have laid its eggs while walking, leaving the young to fend for themselves.
• **DESCRIBED BY** Elmer S. Riggs; 1903.
• **HABITAT** Plains.

*chisel-like teeth at front of mouth*

*long neck made up of 1m- (3ft-) long vertebrae*

*ball-like head of femur*

### MASSIVE BONES
The femur (thigh bone) of *Brachiosaurus* was over 1.8m (6ft) long and massively thick to support the dinosaur's weight. One of the first bones discovered by Elmer S. Riggs, in 1900, was the humerus (upper arm bone). It was over 2.1m (7ft) long, which was so much greater than that of any known humerus, that Riggs thought it was a crushed femur of an *Apatosaurus* (p.76).

| Length 26m (85ft) | Weight 50 tonnes (49½ tons) | Diet Plants |
|---|---|---|

*nostrils on bulge on top of head*

*body sloping downwards from shoulder to hip*

*relatively slim, pillar-like legs*

| Group Ornithiscia | Family Lesothosauridae | Time 208–203mya |
|---|---|---|

# LESOTHOSAURUS

LE-SOO-TOE-SAW-RUS

*Lesothosaurus* ("Lesotho lizard") was an early bipedal herbivorous dinosaur, perhaps the same genus as *Fabrosaurus* (see Glossary). It was small and built for speed, with a lightly-built body, long, slim legs, and a thin, flexible tail. It had pointed front teeth, serrated, arrow-shaped cheek teeth,

THIGH BONE

femoral head

muscle attachment point

large eyes

short arms

long, powerful hind legs

long feet allowed fast running

and its jaws moved only up and down, not from side to side. During chewing, its upper teeth fitted alternately between the lower ones, producing a chopping motion. It may have been an omnivore, and possibly hibernated underground through the driest months of the year.
• **DESCRIBED BY** Peter M. Galton; 1978.
• **HABITAT** Desert plains.

| Length 1m (39in) | Weight 4–7kg (9–15lb) | Diet Leaves, perhaps carrion and insects |
|---|---|---|

| Group Thyreophora | Family Scelidosauridae | Time 208–194mya |
|---|---|---|

# SCELIDOSAURUS

SCEL-EYE-DOH-SAW-RUS

This small, heavy, armoured dinosaur, whose name means "lower hind limb lizard", seems to be one of the earliest and most primitive ornithischians. Its classification as either a primitive stegosaur or ankylosaur is still open to debate. It had impressive defensive armour: its back was covered with bony plates, and studded with a double row of bony spikes. Additional rows of studs ran along its sides, and there was a pair of triple-spiked bony plates behind the neck. The head was small and pointed with a horny beak, and small, leaf-shaped teeth. Although the forelimbs were much shorter than the hind limbs, *Scelidosaurus* seems to have walked on all fours.
• **DESCRIBED BY** Richard Owen; 1861.
• **HABITAT** Woodland.

underside of tail covered by bony studs

three long, one short, clawed digits

longer feet than later thyreophorans

FOSSIL FOOT

| Length 3.5m (11ft) | Weight 250kg (550lb) | Diet Plants |
|---|---|---|

| Group Thyreophora | Family Scutellosauridae | Time 200–195mya |
|---|---|---|

# SCUTELLOSAURUS

SCOO-TELL-OH SAW-RUS

This "little shield lizard" had a long body and slim limbs. Its arms were also relatively long and slender. Over 300 low, bony studs covered its back, flanks, and the base of its tail to form a defensive armour. *Scutellosaurus* probably fed and rested on all fours, but ran away from predators on its hind legs, holding its tail stiffly out behind it to counter-balance the weight of the bony armour.
• **DESCRIBED BY** Edwin H. Colbert; 1981.
• **HABITAT** Woodland.

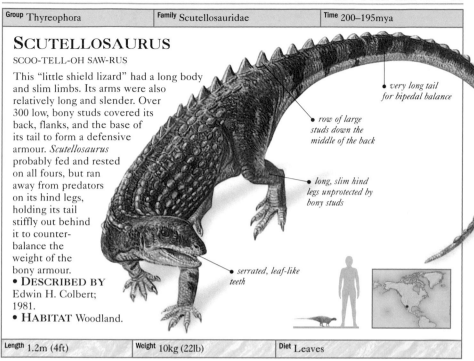

*very long tail for bipedal balance*

*row of large studs down the middle of the back*

*long, slim hind legs unprotected by bony studs*

*serrated, leaf-like teeth*

| Length 1.2m (4ft) | Weight 10kg (22lb) | Diet Leaves |
|---|---|---|

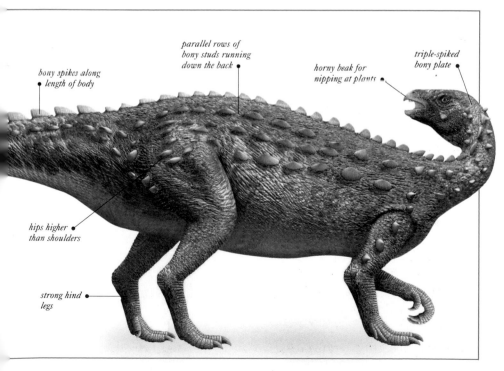

*bony spikes along length of body*

*parallel rows of bony studs running down the back*

*horny beak for nipping at plants*

*triple-spiked bony plate*

*hips higher than shoulders*

*strong hind legs*

| Group Stegosauria | Family Stegosauridae | Time 155–144mya |
|---|---|---|

# STEGOSAURUS

STEG-OH SAW-RUS

*Stegosaurus* ("roof lizard") was the largest plated dinosaur. It had a tiny head, toothless beak, and two rows of bony plates running from behind its neck to halfway along its tail. Some of these plates were over 60cm (24in) high. The tail also had long spikes, each up to 1m (39in) long, the number of which varied between species. The dinosaur's neck was also armoured with many tiny bony studs. The hind legs were twice as long as the forelegs, meaning that the body's highest point was at the hips. *Stegosaurus* had a toothless beak and small, weak cheek teeth, so it probably used gizzard stones to aid digestion.

- **DESCRIBED BY** Othniel C. Marsh; 1877.
- **HABITAT** Woodland.

pointed tip •

very sharp, bony tail spikes •

FOSSIL PLATE

FOSSIL TAIL SPIKE

## PLATES AND SPIKES

Some reconstructions of *Stegosaurus* have the plates arranged in pairs or in a zigzag pattern along the back. However, no one is sure exactly how the plates were arranged.

| Length 6m (20ft) | Weight 2 tonnes (2 tons) | Diet Plants |
|---|---|---|

very small
braincase

plates graduated
in size along
the tail

tail spikes varied
in number
between species

massive
body

long spines on
tail vertebrae

SKELETAL RECONSTRUCTION

covering of skin
or tough horn
over plates

| Group Stegosauria | Family Stegosauridae | Time 156–150mya |
|---|---|---|

# KENTROSAURUS

KEN-TRO-SAW-RUS

This East African contemporary of *Stegosaurus* was smaller than its more famous relative, but as well protected. *Kentrosaurus* ("spiked lizard") had paired rectangular plates running down over the neck, shoulders, and half of the back. Over the hips, the plates gave way to sharp spikes, which ran in pairs down to the tip of the tail. Another pair of long spikes jutted out from the hips on each side. The skull, housing a tiny brain, is known only from fragments, but was probably long and slender with a toothless, horny beak.
• **DESCRIBED BY** Edwin Henning; 1915.
• **HABITAT** Forests.

*pairs of sharp spikes from mid back to tail tip*

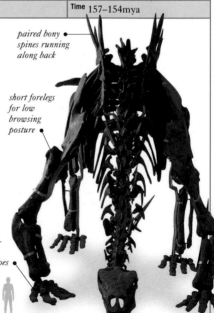

| Length 5m (16ft) | Weight 1.5 tonnes (1½ tons) | Diet Low-lying vegetation |
|---|---|---|

| Group Stegosauria | Family Stegosauridae | Time 157–154mya |
|---|---|---|

# TUOJIANGOSAURUS

TOO-YANG-OH-SAW-RUS

*Tuojiangosaurus* ("Tuojiang lizard") was similar in appearance to *Kentrosaurus*. Fifteen pairs of pointed spines ran down over the neck, shoulders, and back. These became taller and more pointed over the hips and the base of the tail. The end of the tail was armoured with two pairs of long spikes. Unlike *Stegosaurus*, another member of the same family, *Tuojiangosaurus* did not have tall vertebral spines over its hips and lower back. It could probably not rear up to feed from trees, and was a low browser instead. The head was long and low, with small cheek teeth and a horny beak at the front of the snout.
• **DESCRIBED BY** Dong, Li, Zhou and Zhang; 1973.
• **HABITAT** Forests.

*paired bony spines running along back*

*short forelegs for low browsing posture*

*long, forward-facing, clawed toes*

| Length 7m (23ft) | Weight 4.1 tonnes (4 tons) | Diet Low-lying vegetation |
|---|---|---|

paired bony plates
running down neck
and upper back

large body
cavity

small,
sloping
head

relatively long,
sturdily built
hind legs

forelegs much shorter
than hind legs for
low browsing

| Group Ankylosauria | Family Ankylosauridae | Time 156–145mya |
|---|---|---|

# GARGOYLEOSAURUS

GAR-GOYL-EE-OH-SAW-RUS

*Gargoyleosaurus* "gargoyle lizard" was a primitive,
early ankylosaur with body armour formed from
irregular, bony oval plates on the
upper surface of its body and tail.
The hind legs were slightly longer
than the front ones. *Gargoyleosaurus*
had many features unusual among
ankylosaurs, including teeth on both the
upper and lower jaw, a straight nasal passage,
and hollow armour plates. The skull shows
features seen in late Cretaceous ankylosaurs,
including fusion of bone armour to the surface
of the skull and jaw.
• **DESCRIBED BY** Kenneth Carpenter
et al; 1998.
• **HABITAT** Woodland.

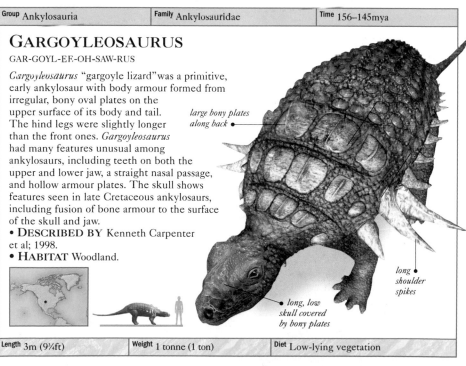

large bony plates
along back

long
shoulder
spikes

long, low
skull covered
by bony plates

| Length 3m (9¾ft) | Weight 1 tonne (1 ton) | Diet Low-lying vegetation |
|---|---|---|

| Group Ornithopoda | Family Heterodontosauridae | Time 208–200mya |

# HETERODONTOSAURUS
### HET-ER-OH-DONT-OH-SAW-RUS

As its name ("different-toothed lizard") suggests, the most remarkable feature of this small bipedal dinosaur was its teeth. *Heterodontosaurus* had three kinds: cutting incisors at the front of the upper jaw, two pairs of large tusk-like teeth, and tall chisel-like teeth used for shredding vegetation. The tusks may have been used for defence, or they may have occurred in males only and been used for sexual display.

- **DESCRIBED BY** Crompton and Charig; 1962.
- **HABITAT** Scrub.

*long tail for counterbalance when running* •

• *tusks possibly only present in males*

*hands capable of grasping and supporting weight for four-legged walking* •

*three long, • forward-facing, clawed toes*

*cutting incisors* •

• *shredding cheek teeth*

**FOSSIL SKULL**

*bony rods stiffened back and tail* •

*horny beak* •

**SKELETON FOSSILIZED IN CLAY**

| Length 1.2m (4ft) | Weight 19kg (42lb) | Diet Leaves, tubers, possibly insects |

| Group Ornithopoda | Family Dryosauridae | Time 156–145mya |
|---|---|---|

# DRYOSAURUS
DRY-OH-SAW-RUS

*Dryosaurus* ("oak lizard") was a lightly built bipedal herbivore, with powerful, slender legs that were much longer than the arms. It was a swift runner. The tail was

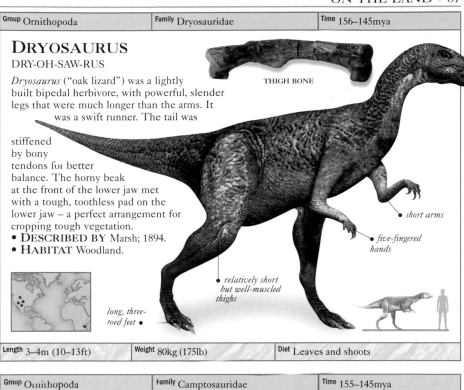

THIGH BONE

stiffened by bony tendons for better balance. The horny beak at the front of the lower jaw met with a tough, toothless pad on the lower jaw – a perfect arrangement for cropping tough vegetation.
• **DESCRIBED BY** Marsh; 1894.
• **HABITAT** Woodland.

short arms

five-fingered hands

relatively short but well-muscled thighs

long, three-toed feet •

| Length 3–4m (10–13ft) | Weight 80kg (175lb) | Diet Leaves and shoots |
|---|---|---|

| Group Ornithopoda | Family Camptosauridae | Time 155–145mya |
|---|---|---|

# CAMPTOSAURUS
KAMP-TOE-SAW-RUS

*Camptosaurus* ("bent lizard") was a bulky plant-eater that browsed on plants and shrubs close to the ground. Its head was long and low, with a sharp, horny beak at the tip of the broad snout. The pubis was shifted back to allow more space for the

sigmoid curve in neck indicating head was held low

tail stiffened by bony ligaments

four-toed hind feet

intestines. Its arms were shorter than its legs, but a large wrist and hoof-like claws on its fingers allowed it to walk on its hands. *Camptosaurus* probably browsed on all fours, rising onto its powerful hind legs to run.
• **DESCRIBED BY** Othniel C. Marsh; 1885.
• **HABITAT** Open woodland.

| Length 5–7m (16–23ft) | Weight 750kg (¾ ton) | Diet Low-growing herbs and shrubs |
|---|---|---|

| Group Mammalia | Family Sinocodontidae | Time 208mya |
|---|---|---|

# SINOCONODON

SINE-OH-CO-DON

*Sinoconodon* ("Chinese spiky tooth") was a small, primitive mammal resembling a modern shrew. Its skull structure, despite retaining some minor synapsid features, showed that it was truly mammalian. In particular, the structures housing the inner ear are similar to those of true mammals. Although the cheek-teeth were permanent, as in living mammals, its other teeth were still replaced, perhaps several times, during its lifetime. The rear of the braincase had expanded and the eye socket was large. *Sinoconodon* was apparently "warm-blooded", and was probably covered in fur. It was a quadruped, with five long, clawed toes on each foot, and a long tail. The snout was long and slim.
• **DESCRIBED BY** Patterson and Olsen; 1961.
• **HABITAT** Woodland.

*long, flexible tail* •

| Length 10–15cm (4–6in) | Weight 30–80g (1–2⅞oz) | Diet Probably mainly insects |
|---|---|---|

| Group Mammaliaformes | Family Docodontidae | Time 150–144mya |
|---|---|---|

# DOCODON

DOH-CO-DON

*probably fur-covered body* •

Docodon ("beam tooth") was a mouse-sized, close mammal relative. So far, this genus is known only from remains of teeth. These had very complex tooth cusp patterns, allowing *Docodon* to chew food effectively. It appears to have been a rodent-like animal, and was probably warm blooded.
• **DESCRIBED BY** Othniel C. Marsh 1880.
• **HABITAT** Forests.

• *five-toed feet*

| Length 10cm (4in) | Weight 20–50g (¾–1¾oz) | Diet Possibly omnivorous |
|---|---|---|

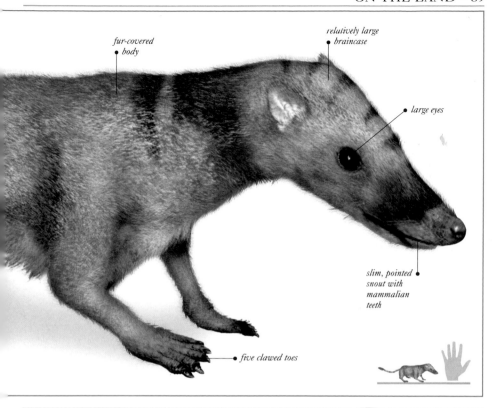

*fur-covered body*

*relatively large braincase*

*large eyes*

*slim, pointed snout with mammalian teeth*

*five clawed toes*

| Group Mammalia | Family Triconodontidae | Time 150 144mya |
| --- | --- | --- |

# TRICONODON

TRY-CON-OH-DON

*Triconodon* ("three-spiked tooth") was a small raccoon- or possum-like primitive mammal. Originally classed in the same group as *Eozostrodon* (p. 51), recent analysis shows that it was a true mammal, perhaps a marsupial. Its teeth were rather unspecialized and versatile, suggesting an omnivorous lifestyle, including insects and small reptiles. The development of a mammalian middle ear seems to have coincided with an increase in brain size.
• **DISCOVERED** Richard Owen; 1859.
• **HABITAT** Woodland.

*molars with three sharp points*

*large teeth at the front of the jaw*

**FOSSIL JAWBONE**

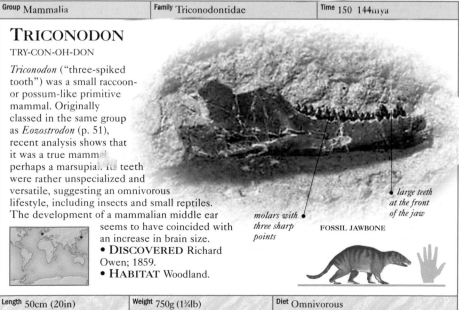

| Length 50cm (20in) | Weight 750g (1¾lb) | Diet Omnivorous |
| --- | --- | --- |

# IN THE WATER

**J**urassic oceans teemed with fish, giant ammonites, and squid, sharks, and the first rays. There were also extensive ranges of coral reefs. The nothosaurs and the placodonts died out at the end of the Triassic Period, and were replaced by the plesiosaurs. These were more adapted for marine life, and lived in both sea and fresh water. There were two main groups: the long-necked plesiosaurs, which had a short body and tail and a long neck with a small head; and the pliosaurs. These were generally larger than the plesiosaurs and had a relatively short neck and large head. The two groups appear to have occupied different hunting niches, with the plesiosaurs feeding in shallow or surface waters, and the pliosaurs hunting at greater depths.

Ichthyosaurs survived into the Jurassic, and many new forms appeared. Some of these reached immense sizes. They all had half-moon shaped tail fins, and swam using their tails for propulsion rather than their paddles. Fossil remains of some ichthyosaurs are quite remarkable – fossil droppings and stomach contents have often been found. This evidence shows that their diet consisted of small fish and cephalopods. Numerous fossils have also been found of young ichthyosaurs inside the body of an adult, or emerging tail-first from an adult's body. This is the same way that modern dolphins give birth.

In the late Jurassic, ichthyosaurs seem to have become rarer, possibly because of competition from the more modern forms of fish that had evolved.

| Group Ichthyosauria | Family Leptopterygidae | Time 209–194mya |
| --- | --- | --- |

## TEMNODONTOSAURUS

TEM-NOH-DON-TOH-SAW-RUS

This large ichthyosaur looked a bit like a modern dolphin. Its body was long, smooth, and streamlined, and it had a long, narrow snout, with many large teeth set into a dental groove. Its tail was large, and it had four long, narrow paddles. Unusually, the rear paddles were almost the same length as the front ones. *Temnodontosaurus* also had a large triangular dorsal fin, as did all advanced ichthyosaurs. Fossil finds of ichthyosaur young preserved inside the body of adults show that these creatures were viviparous – they gave birth to live young in the sea without having to come ashore to lay eggs.

• **DESCRIBED BY** William D. Conybeare; 1922.

• **HABITAT** Shallow seas.

nostrils set far back on snout •

• narrow snout

large teeth set • into groove

| Length 9m (30ft) | Weight 15 tonnes (14¾ tons) | Diet Large squid and ammonites |
| --- | --- | --- |

| Group Ichthyosauria | Family Ichthyosauridae | Time 206–140mya |
|---|---|---|

# ICHTHYOSAURUS

IK-THEE-OH-SAW-RUS

Many hundred complete skeletons of *Ichthyosaurus* have been discovered, making it one of the best-known of all prehistoric animals. It had a high dorsal fin, and broad front paddles. The end section of the tail was angled downward to support the vertical tail fin. *Ichthyosaurus* had massive ear bones, perhaps to pick up underwater vibrations created by potential prey.

• **DESCRIBED BY** Charles Koenig; 1818.

• **HABITAT** Oceans.

*smooth skin*

*half-moon shaped tail fin*

*very short rear paddles*

*small, pointed teeth*

| Length 2m (6½ft) | Weight 90kg (200lb) | Diet Fish |
|---|---|---|

*tapered body*

*aerofoil-shaped front paddles*

*large eyes for clear vision underwater*

*large tail fin for propulsion*

| Group Ichthyosauria | Family Ichthyosauridae | Time 161–145mya |
|---|---|---|

# OPHTHALMOSAURUS

OFF-THAL-MO-SAW-RUS

It is not difficult to see why *Ophthalmosaurus* ("eye lizard") was so-named. Its eyes were the largest of any creature relative to body size. As in other ichthyosaurs, the eyes were surrounded by the sclerotic ring – a circular arrangement of bony plates that prevented the soft tissues from collapsing at high pressures. Some palaeontologists think that *Ophthalmosaurus* had such large eyes because it was a night hunter – others that it swam at very deep depths. *Ophthalmosaurus* had a teardrop-shaped body. The tail had a crescent-shaped fin. The paddles were short and broad.
• **DESCRIBED BY** C.W. Andrews; 1907.
• **HABITAT** Oceans.

*huge eye sockets*

*nostrils set high on snout, close to eyes*

*long, thin snout*

| Length 5m (16ft) | Weight 3 tonnes (3 tons) | Diet Fish, squid, other molluscs |
|---|---|---|

| Group Plesiosauroidea | Family Plesiosauridae | Time 135–120mya |
|---|---|---|

# PLESIOSAURUS

PLEEZ-EE-OH-SAW-RUS

*Plesiosaurus* was built for manoeuvrability rather than speed. It had the typical plesiosaur shape of a short and wide body that tapered towards the tail. Its neck was much longer than the body, and was very flexible. Although its head was relatively small, its jaws were long, and held many sharp, conical teeth. *Plesiosaurus* had four wide paddle-shaped flippers, which it is thought to have used in a combination of rowing (back and forth) and flying (up and down) motions.
• **DESCRIBED BY** H.T. De La Beche, William D. Conybeare; 1821.
• **HABITAT** Oceans.

*small head*

*flexible neck longer than body*

| Length 2.3m (7.6ft) | Weight 90kg (200lb) | Diet Fish, squid-like molluscs |
|---|---|---|

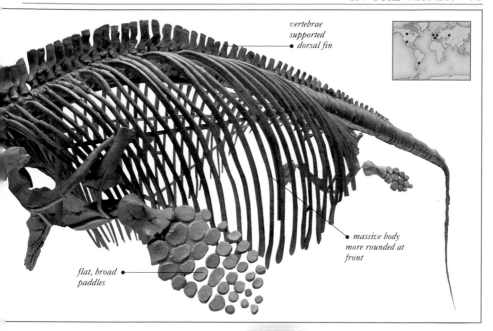

vertebrae
supported
• dorsal fin

massive body
• more rounded at
front

flat, broad •
paddles

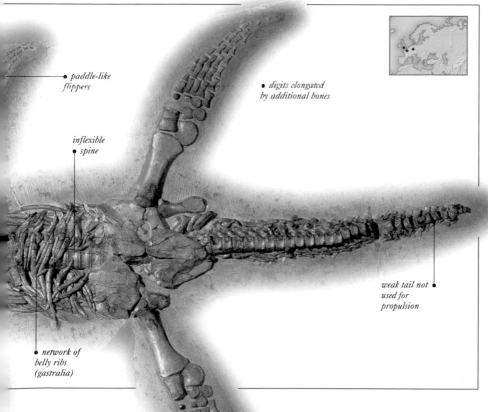

• paddle-like
flippers

• digits elongated
by additional bones

inflexible
• spine

weak tail not •
used for
propulsion

• network of
belly ribs
(gastralia)

| Group Plesiosauroidea | Family Cryptoclididae | Time 165–150mya |
|---|---|---|

# CRYPTOCLIDUS

CRIP-TOH-CLID-US

*Cryptoclidus* was a plesiosaur with a moderately long neck made up of 30 vertebrae. Its small skull had a long snout, with the nostrils set far back. Its jaw contained many sharp, pointed teeth. These interlocked when the jaw was closed to make a fine trap for small fish or shrimp-like prey. *Cryptoclidus* had a relatively short tail, and four hydrofoil-shaped flippers. These are thought to have been moved in steady, vertical strokes to propel the animal along. The belly ribs were moulded into plates that provided protection when *Cryptoclidus* came ashore to lay its eggs.

*long, relatively inflexible neck*

*collar bones formed plates under the body*

• **DESCRIBED BY** Harry G. Seeley; 1892.
• **HABITAT** Shallow oceans.

| Length 4m (13ft) | Weight 8 tonnes (8 tons) | Diet Fish, small marine animals |
|---|---|---|

| Group Pliosauroidea | Family Pliosauridae | Time 165–150mya |
|---|---|---|

# LIOPLEURODON

LIE-OH-PLOOR-OH-DON

*Liopleurodon* was a massive marine carnivore. It had a whale-like appearance, with a large, heavy head, short, thick neck, and a streamlined body. It is thought to have used its front and rear flippers in different swimming motions, with the front pair moving up and down, and the rear ones used in a kicking and turning motion. Its teeth were arranged in a rosette at the front of its mouth. It may have swum with its mouth open, allowing water to pass into its nostrils so that it could smell its prey.

*streamlined body*

• **DESCRIBED BY** H.E. Sauvage; 1873.
• **HABITAT** Oceans.

*rosette of teeth at front of jaw*

*large eyes*

| Length 10–15m (33–49ft) | Weight 20–30 tonnes (19⅝–29½ tons) | Diet Large squid, ichthyosaurs |
|---|---|---|

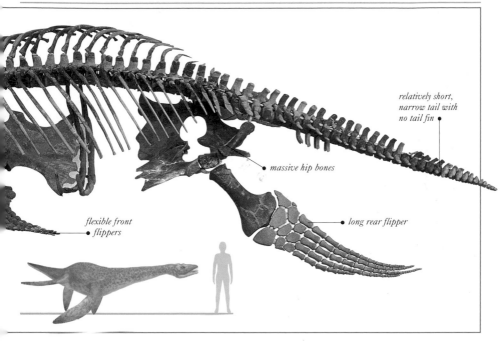

relatively short,
narrow tail with
no tail fin

massive hip bones

flexible front
flippers

long rear flipper

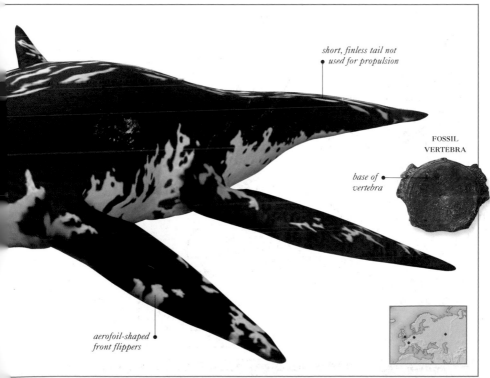

short, finless tail not
used for propulsion

FOSSIL
VERTEBRA

base of
vertebra

aerofoil-shaped
front flippers

| Group Thalattosuchia | Family Metriorhynchidae | Time 178–157mya |
|---|---|---|

## GEOSAURUS

GEE-OH-SAW-RUS

This "earth lizard" was a highly specialized aquatic crocodilian. It had a streamlined shape and had lost the heavy back armour that crocodiles normally have. Its smoother skin meant that *Geosaurus* was more manoeuvrable when swimming, and could move its body, as well as its tail, from side to side to propel itself along. It had two pairs of flippers and a large, fish-like tail fin, which was supported by a steep downward bend of the spine. One fossil specimen of *Geosaurus* was found outlined by a thin film of carbon. This showed the shape of the limbs in life. The hind flippers were longer than the front pair, which were shaped like hydrofoils. The long, slim snout was filled with sharp, pointed teeth.

• **DESCRIBED BY** Baron Georges Cuvier; 1842.
• **HABITAT** Seas.

• *vertical tail fin*

• *long, thin tail*

| Length 3m (9¾ft) | Weight 120kg (265lb) | Diet Fish |
|---|---|---|

| Group Thalattosuchia | Family Metriorhynchidae | Time 157–154mya |
|---|---|---|

## METRIORHYNCHUS

MET-REE-OR-RINE-CUS

An aquatic crocodilian, *Metriorhynchus* is thought to have come ashore only when laying eggs. It had a streamlined shape, although not as streamlined as its relative *Geosaurus*, with a long, slim head, long body, and thin tail. Its skin was smooth, reducing resistance in the water, and it had a vertical, fish-like tail fin. Moving this from side to side propelled *Metriorhynchus* through the water. Its limbs were formed into paddles, with the hindlimbs being larger than the forelimbs. Its snout was long and pointed, and the jaws had long muscles to allow the animal to open its mouth very wide. The teeth were conical.

• **DESCRIBED BY** Hermann von Meyer; 1832.
• **HABITAT** Tropical seas.

• *long snout with nostrils set far forward*

• *front paddles shorter than hind*

• *sharp, conical teeth*

| Length 3m (9¾ft) | Weight 120kg (265lb) | Diet Fish |
|---|---|---|

steep bend in
spine to support
tail fin

FOSSIL SKELETON

short neck

hind flipper

long, slim snout

nostrils at tip
of snout

sharp, pointed
teeth

hydrofoil-shaped
front flippers

smooth skin

tail fin moved
from side to side

flipper-
shaped
hindlimb

sharp downward
bend in tail

well-developed
joint surfaces for
strength when
bending

slim snout

FOSSIL SKULL

FOSSIL VERTEBRA

relatively large
eye sockets

large attachment
sites for jaw
muscles

# IN THE AIR

T he pterosaurs, which had first appeared in the Triassic Period, continued to evolve during the Jurassic, and many new forms appeared. The more advanced pterodactyls, which had a longer neck and skull, and a shorter tail than the rhamphorhynchoids, became well-established by the end of the period. The rhamphorhynchoids did not survive into the Cretaceous.

The discovery in 1971 of a fossil of the rhamphorhynchoid *Sordes* provided strong evidence that pterosaurs had a fast metabolism and were warm-blooded. Impressions in the deposits around the skeleton showed that the body was covered in a fine, dense fur, whereas the tail and wings were not.

Remains of feathered dinosaurs have been found in Jurassic deposits, and in this period, the first true bird, *Archaeopteryx*, appeared. Since its discovery in 1860, there has been great debate about its classification and its ability to fly. Despite early accusations of fraud, the presence of feathers is indisputable. They probably evolved first for insulation, and only later to improve flying efficiency. The action of wing flapping may have originated as an extension of the grabbing forearm motions that small theropods used to capture their prey. Current opinion is that *Archaeopteryx* could sustain powered flight for short distances, but was not a strong flier.

| Group Rhamphorhynchoidea | Family Dimorphodontidae | Time 175–159mya |
| --- | --- | --- |

## DIMORPHODON

DIE-MOR-FOH-DON

The most striking feature of *Dimorphodon* ("two-form tooth") was its enormous puffin-like head. It had a short neck, and a long tail. The tail could only be moved near the base, helping to steer the animal. It was probably a clumsy walker. It has been suggested that it spent most of its time hanging from cliffs or branches, from which it launched itself into flight. *Dimorphodon* had two types of teeth – long front ones and small cheek teeth.
• **DESCRIBED BY** Richard Owen; 1859.
• **HABITAT** Shores.

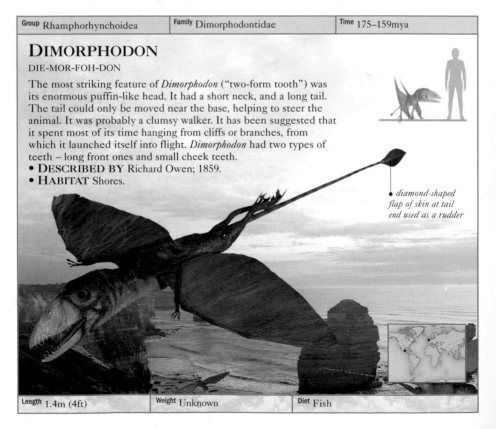

• *diamond-shaped flap of skin at tail end used as a rudder*

| Length 1.4m (4ft) | Weight Unknown | Diet Fish |
| --- | --- | --- |

| Group Rhamphorhynchoidea | Family Rhamphorhynchidae | Time 165–150mya |
|---|---|---|

# RHAMPHORHYNCHUS

RAM-FOR-RINK-US

This pterosaur is well-known from beautifully preserved specimens found along with *Archaeopteryx*. Details of the wing structure and the tail can be seen, and a throat pouch has even been preserved in a few fossils. *Rhamphorhynchus* had long narrow jaws to act as a fish spear. Its sharp teeth pointed outwards. It had a long tail with a diamond-shaped flap of skin at the end, and small legs. The wing membrane stretched down to the ankle.
• **DESCRIBED BY** Hermann von Meyer; 1847.
• **HABITAT** Shores.

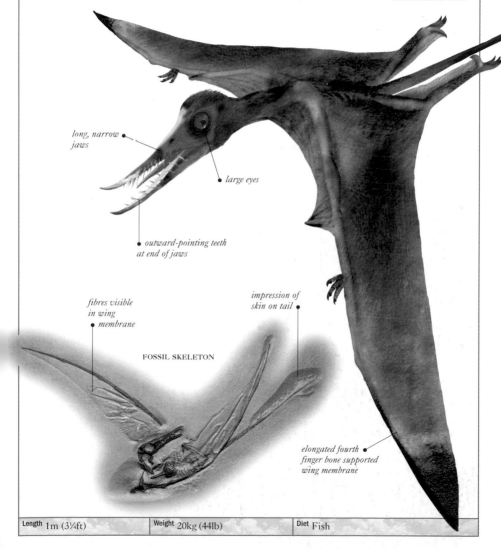

long, narrow
jaws

large eyes

outward-pointing teeth
at end of jaws

fibres visible
in wing
membrane

impression of
skin on tail

FOSSIL SKELETON

elongated fourth
finger bone supported
wing membrane

| Length 1m (3¼ft) | Weight 20kg (44lb) | Diet Fish |
|---|---|---|

| Group Rhamphorhynchoidea | Family Anurognathidae | Time 150–145mya |
|---|---|---|

# ANUROGNATHUS

AN-YOOR-OG-NATH-US

This tiny pterosaur was unlike other rhamphorhynchoids in that it only had a very short tail. In fact, its name means "without tail and jaw". Along with the short tail, its small body size would have made manoeuvring on the wing very easy. Its narrow head had short, yet strong jaws with many peg-like teeth designed for crushing or grinding. Its wings, which reached a maximum span of about 50cm (20in), were composed of a thin flap of skin that stretched from the elongated fourth finger to the ankle. A secondary wing, supported by the pteroid bone, stretched from each wrist to the neck. Some palaeontologists have surmised that *Anurognathus* spent most of their time on the backs of the huge sauropods of the period, hunting for insects from this elevated vantage point.

- **DESCRIBED BY** Doerderline; 1923.
- **HABITAT** Wooded plains.

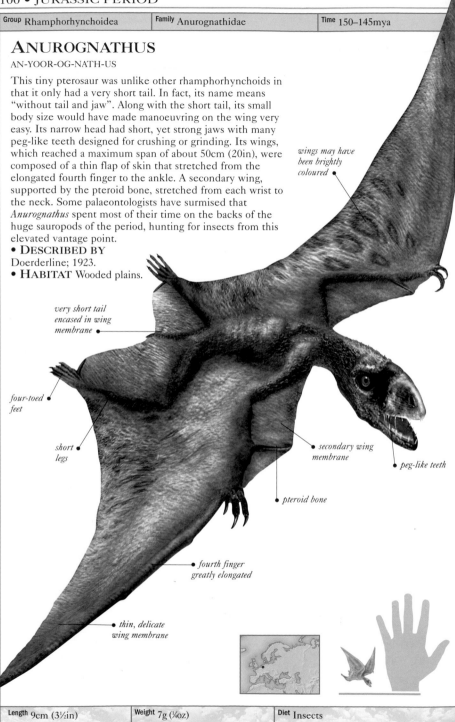

wings may have been brightly coloured

very short tail encased in wing membrane

four-toed feet

short legs

secondary wing membrane

peg-like teeth

pteroid bone

fourth finger greatly elongated

thin, delicate wing membrane

| Length 9cm (3½in) | Weight 7g (¼oz) | Diet Insects |
|---|---|---|

| Group Pterodactyloidea | Family Pterodactylidae | Time 144–150mya |
|---|---|---|

# PTERODACTYLUS

TER-OH-DAK-TIL-US

Many species of *Pterodactylus* ("wing finger") have been discovered – the main differences between them are their size, and the shape and length of the head. All species had the typical pterodactyl features of a short tail, large head, and hollow bones. *Pterodactylus* had a long, curved, pelican-like neck, and a long skull with many small, pointed teeth. Skeletal analysis shows that it was a powerful, active flyer.

• **DESCRIBED BY** Baron Georges Cuvier as Ptero-Dactyle; 1809: name amended by Rafinesque; 1815.

• **HABITAT** Shores.

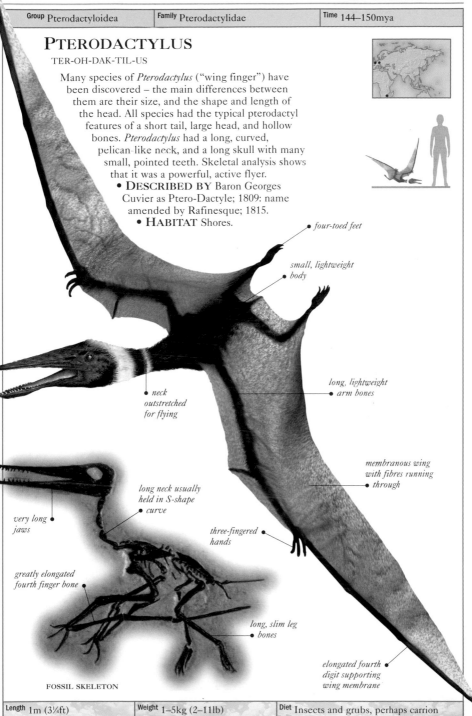

*four-toed feet*

*small, lightweight body*

*neck outstretched for flying*

*long, lightweight arm bones*

*membranous wing with fibres running through*

*long neck usually held in S-shape curve*

*very long jaws*

*three-fingered hands*

*greatly elongated fourth finger bone*

*long, slim leg bones*

*elongated fourth digit supporting wing membrane*

FOSSIL SKELETON

| Length 1m (3¼ft) | Weight 1–5kg (2–11lb) | Diet Insects and grubs, perhaps carrion |
|---|---|---|

| Group Theropoda | Family Archaeopteridae | Time 150mya |
|---|---|---|

# ARCHAEOPTERYX

ARE-KAY-OP-TER-IKS

*Archaeopteryx* ("ancient wing") was about the size of a modern pigeon, with a small head, large eyes, and pointed teeth in its jaws. Its lower leg bones were long and slim, indicating that it could move well on land. Unlike modern birds, *Archaeopteryx* had a flat breastbone, a long, bony tail, and three grasping claws on each wing. However, its feathers, wings, and furcula (wishbone) are characteristics shared by modern birds. Recent analysis shows that *Archaeopteryx* could probably fly, although it was probably not a strong flier. It was almost certainly "warm blooded".

• **DESCRIBED BY** Hermann von Meyer; 1861.
• **HABITAT** Lakeshores or open forests.

*feathered wings for effective flight*

*three clawed digits on elongated hand*

| Length 30cm (12in) | Weight 300–500g (11–18oz) | Diet Insects |
|---|---|---|

feathers attached to
sides of bony tail

impressions of
feathers preserved
in limestone

FOSSIL REMAINS
EMBEDDED IN ROCK

lightly built
body

long, asymmetric wing
feathers typical of birds
capable of true flight

# CRETACEOUS PERIOD

144–65 MILLION YEARS AGO

The climate in the Cretaceous was similar to that in the Jurassic – warm and humid. Sea levels were very high, resulting in large areas of flooding and consequent isolation of landmasses. A major evolutionary development – the appearance of the angiosperms (flowering plants) led to important changes in the landscape and animal life on Earth. Many new insect groups appeared. Dinosaurs continued to flourish, but populations of certain groups, such as sauropods and stegosaurs, were greatly reduced as their staple food supply was taken over by new dinosaur groups, including the advanced ornithopods and ceratopsians. These flourished until the mass extinction event at the end of the period.

**FLOWERING PLANTS**
Late in the Cretaceous, forests were composed of flowering trees, such as birch and magnolia. *Betulites* (above) is an extinct birch species.

4,600mya          4,000mya                              3,000mya

## CRETACEOUS LANDMASSES

During the Cretaceous, continental drift led to the break up of the supercontinents of Laurasia and Gondwana. This process was augmented by the very high sea levels of 200m (640ft). The Atlantic Ocean started to open up between the future South America and Africa, and Antarctica was almost in its modern position. India started to move northwards. There was still a land link between Eurasia and North America.

## CRETACEOUS LIFE

Dinosaurs were still the dominant land animals. They increased in diversity throughout the period, with new groups including the hadrosaurs, horned dinosaurs, and giant tyrannosaurs appearing. Birds continued to evolve and snakes appeared. Mammals were still small, but continued to diversify.

**MAMMAL EVOLUTION**
Mammals remained only minor elements of the fauna. Like the early marsupial *Alphadon* (right) they were shrew- or rabbit-sized animals.

neck frill with
• large openings

• toes adapted
for climbing

**CERATOPSIANS**
The Cretaceous saw the appearance of the frilled ceratopsian dinosaurs, such as *Chasmosaurus* (left). These had brow and nose horns, and a large, bony frill covering the neck and shoulders.

• wide feet

# ON THE LAND

T he Cretaceous Period was the heyday of the dinosaurs. Many new forms of dinosaur evolved, most probably in response to the rapid spread of flowering plants.

Sauropodomorphs were once thought not to have survived the Jurassic–Cretaceous boundary. However, they continued to be present, and remained abundant in the lands that were to become South America, but declined in other areas. Stegosaurs seem to have died out early in the Cretaceous.

Other groups of ornithischian dinosaurs flourished. Ankylosaurs became more numerous and developed extensive armour plating and defensive tail clubs. Ornithopods and hadrosaurs (duck-bills) seem to have formed large herds. The Mid and Late Cretaceous also saw the appearance of the pachycephalosaurs and the ceratopians, such as *Triceratops*. These became more varied as the period progressed.

Theropods also diversified greatly in the Cretaceous. New dinosaur groups that evolved included the immense tyrannosaurs, the highly intelligent dromaeosaurs, such as *Deinonychus*, the bird mimics (ornithomimosaurs), and the oviraptorids. The two latter groups were bird-like in appearance. They had lost their teeth, having a beak instead, and had a varied diet that probably included fruit, small animals, insects, and eggs.

| Group Theropoda | Family Abelisauridae | Time 74–70mya |
|---|---|---|

## ABELISAURUS

AH-BEL-EE-SAW-RUS

This large theropod, named for its discoverer, Roberto Abel, is known only from a single skull. It seems to have been rather a primitive form related to *Carnotaurus*. Its head was large, with a rounded snout, and its teeth were relatively small for a carnivorous dinosaur of its size. Its skull is peculiar in that it has a huge opening at the side just above the jaws, which is much larger than in other dinosaurs. Reconstructions of the rest of its body are necessarily hypothetical. The illustration here is based on the body structure of *Carnotaurus* and similar theropod dinosaurs.

• **DESCRIBED BY** José Bonaparte and F. Novas; 1985.

• **HABITAT** River plains.

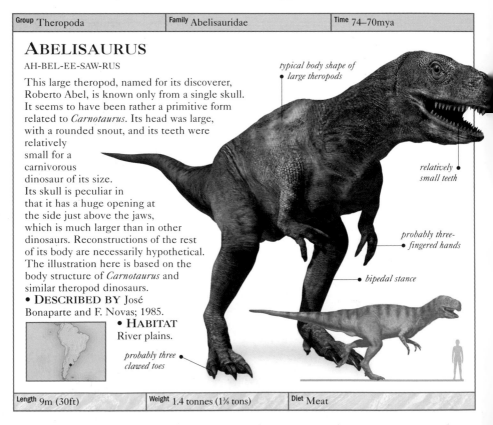

*typical body shape of large theropods*

*relatively small teeth*

*probably three-fingered hands*

*bipedal stance*

*probably three clawed toes*

| Length 9m (30ft) | Weight 1.4 tonnes (1⅜ tons) | Diet Meat |
|---|---|---|

| Group Theropoda | Family Abelisauridae | Time 70mya |
|---|---|---|

# CARNOTAURUS

KAR-NOH-TAW-RUS

The most distinctive feature of *Carnotaurus* ("meat-eating bull") were the broad, triangular horns over its eyes. Otherwise, it looked very like other large theropods. It had long legs and a lightly built body covered in scales and studs. Its forearms were incredibly small. Its three fingers were short and stubby, and the thumbs bore a small spike. Its tail was long, thick, and flexible.

• **DESCRIBED BY** José Bonaparte; 1985.
• **HABITAT** Dry plains, perhaps desert.

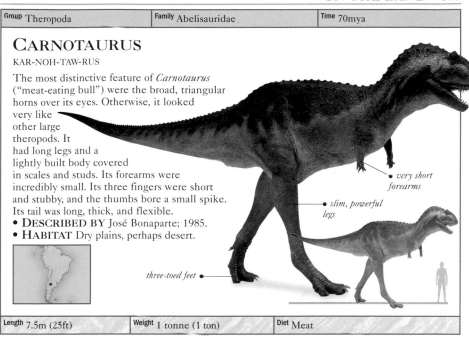

*very short forearms*

*slim, powerful legs*

*three-toed feet*

| Length 7.5m (25ft) | Weight 1 tonne (1 ton) | Diet Meat |
|---|---|---|

| Group Theropoda | Family Carcharodontosauridae | Time 112–90mya |
|---|---|---|

# GIGANOTOSAURUS

GIG-AN-OH-TOE-SAW-RUS

*Giganotosaurus* ("giant southern lizard") is the largest carnivorous dinosaur yet discovered. Its skull was longer than an average man, and held long, serrated teeth. Its hands had three fingers, and it had a slim, pointed tail. Although larger than *Tyrannosaurus*, it was more lightly built than that dinosaur, and seems to have hunted in a different fashion – by slashing at its prey rather than charging and biting head on. Despite its huge size, some paleontologists maintain that, like other large theropods, it may have been able to run relatively fast.

• **DESCRIBED BY** Coria and Salgado; 1995.
• **HABITAT** Warm swamps.

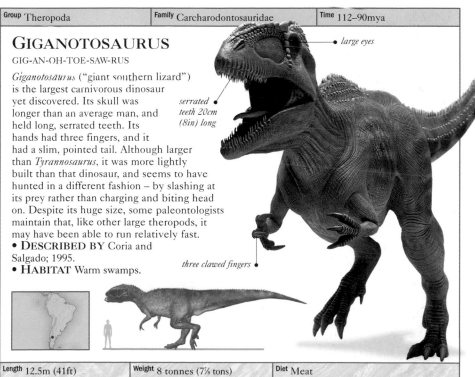

*large eyes*

*serrated teeth 20cm (8in) long*

*three clawed fingers*

| Length 12.5m (41ft) | Weight 8 tonnes (7⅞ tons) | Diet Meat |
|---|---|---|

| Group Theropoda | Family Spinosauridae | Time 98–95mya |
|---|---|---|

# SPINOSAURUS

SPINE-OH-SAW-RUS

*Spinosaurus* ("spine lizard") was an immense theropod with an impressive sail-like structure running all the way down its back. This was held up by blade-like spines sticking out from the vertebrae. The function of the sail is not known. Some palaeontologists believe that it served as a primitive heat-exchanging device, others that it was brightly coloured and was used for sexual display. The herbivorous dinosaur *Ouranosaurus*, which lived in the same region during this period, had a similar structure, so it seems most likely that the sail was an adaptation to the hot climate. *Spinosaurus* had relatively long arms.

- **DESCRIBED BY** Ernst Stromer; 1915.
- **HABITAT** Tropical swamps.

vertical "sail" supported by spines

stiff tail

large, straight teeth

longer than usual arms for a large theropod

powerful hind legs

tooth socket

three long, forward-facing, clawed toes

**FOSSIL TOOTH BATTERY**

| Length 15m (49ft) | Weight 7.1 tonnes (7 tons) | Diet Meat, perhaps fish |
|---|---|---|

| Group Theropoda | Family Spinosauridae | Time 110–100mya |
|---|---|---|

# SUCHOMIMUS

SOOK-OH-MIME-US

This dinosaur, whose name means "crocodile-mimic", had several features that indicate that it ate fish. It had a very long snout, and huge, curved thumb claws that could be used for hooking fish from the water. The jaws had over 100 teeth that pointed slightly backwards, and the end of the snout had a rosette of longer teeth. A low ridge ran along the length of its back. Its arms were relatively long, which would have enabled *Suchomimus* to reach into the water to grasp prey.

• **DESCRIBED BY** Paul C. Sereno; 1998.
• **HABITAT** Lush forests.

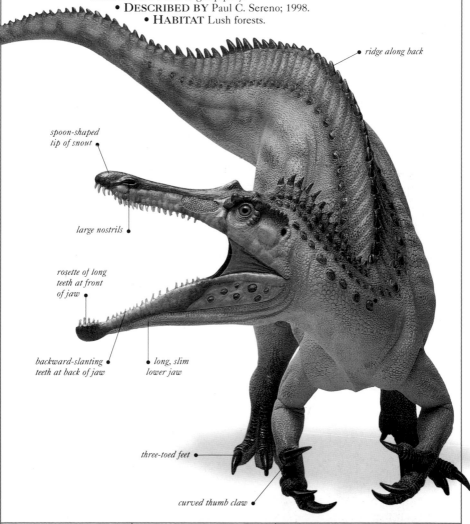

*ridge along back*

*spoon-shaped tip of snout*

*large nostrils*

*rosette of long teeth at front of jaw*

*backward-slanting teeth at back of jaw*

*long, slim lower jaw*

*three-toed feet*

*curved thumb claw*

| Length 11m (36ft) | Weight 5.1 tonnes (5 tons) | Diet Fish, possibly meat |
|---|---|---|

| Group Theropoda | Family Spinosauridae | Time 125mya |
|---|---|---|

# BARYONYX

BAR-EE-ON-ICKS

*Baryonyx* ("heavy claw") was named for one of its unusual features –
its huge, curved thumb claws. Its skull was also an unusual shape for
a theropod, being long and narrow – rather like that of a crocodile.
There was a bony crest on the top of the head, and the jaws were
filled with 96 pointed and serrated teeth. This is twice as many as
theropods usually possessed. The neck was not as flexible as in other
theropods, and could not have been carried in the characteristic S-
bend. Its arms were thick and unusually powerful. These features,
along with the remains of fish found with the skeleton, have led
palaeontologists to surmise that *Baryonyx* fished using its claws
as hooks, in the same way as a modern bear does.

• **DESCRIBED BY** Charig and Milner; 1986.
• **HABITAT** Riverbanks.

## BARYONYX CLAW

sharp, curved thumb
claw 30cm (12in) long

unusually thick,
powerful arm
bones

sharp claws
on other fingers

Although the claws were not found
attached to the skeleton, and it is therefore
not certain that they formed part of the
hand, palaeontologists have reconstructed
*Baryonyx* with the claw in this position
because the length and thickness of the
arms seemed to match its proportions.

| Length 10m (33ft) | Weight 2 tonnes (2 tons) | Diet Fish, perhaps meat |
|---|---|---|

*fenestrae lightened weight of skull*

*long, narrow jaws*

*many small serrated teeth*

BARYONYX SKULL

*bony ridge along spine*

*relatively inflexible neck*

*bony head crest*

| Group Theropoda | Family Deinocheiridae | Time 70–65mya |
|---|---|---|

# DEINOCHEIRUS

DINE-OH-KIRE-US

Little is known about this dinosaur. The only remains so far discovered are two arms 2.4m (8ft) long, which gave rise to the dinosaur's name – "terrible hand". The arms are similar to those of *Ornithomimus*, and are longer than in any other animal except the strange-looking *Therizinosaurus* (p.114). Some experts think that the claws on the hands were too blunt to hunt with. *Deinocheirus* was a bipedal walker. The illustration here is based on what is known about similar dinosaurs.

• **DESCRIBED BY** H. Osmolska and E. Roniewicz; 1970.
• **HABITAT** Desert.

• *body and tail probably similar to other theropods*

• *three fingers on each hand*

*25cm- (10in-) long claws*

| Length 12–15m (43–52ft) | Weight Unknown | Diet Unknown |
|---|---|---|

| Group Theropoda | Family Ornithomimidae | Time 74–65mya |
|---|---|---|

# GALLIMIMUS

GAL-EE-MEEM-US

*Gallimimus* ("chicken mimic") is one of the best-known of the ornithomimids or "bird-mimic" dinosaurs. It had a short body with a long, stiff tail, and slim legs built for running at high speed. Its neck was slender and flexible, and the skull ended in a long, toothless beak. The braincase was relatively large, and *Gallimimus* was probably quite intelligent. Its eyes were large, but it did not have stereoscopic vision.
• **DESCRIBED BY** Osmolska, Roniewicz, Barsbold; 1972.
• **HABITAT** Desert plains.

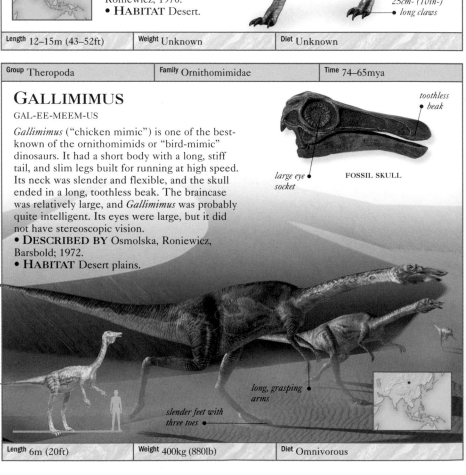

*toothless beak*

*large eye socket*

FOSSIL SKULL

*long, grasping arms*

*slender feet with three toes*

| Length 6m (20ft) | Weight 400kg (880lb) | Diet Omnivorous |
|---|---|---|

| Group Theropoda | Family Ornithomimidae | Time 76–65mya |
|---|---|---|

# ORNITHOMIMUS

OR-NITH-OH-MEEM-US

This "bird mimic" is typical of its family. It had slim arms and long, slim legs. Its tail made up more than

• impression of toes

FOSSIL FOOTPRINTS

half of its length, and was kept stiff by a network of ligaments. Its small head had a toothless beak, and was held upright by an S-shaped bend in the long, flexible neck. The brain cavity was relatively large. *Ornithomimus* ran with its body held horizontally and its tail outstretched for balance. Its top speed has been estimated at up to 30mph (50kph).

• **DESCRIBED BY** Othniel C. Marsh; 1890.

• **HABITAT** Swamps, forests.

• large eyes on side of head

• three clawed fingers on each hand

• long bones in feet

| Length 3.5m (11ft) | Weight 175kg (385lb) | Diet Omnivorous |
|---|---|---|

| Group Theropoda | Family Ornithomimidae | Time 76–74mya |
|---|---|---|

# STRUTHIOMIMUS

STRUTH-EE-OH-MEEM-US

For many years after its first discovery, *Struthiomimus* ("ostrich mimic") was thought to be the same dinosaur as *Ornithomimus*. The two dinosaurs are remarkably similar – the main difference is that *Struthiomimus* had longer arms with stronger fingers. In addition, its thumbs did not oppose the fingers. This reduced the

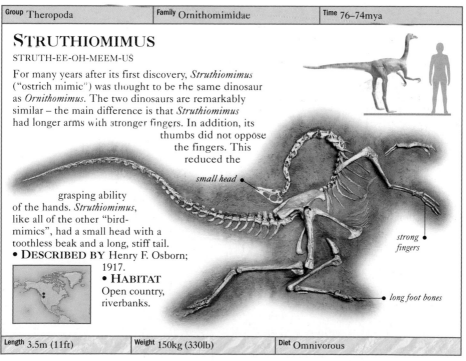

small head •

grasping ability of the hands. *Struthiomimus*, like all of the other "bird-mimics", had a small head with a toothless beak and a long, stiff tail.

• **DESCRIBED BY** Henry F. Osborn; 1917.

• **HABITAT** Open country, riverbanks.

strong • fingers

• long foot bones

| Length 3.5m (11ft) | Weight 150kg (330lb) | Diet Omnivorous |
|---|---|---|

| Group Theropoda | Family Therizinosauridae | Time 85–70mya |
|---|---|---|

# THERIZINOSAURUS

THER-IZ-IN-OH-SAW-RUS

One of the strangest dinosaurs, the reconstruction of *Therizinosaurus* ("scythe lizard") is based on finds of other members of the family. Little is known of it apart from its incredibly long arms. These had three fingers that ended in curved, flat-sided claws, the first of which was longer than a man's arm. The claws seem too blunt for use in attack. Suggestions for their function have included that they were used in courtship, for raking plants, or for ripping open termite nests. This bipedal dinosaur may have occasionally rested on all fours. *Therizinosaurus* seems to have been related to *Oviraptor*.

- **DESCRIBED BY** E. A. Maleev; 1954.
- **HABITAT** Woodland.

*fine, hairy feathers may have covered the skin*

*toothless beak*

FOSSIL SCYTHE CLAW

*claws up to 60cm (24in) long*

*three clawed fingers*

| Length 11m (36ft) | Weight Unknown | Diet Meat, or possibly plants or insects |
|---|---|---|

| Group Theropoda | Family Oviraptoridae | Time 85–75mya |
|---|---|---|

# OVIRAPTOR

OV-EE-RAP-TOR

This dinosaur, whose name means "egg thief", seems to have been very closely related to birds, and was probably feathered. Its most distinctive feature was its head, which was short and deep, with a stumpy beak. It had no teeth, but there were two bony projections on the upper palate of the mouth. The jaws were so powerful that they could have crushed objects as hard as bones. The first specimen (see below left) of *Oviraptor* was discovered preserved with eggs, thought to be those of *Protoceratops*, and this led to its name. Later research proved that this *Oviraptor* was actually sitting on its own nest. This dinosaur may have had feathers, but some reconstructions, such as that of the head below right, show it without them.

- **DESCRIBED BY** Henry F. Osborn; 1924.
- **HABITAT** Semi-desert.

horn-like crest
• on snout

large eyes

short beak •

clutch of eggs

FOSSILIZED
NEST SITE

DETAIL OF
HEAD

bird-like feet

| Length 2.5m (8ft) | Weight 35kg (77lb) | Diet Uncertain |
|---|---|---|

| Group Theropoda | Family Tyrannosauridae | Time 67–65mya |
| --- | --- | --- |

# TYRANNOSAURUS

TIE-RAN-OH-SAW-RUS

*Tyrannosaurus* ("tyrant lizard") was one of the largest terrestrial carnivores ever. It was a heavily-built theropod, with thick, long, powerful legs and a large, deep head. Palaeontologists are still hotly debating whether it was an active predator or simply a scavenger, and how fast it actually was. Arguments against predation include its small eyes and arms, and presumed slow speed. Evidence supporting scavenging includes the fact that *Tyrannosaurus* had very large olfactory lobes (the area in the brain used for processing odours), and that its legs were built for walking long distances. Recent analysis indicates its top speed may have been as slow as 10mph.

• **DESCRIBED BY** Henry F. Osborn; 1905.
• **HABITAT** Open forests, coastal forested swamps.

*15cm- (6in-) long, serrated teeth*

*large fenestrae to lighten skull*

*12 back vertebrae with holes to reduce weight*

*tail made up of about 40 vertebrae*

*58 teeth*

*relatively slim, bird-like foot*

*saurischian hip*

## TYRANNOSAURUS SKELETON

The first skeletal reconstruction of *Tyrannosaurus* was prepared in 1915, showing the dinosaur standing upright with its tail along the ground. Recent analysis has shown that the backbone was held horizontally, with the body perfectly balanced at the hips.

| Length 12m (40ft) | Weight 6.7 tonnes (6⅔ tons) | Diet Hadrosaurs, ceratopsians |
| --- | --- | --- |

**NEW DISCOVERY**
In 1990 a new
specimen of
*Tyrannosaurus* was
discovered in South
Dakota, USA. The
skeleton was at least
70 per cent complete,
and is the largest
specimen yet found.

pebbled skin
texture

tail held stiffly
for balance

tail heavily
muscled at base

long, heavily
muscled legs

| Group Theropoda | Family Dromaeosauridae | Time 110–100mya |

# DEINONYCHUS

DIE-NON-EE-KUS

One of the most fearsome predators of the Cretaceous, *Deinonychus* ("terrible claw") was named for the sickle-shaped claws on the second toe of each foot. These were used alternately to slash at prey as the dinosaur stood on one leg. A group found preserved with the skeleton of a large *Tenontosaurus* (see p.208) suggests that *Deinonychus* was a pack hunter.

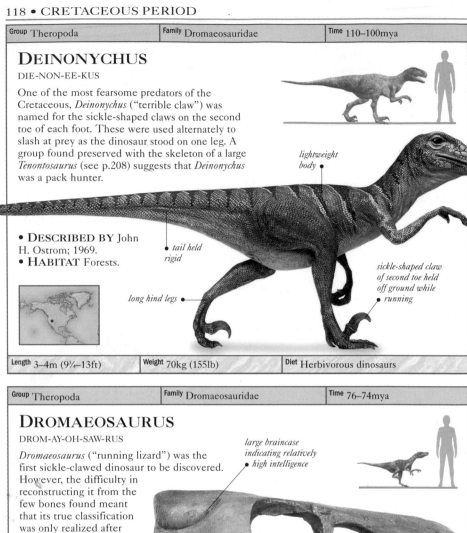

*lightweight body*

- **DESCRIBED BY** John H. Ostrom; 1969.
- **HABITAT** Forests.

*tail held rigid*

*long hind legs*

*sickle-shaped claw of second toe held off ground while running*

| Length 3–4m (9¾–13ft) | Weight 70kg (155lb) | Diet Herbivorous dinosaurs |

| Group Theropoda | Family Dromaeosauridae | Time 76–74mya |

# DROMAEOSAURUS

DROM-AY-OH-SAW-RUS

*Dromaeosaurus* ("running lizard") was the first sickle-clawed dinosaur to be discovered. However, the difficulty in reconstructing it from the few bones found meant that its true classification was only realized after *Deinonychus* was described. This dinosaur was smaller than *Deinonychus*, but otherwise very similar. Its body was slender, with long limbs and a large head. Its sharp claws would have been effective slashing weapons.

- **DESCRIBED BY** Matthew, Brown; 1922.
- **HABITAT** Forests, plains.

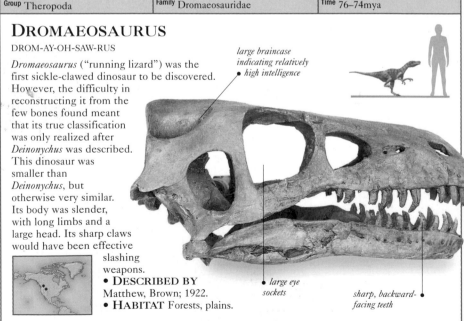

*large braincase indicating relatively high intelligence*

*large eye sockets*

*sharp, backward-facing teeth*

| Length 1.8m (5½ft) | Weight 15kg (33lb) | Diet Herbivorous dinosaurs |

| Group Theropoda | Family Dromaeosauridae | Time 85–80mya |
|---|---|---|

# SAURORNITHOIDES

SAWR-OR-NITH-OID-EEZ

Only the skull, a few arm bones, and teeth of *Saurornithoides* ("lizard bird form") have been found to date, and its classification as a dromaeosaur is therefore uncertain. Its long, narrow skull had a relatively large braincase. Its long, powerful arms ended in three-fingered hands capable of grasping prey.
• **DESCRIBED BY** Osborn; 1924.
• **HABITAT** Plains.

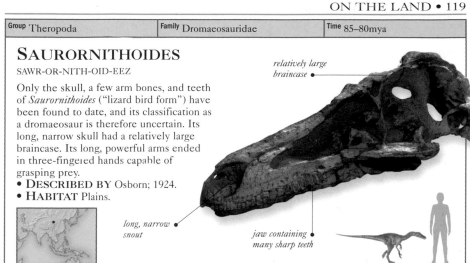

*relatively large braincase*

*long, narrow snout*

*jaw containing many sharp teeth*

| Length 2m–3.5 (6½–11ft) | Weight 13–27kg (29–60lb) | Diet Meat |
|---|---|---|

| Group Theropoda | Family Troodontidae | Time 74–65mya |
|---|---|---|

# TROODON

TROH-OH-DON

*Troodon* ("wounding tooth") was named for its sharp, serrated teeth. Its remains are very rare, and no complete skeleton has been found to date. Its reconstruction is based on the fossils found and details known from similar, closely related dinosaurs. It was probably an efficient hunter. It had long, slim hind legs, a large sickle-shaped claw on both second toes, and three long, clawed fingers that were capable of grasping prey. The sickle claws were smaller than in *Deinonychus* (opposite) and *Velociraptor* (see p.120). This has led some palaeontologists to suggest that they were mainly used for defence. The shape of the teeth has prompted debate on whether it was omnivorous. *Troodon* could undoubtedly run quickly on its long legs, with its stiff tail held out behind for balance. Analysis of the slim skull shows that it had keen eyesight and may have had good hearing. Its braincase was also very large in proportion to its body size, indicating an unusually high level of intelligence for a dinosaur. *Troodon* eggs have been found in fossil nests.
• **DESCRIBED BY** Joseph Leidy; 1856.
• **HABITAT** Plains.

*large, keen eyes*

*slim, lightly built body*

*three-fingered hands*

*sickle-shaped claws on second toes*

| Length 2m (6½ft) | Weight 50kg (110lb) | Diet Meat, carrion |
|---|---|---|

| Group Theropoda | Family Dromaeosauridae | Time 85–80mya |
|---|---|---|

# VELOCIRAPTOR

VEL-O-SEE-RAP-TOR

Many well-preserved skeletons of *Velociraptor* ("fast thief") have been found, making it the best-known member of its family. The main feature that sets it apart from other members of the family is its low, long, flat-snouted head. *Velociraptor* must have been a formidable predator: its jaws held about 80 very sharp teeth, and the second toe of each foot ended in a slashing, sickle-shaped claw. The neck was S-shaped, and the hands bore three clawed fingers. It is probable that *Velociraptor* hunted in packs. Traditionally reconstructed with scaly skin, recent analysis has shown that this dinosaur was probably at least partly covered in a downy coat or primitive feathers.
• **DESCRIBED BY** Henry F. Osborn; 1924.
• **HABITAT** Woodland.

**PRESERVED IN DEATH**
One of the most famous fossil finds is a *Velociraptor* and *Protoceratops* locked together in battle at the time of their deaths.

*stiff tail held outstretched for balance*

*slim legs with long shins for speed*

| Length 1.8m (6ft) | Weight 15kg (33lb) | Diet Lizards, mammals, smaller dinosaurs |
|---|---|---|

large eye socket

long, slim jaws
with pointed,
recurved teeth

FOSSIL SKULL

probable downy
covering over
much of body

three-fingered
grasping hands
with claws

large, sickle-shaped
second claw

| Group Theropoda | Family Not yet assigned | Time 120–136mya |
|---|---|---|

# CAUDIPTERYX

CORD-IP-TER-IKS

The discovery of this small, feathered dinosaur provided firm evidence of a theropod ancestry for birds. *Caudipteryx* ("tail feather") was a theropod with feathers covering its arms, most of its body, and its short tail. The feathers varied in structure – some were downy, and others were structured quills with shafts and veins. The feathers were symmetrical, showing that this animal did not fly. Some palaeontologists regard *Caudipteryx's* feathers as an example of convergent evolution, since this dinosaur lived after the time of *Archaeopteryx*. Others contend that *Caudipteryx* was a true bird that had lost the power of flight.
 • **DESCRIBED BY** Ji Q., Currie, Norell, Ji S.; 1998.
 • **HABITAT** Lakesides.

pointed beak with cluster of teeth at front of upper jaw

small, short skull with no teeth in lower jaw

fan of feathers on tail with bands of dark and light

long, slim legs best-suited to running

short arms with symmetrical feathers

three clawed fingers on hands

bird-like feet with three forward-facing clawed toes

| Length 90cm (35in) | Weight 10kg (22lb) | Diet Plants |
|---|---|---|

| Group Sauropoda | Family Titanosauridae | Time 90mya |
|---|---|---|

# ARGENTINOSAURUS

AR-GEN-TEEN-OH-SAW-RUS

Only a few bones of *Argentinosaurus* (Argentina lizard) have been found to date, including some enormous vertebrae from the back, which were over 1.5m (5ft) wide in cross-section. Other bones found were the sacrum, a tibia (shin bone), and a few ribs. Because of the sparsity of fossil evidence, very little is known about *Argentinosaurus*. However, it appears to have been the longest dinosaur ever found. It is thought to have been a titanosaur, which had some body structures similar to those of *Diplodocus* (p.76).

As in other titanosaurs, the neck and tail would have been very long and thin, and the skull is likely to have been small and triangular.

• **DESCRIBED BY** José Bonaparte and R. Coria; 1993.

• **HABITAT** Forested areas.

**DISCOVERY IN ARGENTINA**
The first bone of *Argentinosaurus* was found on an Argentinian sheep ranch in 1988.

long, slim neck

body thought to resemble that of other titanosaurs

long, whiplash tail

elephant-like, thick limbs with clawed toes

| Length 40m (130ft) | Weight 100 tonnes (98 tons) | Diet Conifers |
|---|---|---|

| Group Sauropoda | Family Titanosauridae | Time 83–65mya |
|---|---|---|

# TITANOSAURUS

TI-TAN-OH-SAW-RUS

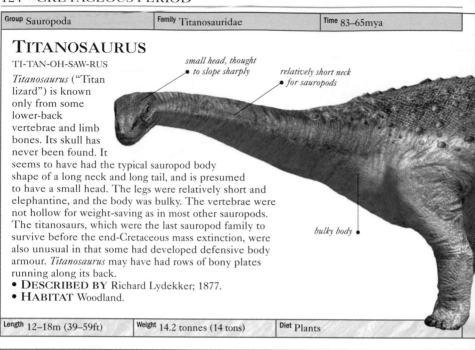

small head, thought to slope sharply

relatively short neck for sauropods

bulky body

*Titanosaurus* ("Titan lizard") is known only from some lower-back vertebrae and limb bones. Its skull has never been found. It seems to have had the typical sauropod body shape of a long neck and long tail, and is presumed to have a small head. The legs were relatively short and elephantine, and the body was bulky. The vertebrae were not hollow for weight-saving as in most other sauropods. The titanosaurs, which were the last sauropod family to survive before the end-Cretaceous mass extinction, were also unusual in that some had developed defensive body armour. *Titanosaurus* may have had rows of bony plates running along its back.
• **DESCRIBED BY** Richard Lydekker; 1877.
• **HABITAT** Woodland.

| Length 12–18m (39–59ft) | Weight 14.2 tonnes (14 tons) | Diet Plants |
|---|---|---|

| Group Sauropoda | Family Titanosauridae | Time 83–65mya |
|---|---|---|

# SALTASAURUS

SALT-AH-SAW-RUS

long, flexible tail

*Saltasaurus* was named for the province in Argentina where it was first found, and was the first sauropod for which evidence of armour was found. The fossil remains consisted of a group of partial skeletons surrounded by thousands of bony plates. Most of these plates were tiny, but others were larger and may have ended in bony spikes. It is likely that these bony plates covered the back and sides of the dinosaur to form a protective covering. *Saltasaurus* also had a very flexible tail, and it may have been able to rear up on its hind legs using the tail as a prop to feed on leaves. Further evidence for this theory comes from the breadth of the upper tail bones and its strong hips. The neck and tail were long, and the head was small, with a high skull.
• **DESCRIBED BY** Bonaparte and Powell; 1980.
• **HABITAT** Woodland.

| Length 12m (39ft) | Weight 20 tonnes (19¾ tons) | Diet Plants |
|---|---|---|

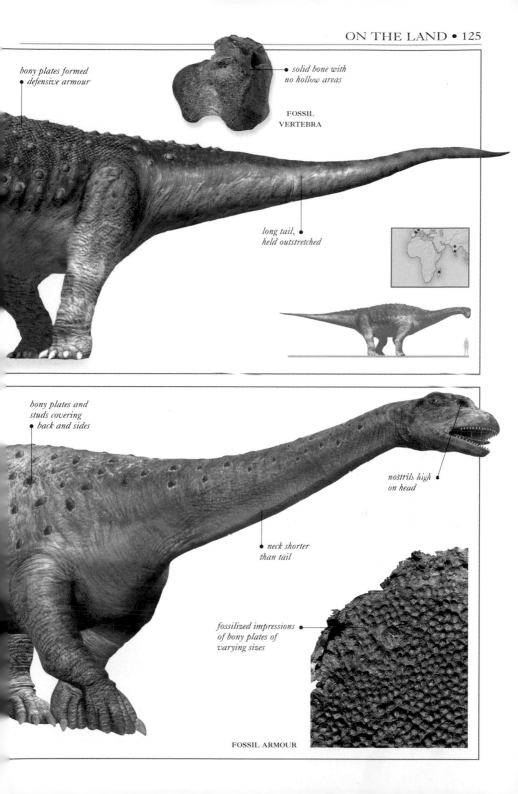

bony plates formed
• defensive armour

• solid bone with
no hollow areas

FOSSIL
VERTEBRA

long tail, •
held outstretched

bony plates and
studs covering
• back and sides

nostrils high •
on head

• neck shorter
than tail

fossilized impressions •
of bony plates of
varying sizes

FOSSIL ARMOUR

| Group Ceratopsia | Family Psittacosauridae | Time 120–100mya |
|---|---|---|

# PSITTACOSAURUS

SIT-OH-KOH-SAW-RUS

Its characteristic square skull and curved beak were the features that led to this dinosaur being given its name, which means "parrot lizard". Its cheek bones formed a pair of horns, believed to have been used for fighting or sexual display. Its hind legs were long and thin, suggesting that it was a fast bipedal runner. The long toes with blunt claws were perhaps used for digging. Its long tail was stiffened by bony tendons along its length.
• **DESCRIBED BY** Henry F. Osborn; 1923.
• **HABITAT** Desert and scrubland.

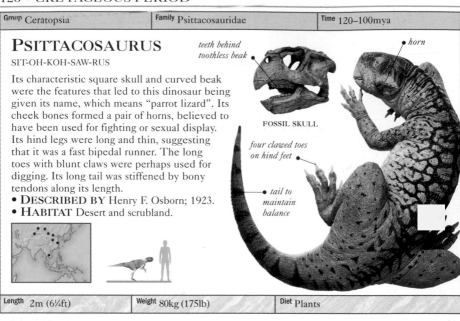

*teeth behind toothless beak*

*horn*

FOSSIL SKULL

*four clawed toes on hind feet*

*tail to maintain balance*

| Length 2m (6¼ft) | Weight 80kg (175lb) | Diet Plants |
|---|---|---|

| Group Ceratopsia | Family Ceratopsidae | Time 85–80mya |
|---|---|---|

# PROTOCERATOPS

PRO-TOE-KER-A-TOPS

*Protoceratops* ("before the horned faces") is very well-known from the many specimens discovered. It had a broad neck frill at the back of its skull, which was larger and taller in males. There was a small nasal horn between the eyes and two pairs of teeth in the upper jaw. Its legs were long and slender, so it was probably a fast runner.
• **DESCRIBED BY** Walter Granger and William K. Gregory; 1923.
• **HABITAT** Scrubland and desert.

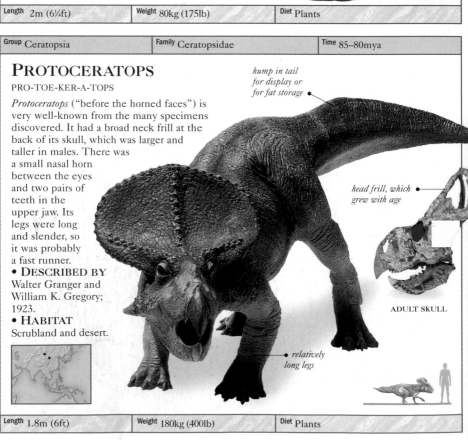

*hump in tail for display or for fat storage*

*head frill, which grew with age*

ADULT SKULL

*relatively long legs*

| Length 1.8m (6ft) | Weight 180kg (400lb) | Diet Plants |
|---|---|---|

| Group Ceratopsia | Family Ceratopsidae | Time 76–74mya |
|---|---|---|

# CENTROSAURUS

SEN-TROH-SAW-RUS

*Centrosaurus* ("horned lizard") used to be known by the name *Monoclonius*, and was tentatively renamed *Eucentrosaurus* in 1989. Its most distinctive feature was the long horn on the snout. There were also two small brow horns and a neck frill standing up behind the head. This had a wavy edge and was frilled with spines. *Centrosaurus* had a massive body, quite a short tail, and sturdy legs.
• **DESCRIBED BY** Lawrence M. Lambe (under name *Monoclonius*); 1904.
• **HABITAT** Woodland.

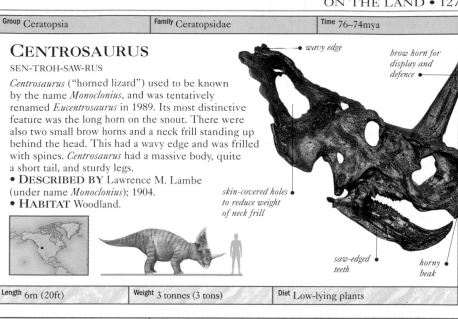

*wavy edge*

*brow horn for display and defence*

*skin-covered holes to reduce weight of neck frill*

*saw-edged teeth*

*horny beak*

| Length 6m (20ft) | Weight 3 tonnes (3 tons) | Diet Low-lying plants |
|---|---|---|

---

| Group Ceratopsia | Family Ceratopsidae | Time 76–70mya |
|---|---|---|

# STYRACOSAURUS

STY-RAK-OH-SAW-RUS

One of the most spectacular of the horned lizards, *Styracosaurus* ("spiked lizard") had six long spikes on the back edge of its neck frill, and smaller spikes around them. There was a large horn on the snout that pointed upwards and forwards. Its snout was very deep, and its nostrils seem to have been unusually large, although the reason for this is unknown. All four feet had five fingers or toes with claw-like hooves. Its teeth grew continuously to replace worn ones, and had a shearing action for slicing through tough plant material.
• **DESCRIBED BY** Lawrence M. Lambe; 1913.
• **HABITAT** Open woodland.

*holes in neck frill to reduce weight*

*defensive spikes*

FOSSIL SKULL

*defensive horn on snout*

| Length 5.2m (17ft) | Weight 2.8 tonnes (2¾ tons) | Diet Ferns and cycads |
|---|---|---|

| Group Ceratopsia | Family Ceratopsidae | Time 76–74mya |
|---|---|---|

# CHASMOSAURUS

KAZ-MOH-SAW-RUS

*Chasmosaurus* ("cleft lizard") was a typical frilled, horned dinosaur. It had a large body with four stocky legs. Its most distinctive feature – its enormous neck frill – was likely to have been brightly coloured in life for sexual display. The frill was so long that it reached over the shoulders. Its bony structure was lightened by two large holes that were covered with skin. Triangular, bony protrusions ran along the edge of the frill. *Chasmosaurus* had a small nose horn, and two blunt brow horns, which were of different lengths in different species or sexes. There was also a parrot-like beak at the front of the snout. The skin was covered in knob-like bumps with five or six sides.

- **DESCRIBED BY** Lawrence Lambe; 1914.
- **HABITAT** Woodland.

bony protrusions along frill edge

large nasal cavity

FRONT VIEW OF SKULL

hips firmly attached by eight sacral vertebrae

neck frill held upright, possibly to scare predators

short tail

blunt hooves

five short toes on all four feet

horny, parrot-like beak

| Length 5m (16ft) | Weight 2.5 tonnes (2½ tons) | Diet Cycads, palms, other plants |
|---|---|---|

| Group Ceratopsia | Family Ceratopsidae | Time 75–65mya |
|---|---|---|

# PENTACERATOPS

PEN-TAH-SER-A-TOPS

*Pentaceratops* ("five-horn face") was so named because it was originally thought to have had five horns on its face. In fact, it had the usual three horns – a straight horn on the snout and two curved brow horns. The two smaller "horns" were simply outgrowths of the cheekbones. *Pentaceratops'* most unusual feature is the size of its head – a skull reconstructed in 1998 was over 3m (10ft) long. Its neck frill was also enormous, and edged with triangular, bony projections. The body was stockily built, with a short, pointed tail.

- **DESCRIBED BY** Henry F. Osborn; 1923.
- **HABITAT** Wooded plains.

SKULL FRAGMENT

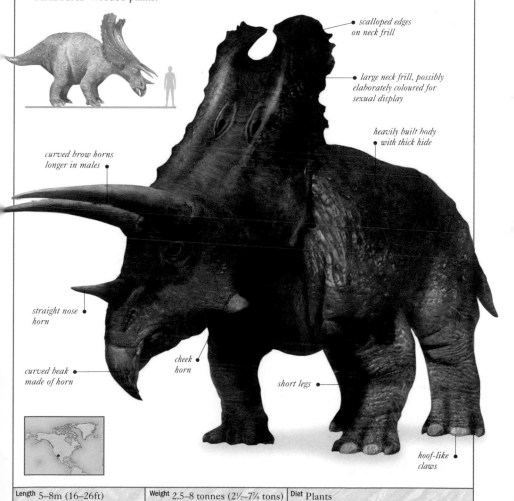

scalloped edges on neck frill

large neck frill, possibly elaborately coloured for sexual display

heavily built body with thick hide

curved brow horns longer in males

straight nose horn

cheek horn

curved beak made of horn

short legs

hoof-like claws

| Length 5–8m (16–26ft) | Weight 2.5–8 tonnes (2½–7⅞ tons) | Diet Plants |
|---|---|---|

| Group Ceratopsia | Family Ceratopsidae | Time 70–65mya |
|---|---|---|

# TRICERATOPS

TRY-SER-A-TOPS

Probably the best-known of the horned dinosaurs, *Triceratops* ("three-horned face") lived throughout the lands that now form North America at the end of the Cretaceous Period. The nose horn was short and thick, and the two long brow horns, each over 1m (3¼ft) long, curved forwards and slightly outwards over the snout. There were pointed studs set around the edge of the neck frill for further protection and ornamentation. Many of the fossil skulls found have evidence of scarring. This suggests that *Triceratops* may have fought in territorial or mating battles by locking horns with rivals.
• **DESCRIBED BY** Othniel C. Marsh; 1889.
• **HABITAT** Woodland.

*bony studs around margin of frill*

| Length 9m (30ft) | Weight 4.5–10 tonnes (4⅜–9⅞ tons) | Diet Plants |
|---|---|---|

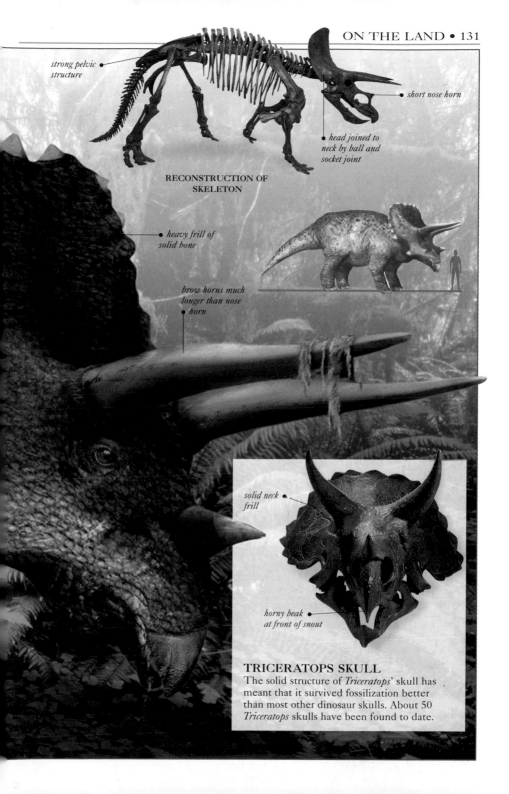

strong pelvic
structure

short nose horn

head joined to
neck by ball and
socket joint

RECONSTRUCTION OF
SKELETON

heavy frill of
solid bone

brow horns much
longer than nose
horn

solid neck
frill

horny beak
at front of snout

## TRICERATOPS SKULL

The solid structure of *Triceratops*' skull has
meant that it survived fossilization better
than most other dinosaur skulls. About 50
*Triceratops* skulls have been found to date.

| Group Ankylosauria | Family Nodosauridae | Time 115–91mya |
| --- | --- | --- |

# ACANTHOPHOLIS

A-CAN-THUH-FOE-LIS

*Acanthopholis* ("spiny scales") is a poorly known nodosaur with a low-slung, bulky body. Its formidable armour was formed from rows of oval plates (scutes) set into the skin. It also had long, bony spikes jutting out of its neck and shoulder area along the spine.

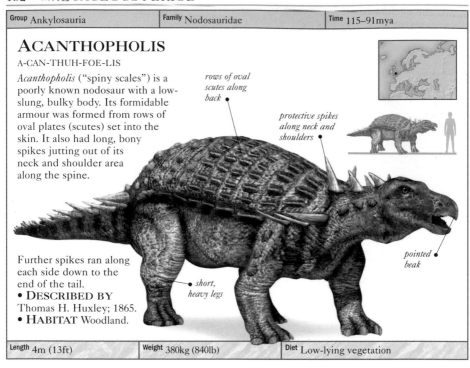

*rows of oval scutes along back*

*protective spikes along neck and shoulders*

*pointed beak*

Further spikes ran along each side down to the end of the tail.
• **DESCRIBED BY** Thomas H. Huxley; 1865.
• **HABITAT** Woodland.

*short, heavy legs*

| Length 4m (13ft) | Weight 380kg (840lb) | Diet Low-lying vegetation |
| --- | --- | --- |

| Group Ankylosauria | Family Anklyosauridae | Time 76–74mya |
| --- | --- | --- |

# EDMONTONIA

ED-MON-TONE-EE-AH

This ankylosaur (whose name means "from Edmonton") had a bulky body, four short, thick legs, wide feet, and a short neck. The back and tail were covered with rows of bony plates (scutes) and spikes. The shoulders of this dinosaur were particularly well-armoured with long spikes and large scutes. Fossil scutes that have been found are not symmetrical, meaning that they would not have projected straight out from the hide, but at an angle. *Edmontonia*'s skull was long and flat, with large nasal cavities and weak jaws. The front of the snout was formed into a horny, toothless beak, with small, weak cheek teeth inside the mouth. Some palaeontologists have suggested that *Edmontonia* may have used its shoulder spines for fighting with others of its own kind, as modern deer species do. It is also possible that the large spines were used for sexual display or for dominance signalling.
• **DESCRIBED BY** C.M. Sternberg; 1928.
• **HABITAT** Woodland.

*sloping back*

*short neck protected by bony scutes*

*long skull*

*double shoulder spike*

*horny beak*

| Length 6m (20ft) | Weight 3.5 tonnes (3½ tons) | Diet Low-lying vegetation |
| --- | --- | --- |

| Group Ankylosauria | Family Nodosauridae | Time 119 –113mya |

# MINMI

MIN-ME

This small, heavily-built and thickly armoured ankylosaur, named for Minmi Crossing in Australia had rows of small, bony plates running down its back and triangular spikes over the hips. There were also large bony plates over the neck and shoulders. Unlike other ankylosaurs, there were horizontal plates of bone running along each side of the vertebrae. The head was box-shaped, with a very narrow snout ending in a horny beak. Four small horns jutted out from the back of the face.

• **DESCRIBED BY** Ralph E. Molnar; 1980.
• **HABITAT** Scrubby and wooded plains.

*horizontal plates of bone alongside each vertebra*

*short neck*

*wide feet*

*short, sturdy legs*

| Length 3m (9¾ft) | Weight Unknown | Diet Low-lying vegetation |

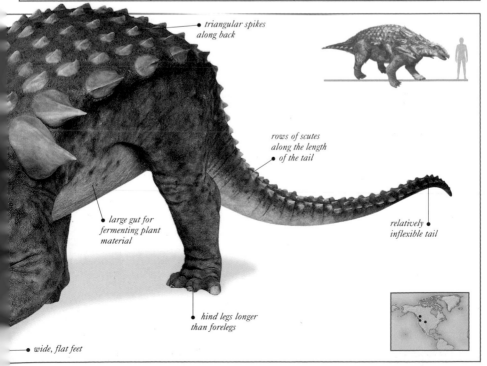

*triangular spikes along back*

*rows of scutes along the length of the tail*

*large gut for fermenting plant material*

*relatively inflexible tail*

*hind legs longer than forelegs*

*wide, flat feet*

| Group Ankylosauria | Family Nodosauridae | Time 131–124mya |
|---|---|---|

# GASTONIA

GAS-TONE-EE-A

*Gastonia* (named after Robert Gaston) had a mixture of ankylosaur and nodosaur features. This herbivore's defensive armour was impressive: there were four horns on the head, and bony rings covering the neck; rows of spikes covered the back and the flanks, and fused, bony armoured plates protected the hips. The tail, which could lash from side to side, had rows of triangular blades along each side. The long spikes running along each side of the spine curved up and outwards, forming a formidable defensive shield against attack by predators.
• **DESCRIBED BY** J.I. Kirkland; 1998.
• **HABITAT** Woodland.

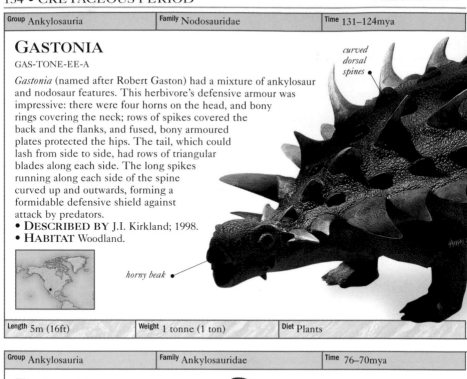

*curved dorsal spines*

*horny beak*

| Length 5m (16ft) | Weight 1 tonne (1 ton) | Diet Plants |
|---|---|---|

| Group Ankylosauria | Family Ankylosauridae | Time 76–70mya |
|---|---|---|

# EUOPLOCEPHALUS

YOU-OH-PLO-KEF-AH-LUSS

Built like a military tank, the back of *Euoplocephalus* ("well-armoured head") was embedded with bands of armour and bony studs. Fused plates covered the neck, and triangular horns protected the shoulders, base of tail, and the face. A large ball of fused bone at the end of the tail acted as a club that could be swung at attacking predators.
• **DESCRIBED BY** Lawrence Lambe as *Stereocephalus*; 1910.
• **HABITAT** Woodland.

*strong hips fused to backbone*

TAIL CLUB

| Length 6m (20ft) | Weight 2 tons (2 tonnes) | Diet Plants |
|---|---|---|

skull highest in front of eyes

tail with spikes along edges, but no tail club

small cheek teeth behind horny beak

eye socket

longer hind legs than front legs

INCOMPLETE FOSSIL SKULL

bony spikes and studs along back

bony plates covering neck

FOSSIL ARMOUR

secondary bony eyelids protected eyes

skull highest in front of eyes

short, stumpy limbs

large nasal cavity

FOSSIL SKULL

| Group Ankylosauria | Family Ankylosauridae | Time 74–67mya |
|---|---|---|

# ANKYLOSAURUS

AN-KIE-LOH-SAW-RUS

*Ankylosaurus* ("fused lizard") has aptly been described as a
living tank. Its stocky body, neck, and head were protected
by thick bands of armour-plating. The skin was thick and
leathery, and was studded with hundreds of oval bony
plates and rows of spikes. A pair of long spikes stuck out
from the back of the head, and the cheekbones were drawn
out into another pair of spikes on the face. The tail was
armed with a bony club, which could be swung with great
force. The legs were strong, although short, and the body
was wide and squat. The face was also broad, with a
blunt snout that ended in a toothless beak.

- **DESCRIBED BY** Barnum Brown; 1908.
- **HABITAT** Woodland.

terminal plate

lateral plate

bony tendons to support end of tail

FOSSIL TAIL CLUB

nostril

head spike

FOSSIL SKULL

teeth

bony spikes

end of tail held out stiffly

horny beak

large, bony tail club

unprotected underbelly

feet with five short toes

front legs shorter than hind legs

| Length 7.5–10.5m (25–35ft) | Weight 4.5–7 tonnes (4⅜–6⅞ tons) | Diet Large herbivorous dinosaurs |
|---|---|---|

| Group Ornithopoda | Family Hypsilophodontidae | Time 125–120mya |
|---|---|---|

# HYPSILOPHODON

HIP-SILL-OH-FO-DON

This primitive ornithischian, whose name means "high-ridge tooth", is generally believed to have been a fully terrestrial dinosaur that was capable of running at high speeds. It walked on its hindlegs; its short thigh bones and long shins meant that it was capable of taking long strides. The tail, stiffened by a network of bony ligaments, helped to balance the animal as it ran. Its small head had a horny beak and large eyes. The jaws held 28 or 30 cheek teeth that were self-sharpening, and the mouth had cheek pouches that could be used for storing food. Groups of fossils found together in bone beds suggest that this was a herding dinosaur.

- **DESCRIBED BY** Thomas H. Huxley; 1869.
- **HABITAT** Forests.

small beak

slim tail held out straight behind body

short, relatively weak forelimbs

slightly built skeleton

possibly two rows of bony plates down back

five-fingered hands

four-toed feet, one with claw

| Length 2m (6½ft) | Weight 68kg (150lb) | Diet Plants |
|---|---|---|

| Group Ornithopoda | Family Iguanodontidae | Time 135–125mya |

# IGUANODON

IG-WAH-NOH-DON

Originally thought to have been entirely quadrupedal, *Iguanodon* ("iguana tooth") is now thought to have been primarily quadrupedal, but also capable of bipedal walking. Its hind legs were thick and column-like, while the front legs were considerably shorter and thinner. The middle three fingers on each hand were joined together by a pad of skin and the fifth finger could curl to grasp food. The thumb was armed with a vicious, long spike. *Iguanodon* could chew food; it had a hinged upper jaw that allowed the teeth in the upper jaw to grind over those in the lower jaw.

- **DESCRIBED BY** Gideon A. Mantell; 1825.
- **HABITAT** Woodland.

*body held horizontally and • balanced at hips*

*deep tail held stiffly out for • balance*

| Length 9m (30ft) | Weight 4–5 tonnes (3⅞–4⅞ tons) | Diet Plants |

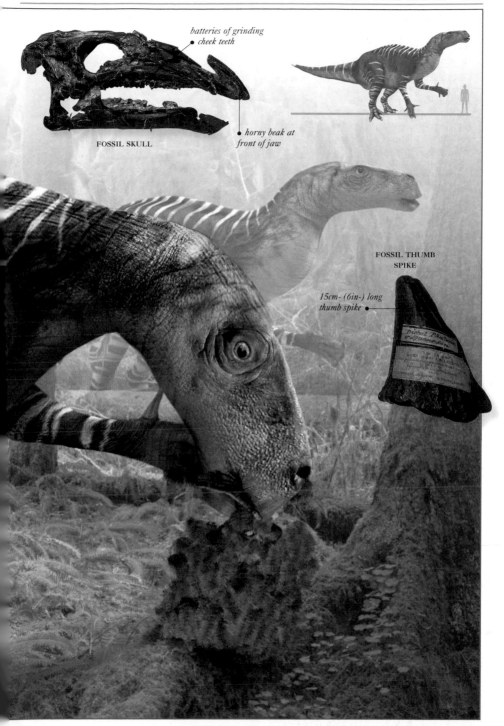

*batteries of grinding cheek teeth*

FOSSIL SKULL

*horny beak at front of jaw*

FOSSIL THUMB SPIKE

*15cm- (6in-) long thumb spike*

| Group Ornithopoda | Family Iguanodontidae | Time 115–100mya |
|---|---|---|

# OURANOSAURUS

OO-RAH-NOH-SAW-RUS

The most remarkable feature of *Ouranosaurus*, whose name means "brave lizard", was the row of spines growing out from the spinal and caudal vertebrae. They ran from the shoulders to halfway along the tail. Some palaeontologists think they supported a sail that acted as a heat controller in the hot conditions in which it lived. Others suggest that *Ouranosaurus* may have had a fatty hump as modern bisons do (and as illustrated here). *Ouranosaurus* had a pair of bony bumps between the eyes, and a horny beak.

• **DESCRIBED BY** Philippe Taquet; 1976.
• **HABITAT** Tropical plains and forest.

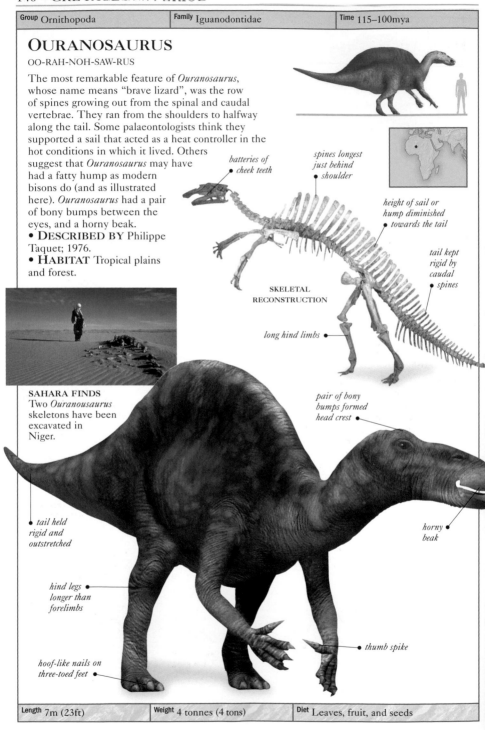

*batteries of cheek teeth*

*spines longest just behind shoulder*

*height of sail or hump diminished towards the tail*

*tail kept rigid by caudal spines*

**SKELETAL RECONSTRUCTION**

*long hind limbs*

**SAHARA FINDS**
Two *Ouranousaurus* skeletons have been excavated in Niger.

*pair of bony bumps formed head crest*

*tail held rigid and outstretched*

*horny beak*

*hind legs longer than forelimbs*

*thumb spike*

*hoof-like nails on three-toed feet*

| Length 7m (23ft) | Weight 4 tonnes (4 tons) | Diet Leaves, fruit, and seeds |
|---|---|---|

| Group Ornithopoda | Family Hadrosauridae | Time 80–74mya |

# HADROSAURUS

HAD-ROW-SAW-RUS

*Hadrosaurus* ("sturdy lizard") was one of the first dinosaurs discovered in North America. Its skull had a toothless, horny beak used for nipping off vegetation, and hundreds of blunt cheek teeth. These were continually replaced as they wore down from chewing tough plant material. Although its forelimbs were much shorter than its hind legs, *Hadrosaurus* spent most of its time browsing on all fours. It walked with its tail held outstretched for balance.

- **DESCRIBED BY** Joseph Leidy; 1859.
- **HABITAT** Swamps and forests.

snout crest of solid bone

beak would have been covered with horny skin

batteries of grinding cheek teeth

| Length 9m (30ft) | Weight 7 tonnes (6⅞ tons) | Diet Leaves and twigs |

---

| Group Ornithopoda | Family Hadrosauridae | Time 80–74mya |

# MAIASAURA

MAY-A-SAW-RA

This dinosaur's name means "good earth-mother lizard". It was so named because remains were found close to fossilized nests scooped out of mud. The nests were each about 2m (6½ft) across and contained eggs arranged in circular layers. Remains of juvenile dinosaurs at various stages of development showed that the parents brought food to their young at the nest site for a considerable time. It appears that *Maiasaura* migrated and nested each year in large herds. It had numerous cheek teeth adapted to grinding tough plant material.

- **DESCRIBED BY** John R. Horner, R. Makela; 1979.
- **HABITAT** Coastal plains.

NEST-SITE RECONSTRUCTION

large eye sockets characterize juvenile

stiff, narrow tail

long hind legs

hundreds of grinding cheek teeth

SKELETON OF JUVENILE

| Length 9m (30ft) | Weight 5 tonnes (4⅞ tons) | Diet Leaves |

| Group Ornithopoda | Family Hadrosauridae | Time 76–74mya |
|---|---|---|

# CORYTHOSAURUS

KOH-RITH-OH-SAW-RUS

*Corythosaurus* ("Corinthian helmet lizard") was named for the distinctive hollow crest on top of its head. This seems to have been larger in males. The crest was made up of greatly altered nasal bones, and the hollows were expanded nasal passages. Models of the crest have been made, which produce a booming foghorn-like sound when blown through, adding to the current theory that the crest served as a resonating device for signalling amongst herds. *Corythosaurus* was a low browser that spent most of its time on all fours. It had a broad toothless beak.

• **DESCRIBED BY**
Barnum Brown; 1914.
• **HABITAT**
Forests.

*spectacular head crest*

*vertebral spines possibly supported narrow skin frill*

*sigmoid neck held head close to ground*

| Length 10m (33ft) | Weight 4.5 tonnes (4⅖ tons) | Diet Leaves, seeds, pine needles |
|---|---|---|

| Group Ornithopoda | Family Hadrosauridae | Time 76–74mya |
|---|---|---|

# PARASAUROLOPHUS

PA-RA-SAW-ROL-OFF-US

This dinosaur, whose name means "beside *Saurolophus*", is instantly recognizable from its trombone-like head crest. This was up to 1.8m (6ft) long, and was probably used for display and as a resonating device for sound signalling. The crest was longer in males than in females. A frill of skin may have joined the crest to the neck.

• **DESCRIBED BY**
William A. Parks; 1922
• **HABITAT** Woodland.

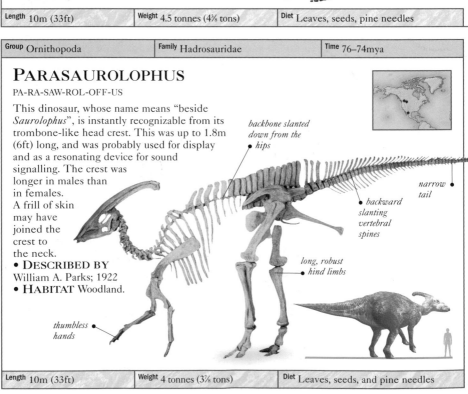

*backbone slanted down from the hips*

*narrow tail*

*backward slanting vertebral spines*

*long, robust hind limbs*

*thumbless hands*

| Length 10m (33ft) | Weight 4 tonnes (3⅞ tons) | Diet Leaves, seeds, and pine needles |
|---|---|---|

tall vertebral spines and
• chevrons in tail area

top vertebral
spines slanted
backwards •

tail stiffened •
by network
of bony
ligaments

relatively •
short toes

**DETAIL OF HIP REGION**
The network of bony rods on
*Corythosaurus*'s tail kept the
backbone immobile.

---

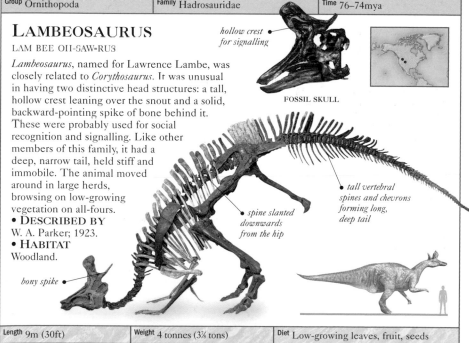

| Group Ornithopoda | Family Hadrosauridae | Time 76–74mya |
|---|---|---|

# LAMBEOSAURUS

LAM BEE OH-SAW-RUS

*Lambeosaurus*, named for Lawrence Lambe, was
closely related to *Corythosaurus*. It was unusual
in having two distinctive head structures: a tall,
hollow crest leaning over the snout and a solid,
backward-pointing spike of bone behind it.
These were probably used for social
recognition and signalling. Like other
members of this family, it had a
deep, narrow tail, held stiff and
immobile. The animal moved
around in large herds,
browsing on low-growing
vegetation on all-fours.
• **DESCRIBED BY**
W. A. Parker; 1923.
• **HABITAT**
Woodland.

hollow crest •
for signalling

**FOSSIL SKULL**

tall vertebral •
spines and chevrons
forming long,
deep tail

spine slanted •
downwards
from the hip

bony spike •

| Length 9m (30ft) | Weight 4 tonnes (3⅞ tons) | Diet Low-growing leaves, fruit, seeds |
|---|---|---|

| Group Pachycephalosauria | Family Pachycephalosauridae | Time 74–65mya |
|---|---|---|

# PACHYCEPHALOSAURUS

PACK-EE-KEF-AL-OH-SAW-RUS

It is easy to see why *Pachycephalosaurus* ("thick-headed lizard") was so named. The top of the dinosaur's skull was thickened into a dome of solid bone 25cm (10in) thick. It is thought that *Pachycephalosaurus* used its head as a battering ram for defence or in territorial fighting. It had a beak, and clusters of bony knobs surrounded the snout. Further groups of round knobs encircled the back of the head. Its relatively slim leg and foot bones indicate that this dinosaur may have been able to run more quickly than its heavy build might suggest. *Pachycephalosaurus* is the largest member of the Pachycephalosauridae family of dinosaurs discovered so far, and was the last to exist before the extinction of the dinosaurs at the end of the Cretaceous Period.

- **DESCRIBED BY** Barnum Brown and Erich Schlaiker; 1943.
- **HABITAT** Forests.

*greatly thickened bone on top of skull forming a dome*

*curved, fang-like teeth at front of mouth*

*bony protuberances around back of head*

SKULL

*small horny bumps covering the nose*

*straight tail stiffened by ligaments*

*five-fingered hands*

*long, slim legs*

*three-toed feet*

*long claws*

| Length 5m (16ft) | Weight 2 tonnes (2 tons) | Diet Leaves, fruit, perhaps small animals |
|---|---|---|

| Group Pachycephalosauria | Family Pachycephalosauridae | Time 76–74mya |
|---|---|---|

# STEGOCERAS

STEG-OH-SER-AS

A fast runner, *Stegoceras* (meaning "roof horn") had a body designed to withstand vigorous head-butting activity. When charging, its head was lowered at right angles, balanced by its neck, body, and tail held in a straight line. The skullcap was thickened into a dome of solid bone, and the grain of bone was angled to the surface, enabling it to withstand impact more effectively. Two types of skull have been found – ones with low, flat domes, and others with tall, rounded ones. These variations may indicate sexual differences. Stegoceras had small, serrated teeth that were ideal for shredding plant material.

- **DESCRIBED BY** Lawrence M. Lambe; 1902.
- **HABITAT** Upland forests.

*ridge of bone over eye and round back of head*

*skullcap thickened into dome of bone*

*slightly curved, serrated teeth*  FOSSIL SKULL

*domed skull*

*neck designed to be held horizontally when charging*

*expanded chamber at base of tail had unknown function*

*bony frill extended from back of skull*

*long, slim arms*

*three long, forward-facing, clawed toes*

| Length 2m (6½ft) | Weight 54kg (120lb) | Diet Leaves, fruit |
|---|---|---|

| Group Crocodylia | Family Eusuchia | Time 85–66mya |
|---|---|---|

# DEINOSUCHUS

DEI-NOH-SOOK-US

Only the skull of this "terrible crocodile" has been found, but the size of that suggests that *Deinosuchus* was one of the largest crocodilians ever to have existed. Palaeontologists are still debating its size, body proportions, and way of life. Like other members of its group, *Deinosuchus* had a secondary bony palate, allowing it to open its mouth underwater without swallowing water. It probably fed on fish and land-dwelling animals as they came close to river banks.

*large eye sockets*

*mouth with two bony palates*

*long sharp teeth*

*2m- (6½ft-) long skull*

• **DESCRIBED BY** John H. Ostrom; 1969.
• **HABITAT** Swamps.

| Length 15m (49ft) | Weight Unknown | Diet Fish, medium to large dinosaurs |
|---|---|---|

| Group Theria | Family Placentalia | Time 83.5–71mya |
|---|---|---|

# ZALAMBDALESTES

ZAH-LAMB-DAL-ES-TEES

*Zalambdalestes* was a shrew-like mammal, with a long tail and powerful hind legs that were longer than the front ones. The legs had elongated foot bones, and the hands were small, with non-opposable fingers. This suggests that *Zalambdalestes* was probably not a tree dweller. The eyes were very large, and the snout turned up sharply at the end. The incisors were long and sharp. The recent discovery of an epipubic bone (present only in non-placental mammals) in a skeleton of *Zalambdalestes* means its classification as a placental mammal is in dispute.

*small brain cavity*

*sensitive, long, upturned snout*

• **DESCRIBED BY** W.K. Gregory, G.G. Simpson; 1926.
• **HABITAT** Prairie.

| Length 20cm (8in) | Weight 25g (1oz) | Diet Insects |
|---|---|---|

| Group Theria | Family Marsupialia | Time 70mya |
|---|---|---|

# ALPHADON

AL-FA-DON

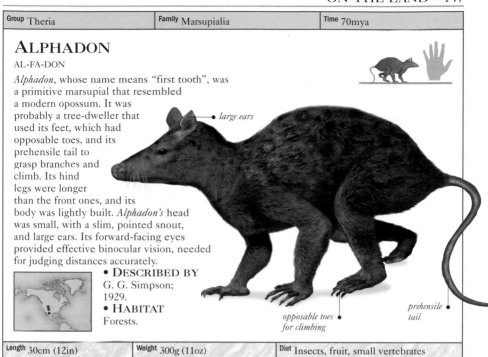

*Alphadon*, whose name means "first tooth", was a primitive marsupial that resembled a modern opossum. It was probably a tree-dweller that used its feet, which had opposable toes, and its prehensile tail to grasp branches and climb. Its hind legs were longer than the front ones, and its body was lightly built. *Alphadon's* head was small, with a slim, pointed snout, and large ears. Its forward-facing eyes provided effective binocular vision, needed for judging distances accurately.

- **DESCRIBED BY** G. G. Simpson; 1929.
- **HABITAT** Forests.

large ears

opposable toes for climbing

prehensile tail

| Length 30cm (12in) | Weight 300g (11oz) | Diet Insects, fruit, small vertebrates |
|---|---|---|

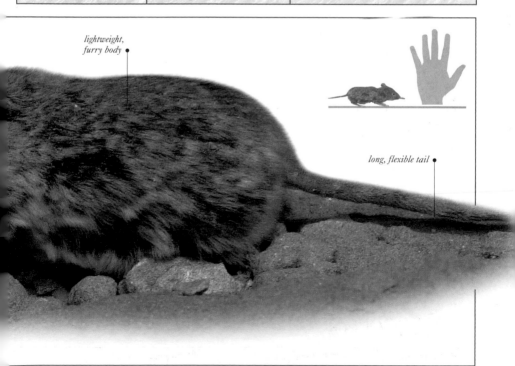

lightweight, furry body

long, flexible tail

# IN THE WATER

D uring the Cretaceous Period, oceans were generally warm, and there was a consequent increase in plankton growth, leading to greater diversity and larger sizes in marine species. Teleost fish, a group of advanced bony fish, which had first appeared during the Jurassic Period, now outnumbered the more primitive forms. Some species in this group, such as *Xiphactinus*, grew to 5m (16ft) or more in length. The ammonoids, which were the largest group of marine predators, were also abundant and grew to great sizes.

However, reptiles remained the largest marine carnivores. Plesiosaurs were still present in moderately large numbers, but ichthyosaurs had become rare by the end of the Jurassic, possibly due to competition from sharks.

The ecological niche vacated by the ichthyosaurs at the beginning of the Cretaceous was filled by the mosasaurs (a group of large marine reptiles distantly related to monitor lizards). During this period, they became the dominant carnivores in many marine environments around the world. They hunted squid, ammonoids, fish, and other mosasaurs. Like ichthyosaurs, mosasaurs gave birth to live young. Other large marine carnivores of the Cretaceous Period included giant turtles, such as *Archelon*, and sharks, such as *Cretoxyrhina*.

| Group Cryptodira | Family Protostegidae | Time 75mya |
|---|---|---|

## ARCHELON

AR-KAY-LON

This marine animal, whose name means "ruling turtle", was twice the length of modern species. It had a wide, flattened shell. This was was formed from belly ribs (gastralia) that grew out from the body wall. The shell was composed of a leathery covering or horny plates over a framework of bony struts that may have been visible underneath.

• **DESCRIBED BY** Wieland; 1895.
• **HABITAT** Oceans.

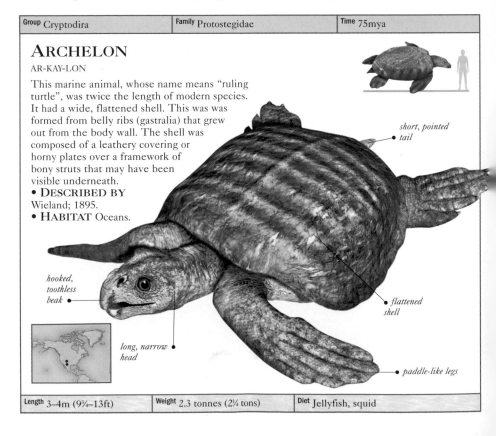

*short, pointed tail*

*hooked, toothless beak*

*long, narrow head*

*flattened shell*

*paddle-like legs*

| Length 3–4m (9¾–13ft) | Weight 2.3 tonnes (2¼ tons) | Diet Jellyfish, squid |
|---|---|---|

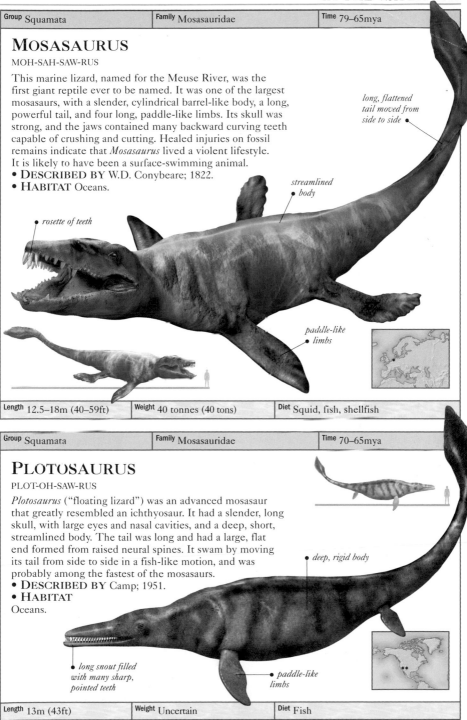

| Group Squamata | Family Mosasauridae | Time 79–65mya |
|---|---|---|

# MOSASAURUS

MOH-SAH-SAW-RUS

This marine lizard, named for the Meuse River, was the first giant reptile ever to be named. It was one of the largest mosasaurs, with a slender, cylindrical barrel-like body, a long, powerful tail, and four long, paddle-like limbs. Its skull was strong, and the jaws contained many backward curving teeth capable of crushing and cutting. Healed injuries on fossil remains indicate that *Mosasaurus* lived a violent lifestyle. It is likely to have been a surface-swimming animal.
• **DESCRIBED BY** W.D. Conybeare; 1822.
• **HABITAT** Oceans.

long, flattened tail moved from side to side

streamlined body

rosette of teeth

paddle-like limbs

| Length 12.5–18m (40–59ft) | Weight 40 tonnes (40 tons) | Diet Squid, fish, shellfish |
|---|---|---|

| Group Squamata | Family Mosasauridae | Time 70–65mya |
|---|---|---|

# PLOTOSAURUS

PLOT-OH-SAW-RUS

*Plotosaurus* ("floating lizard") was an advanced mosasaur that greatly resembled an ichthyosaur. It had a slender, long skull, with large eyes and nasal cavities, and a deep, short, streamlined body. The tail was long and had a large, flat end formed from raised neural spines. It swam by moving its tail from side to side in a fish-like motion, and was probably among the fastest of the mosasaurs.
• **DESCRIBED BY** Camp; 1951.
• **HABITAT** Oceans.

deep, rigid body

long snout filled with many sharp, pointed teeth

paddle-like limbs

| Length 13m (43ft) | Weight Uncertain | Diet Fish |
|---|---|---|

| Group Squamata | Family Mosasauridae | Time 85–78mya |
|---|---|---|

# TYLOSAURUS

TIE-LOW-SAW-RUS

This large sea lizard was one of the later members of the mosasaur family, and a fearsome predator. It had teeth on its palate bones as well as those in its long jaws. Its skull bones could move quite freely at the joints, allowing it to expand its jaws to swallow large prey. The snout was hard and bony at the tip (its name means "knob lizard"), leading some paleontologists to surmise that it may have rammed its prey. *Tylosaurus* probably swam by moving its deep, narrow tail in a side-to-side motion and steering with its large, wing-shaped flippers.
• **DESCRIBED BY** Othniel C. Marsh; 1872.
• **HABITAT** Shallow seas.

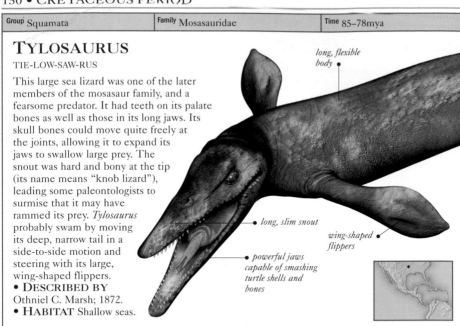

*long, flexible body*

*long, slim snout*

*wing-shaped flippers*

*powerful jaws capable of smashing turtle shells and bones*

| Length 11m (36ft) | Weight 7 tonnes (6⅞ tons) | Diet Turtles, fish, other mosasaurs |
|---|---|---|

| Group Plesiosauroidea | Family Pliosauridae | Time 110mya |
|---|---|---|

# KRONOSAURUS

CRO-NO-SAW-RUS

*Kronosaurus* ("Kronos lizard") was a giant marine reptile, classed as a pliosaur because of its enormous head, compact body, and short neck and tail. Fossilized stomach contents show that *Kronosaurus* lived rather like a modern shark, devouring anything that came its way. Its head alone was 3m (9¾ft) long, and its sharp, pointed teeth were about 25cm (10in) long. Its snout was long and triangular. It had two pairs of flippers, the rear ones being longer than the front pair. There may have been a fin at the top of the tail to help steer the animal. The body of *Kronosaurus* was kept stiff as it swam by tightly linked belly ribs (gastralia).
• **DESCRIBED BY** Heber A. Longman; 1924.
• **HABITAT** Deep oceans.

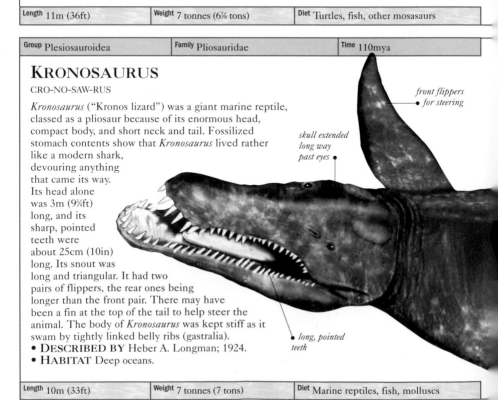

*front flippers for steering*

*skull extended long way past eyes*

*long, pointed teeth*

| Length 10m (33ft) | Weight 7 tonnes (7 tons) | Diet Marine reptiles, fish, molluscs |
|---|---|---|

high but narrow
tail for effective
propulsion

high vertebral
spines on tail

bones in body
had fat-filled
spaces

FRONT
FLIPPER
BONES

FOSSIL SKELETON

finger bone

mobile skull bones
allowed for swallowing
large prey

compact
body

vertebral
spine

short tail

large rear flippers

| Group Plesiosauria | Family Elasmosauridae | Time 69–66mya |
|---|---|---|

# ELASMOSAURUS

EH-LAZ-MOH-SAW-RUS

*Elasmosaurus* ("ribbon lizard") was the longest known plesiosaur. More than half of its body length consisted of the greatly elongated neck. This had 71 vertebrae, whereas earlier plesiosaurs had only 28. The length and structure of its neck meant that *Elasmosaurus* would have been able to bend it around its body sideways to feed. However, calculations of the water resistance it would have met have led some palaeontologists to suggest an alternative method of feeding. It is possible that *Elasmosaurus* paddled along on the surface, holding its neck high to spot prey in the water. The long neck would then have been plunged into the water to catch it.

*Elasmosaurus'* body was similar to that of other plesiosaurs: it had four long, paddle-like flippers, a tiny head, sharp teeth in strong jaws, and a short, pointed tail.

• **DESCRIBED BY** E.D. Cope; 1868.
• **HABITAT** Oceans.

*greatly elongated*
*• neck*

*tiny head and mouth*
*• with small, sharp teeth*

| Length 14m (46ft) | Weight 3 tons (3 tonnes) | Diet Fish, squid, shellfish |
|---|---|---|

front flippers
slightly
longer than
hind ones •———

• short, stiff body

short pointed •
tail

## LEPIDOTES

*Elasmosaurus* feasted on large fish
such as *Lepidotes* (right) and
many other forms of marine life
that abounded in the Cretaceous
oceans. *Lepidotes* was almost the
length of a human and was itself
a voracious predator of smaller
marine creatures, such as
shellfish, which it crunched with
its strong teeth.

bony rays
supported
each fin •

rigid overlapping
• scales

# IN THE AIR

**B**y the early Cretaceous Period, bird species had greatly radiated and diversified. Most of these early birds still had very primitive features, such as teeth. However, by the Late Cretaceous they were looking far more like modern birds. Some species of wading and diving birds had even lost the ability to fly.

Cretaceous skies still seem to have been dominated by the pterosaurs, at least until later on in the period. In the Cretaceous these reached immense sizes. It was at this time that the largest flying animal ever existed. This was the pterosaur *Quetzalcoatlus*, which has a wingspan as large as a modern small glider.

The fossil record suggests that the diversity of pterosaurs declined in the Late Cretaceous, and by the end of the period, only a few species were left. To date, no fossil remains have been found of these creatures from sediments younger than the Cretaceous, so it seems likely that they died out along with the dinosaurs in the end-Cretaceous extinction. However, the reasons why birds survived while the pterosaurs did not are unclear.

It is possible that the increasing numbers and diversity of birds had some impact on pterosaur populations and evolution. Birds may have filled ecological niches the pterosaurs vacated through normal extinction processes and thus slowly displaced pterosaurs. However, for most of the Cretaceous Period, it seems that pterosaurs and birds overlapped only to a small extent, with the two groups apparently co-existing quite easily.

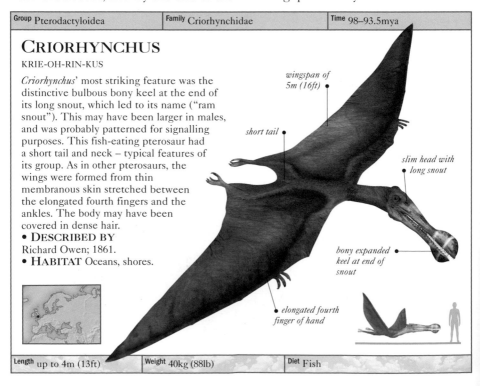

| Group Pterodactyloidea | Family Criorhynchidae | Time 98–93.5mya |
|---|---|---|

## CRIORHYNCHUS

KRIE-OH-RIN-KUS

*Criorhynchus'* most striking feature was the distinctive bulbous bony keel at the end of its long snout, which led to its name ("ram snout"). This may have been larger in males, and was probably patterned for signalling purposes. This fish-eating pterosaur had a short tail and neck – typical features of its group. As in other pterosaurs, the wings were formed from thin membranous skin stretched between the elongated fourth fingers and the ankles. The body may have been covered in dense hair.

• **DESCRIBED BY** Richard Owen; 1861.
• **HABITAT** Oceans, shores.

wingspan of 5m (16ft)

short tail

slim head with long snout

bony expanded keel at end of snout

elongated fourth finger of hand

| Length up to 4m (13ft) | Weight 40kg (88lb) | Diet Fish |
|---|---|---|

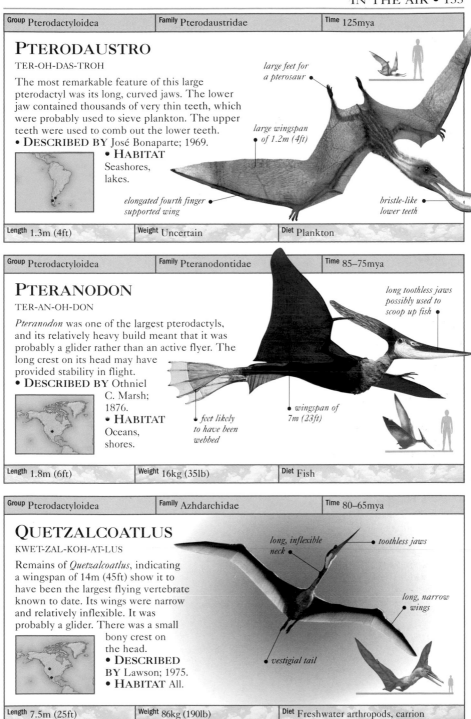

| Group Pterodactyloidea | Family Pterodaustridae | Time 125mya |

# PTERODAUSTRO

TER-OH-DAS-TROH

The most remarkable feature of this large pterodactyl was its long, curved jaws. The lower jaw contained thousands of very thin teeth, which were probably used to sieve plankton. The upper teeth were used to comb out the lower teeth.
• **DESCRIBED BY** José Bonaparte; 1969.
• **HABITAT** Seashores, lakes.

*large feet for a pterosaur*

*large wingspan of 1.2m (4ft)*

*elongated fourth finger supported wing*

*bristle-like lower teeth*

| Length 1.3m (4ft) | Weight Uncertain | Diet Plankton |

| Group Pterodactyloidea | Family Pteranodontidae | Time 85–75mya |

# PTERANODON

TER-AN-OH-DON

*Pteranodon* was one of the largest pterodactyls, and its relatively heavy build meant that it was probably a glider rather than an active flyer. The long crest on its head may have provided stability in flight.
• **DESCRIBED BY** Othniel C. Marsh; 1876.
• **HABITAT** Oceans, shores.

*long toothless jaws possibly used to scoop up fish*

*feet likely to have been webbed*

*wingspan of 7m (23ft)*

| Length 1.8m (6ft) | Weight 16kg (35lb) | Diet Fish |

| Group Pterodactyloidea | Family Azhdarchidae | Time 80–65mya |

# QUETZALCOATLUS

KWET-ZAL-KOH-AT-LUS

Remains of *Quetzalcoatlus*, indicating a wingspan of 14m (45ft) show it to have been the largest flying vertebrate known to date. Its wings were narrow and relatively inflexible. It was probably a glider. There was a small bony crest on the head.
• **DESCRIBED BY** Lawson; 1975.
• **HABITAT** All.

*long, inflexible neck*

*toothless jaws*

*long, narrow wings*

*vestigial tail*

| Length 7.5m (25ft) | Weight 86kg (190lb) | Diet Freshwater arthropods, carrion |

| Group Aves | Family Confuciusornithidae | Time 150–120mya |
|---|---|---|

# CONFUCIUSORNIS

CON-FUSH-EE-US-OAR-NIS

*Confuciusornis* ("Confucius bird") was the first bird known to have a true, horny beak. It had a mixture of primitive features (clawed wing fingers and a flat breastbone) and modern adaptations, such as a deeper chest and shortened tail core. The foot claws were highly curved, and the large toe was reversed, indicating that it was a tree-dweller. Males had long tail feathers.

*three wing fingers with curved claws*

*toothless, horny beak with slight upward curve*

Its beak turned up slightly at the end, leading to debate about its diet. *Confuciusornis* was most probably a side-shoot from the modern bird lineage.
• **DESCRIBED BY** Lianhai Hou; 1997.
• **HABITAT** Woodland.

| Length 31cm (1ft) | Weight Unknown | Diet Seeds, possibly fish |
|---|---|---|

| Group Aves | Family Hesperornithidae | Time 75mya |
|---|---|---|

# HESPERORNIS

HESS-PER-OAR-NISS

This large, toothed seabird lived a lifestyle very similar to that of modern penguins. It had lost the power of flight, and its vestigial wings were tiny and stubby.

*long neck that could be held in S-shape over shoulders*

The head was long and low, with a long beak armed with sharp, pointed teeth for catching fish and other small marine creatures. *Hesperornis* ("western bird") was probably a powerful swimmer, using its large, webbed feet for propulsion, but may have moved clumsily on land. It probably nested on seashores.

*legs set far back*

*splint-like bones supported tiny wings*

*long, pointed, toothed beak*

• **DESCRIBED BY** Othniel C. Marsh; 1872.
• **HABITAT** Seashores.

| Length 2m (6½ft) | Weight Unknown | Diet Fish, squid |
|---|---|---|

| Group Aves | Family Ichthyornithidae | Time 135–70mya |
|---|---|---|

# ICHTHYORNIS

IK-THEE-OAR-NISS

When the jaw of this toothed, primitive bird was re-examined in 1952, it was thought for a time, incorrectly, to belong to a juvenile mosasaur. The jaws and teeth of *Ichthyornis* ("fish bird") are indeed similar to those of a marine reptile. *Ichthyornis* was a seabird, similar in size and build to a modern seagull, but its head and beak were much larger. It had a well-developed, keeled breastbone, and a deep chest, suggesting it may have been a strong flyer. Its webbed feet had claws.

• **DESCRIBED BY** Othniel C. Marsh; 1872.
• **HABITAT** Seashores.

*proportionately large head*

*long, horny bill filled with sharp teeth*

*webbed feet with short claws*

| Length 20cm (8in) | Weight Unknown | Diet Fish |
|---|---|---|

| Group Theropoda | Family Alvezsauria | Time 85–75mya |
|---|---|---|

# SHUVUUIA

SHU-VOO-EE-A

Since its discovery, *Shuvuuia* (its name is derived from "shuvuu", the Mongolian word for bird) has provoked great debate as to whether it was a dinosaur-like bird, or a bird-like dinosaur. It did look superficially like a dinosaur, but examination of its skull shows it to have been more closely related to modern birds than, for example, *Archaeopteryx*. Although *Shuvuuia* did not have a true beak, its slender jaws bore tiny teeth, and it may have been able to raise its upper jaw in relation to the braincase, a facility only modern birds have. Chemical analysis also shows that it was feathered. The legs were long and slim, suggesting that it may have been a fast runner. The forelimbs were short and stubby, and ended in a single, clawed digit.

• **DESCRIBED BY** Chiappe, Norell, and Clark; 1998.
• **HABITAT** Plains.

*head very like that of modern birds*

*long, slender neck*

*claw on digit may have been used for opening termite nests*

*long, slim legs*

*feet with three forward-facing, clawed toes*

| Length 1m (3½ft) | Weight 2.5kg (5½lb) | Diet Insects, small reptiles |
|---|---|---|

# CENOZOIC ERA
## AFTER THE DINOSAURS

The Cenozoic Era (comprising the Tertiary
and Quaternary Periods) followed the end-
Cretaceous mass extinction event, which
marked the disappearance of the dinosaurs,
pterosaurs, some birds and mammals, and
many marine species.

During the Early Tertiary (Paleocene,
Eocene, and Oligocene Epochs)—the
surviving mammals and birds diversified
rapidly to take over the ecological niches left
vacant by the dinosaurs. During the Late
Tertiary (Miocene and Pliocene Epochs) the
spread of grasslands led to the evolution of
modern forms of grazing mammals.

By the Quaternary Period (Pleistocene and
Holocene Epochs), animal and plant life
generally resembled modern forms, although
some species that were adapted to recurring
ice ages did not survive into modern times.

# EARLY TERTIARY PERIOD

65–23.5 MILLION YEARS AGO

The Early Tertiary, including the Palaeocene, Eocene, and Oligocene epochs, was the beginning of the "Age of Mammals". Many ecological niches had been left vacant by the end-Cretaceous mass extinction of dinosaurs, and mammal and bird populations evolved and expanded rapidly to fill the gaps. Climates worldwide were warm or hot, with high rainfall. Vast areas of swampy forest and tropical rainforest developed. Towards the mid Tertiary, a large ice cap formed over the South Pole. This resulted in a fall in sea levels, and the climate became much cooler. Tropical forests disappeared in temperate regions and were replaced by woodlands dominated by deciduous and coniferous trees.

### EARLY TERTIARY LIFE

Despite the rapid evolution of mammals into many ecological niches, large herbivores only appeared at the end of the Palaeocene (about 53mya). There were no large mammalian carnivores at all – their niche was filled by very large, flightless birds, such as *Gastornis* (p.167). The reptile groups, including crocodiles and lizards, that had survived the end-Cretaceous extinction flourished in the warm, swampy conditions, as did smaller amphibians.

### ICARONYCTERIS

The first bats, such as *Icaronycteris* (right), first appeared in the Palaeocene. They filled the niche left by insectivorous pterosaurs, and like them, had wings formed from membranous skin.

• *wings supported on all fingers*

• *feet thought to have been webbed for swimming*

### AMBULOCETUS

As well as diversifying on the land, mammals took to the oceans. The ancestors of whales, such *Ambulocetus* (left), evolved from pig-like mammals. These primitive animals showed few adaptations to marine life.

4,600mya        4,000mya                    3,000mya

## EARLY TERTIARY LANDMASSES

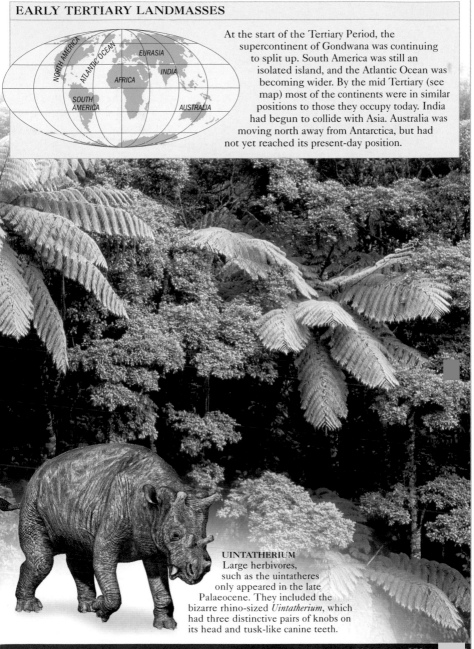

At the start of the Tertiary Period, the supercontinent of Gondwana was continuing to split up. South America was still an isolated island, and the Atlantic Ocean was becoming wider. By the mid Tertiary (see map) most of the continents were in similar positions to those they occupy today. India had begun to collide with Asia. Australia was moving north away from Antarctica, but had not yet reached its present-day position.

On the map: NORTH AMERICA, ATLANTIC OCEAN, EURASIA, INDIA, AFRICA, SOUTH AMERICA, AUSTRALIA

**UINTATHERIUM**
Large herbivores, such as the uintatheres only appeared in the late Palaeocene. They included the bizarre rhino-sized *Uintatherium*, which had three distinctive pairs of knobs on its head and tusk-like canine teeth.

2,000mya        1,000mya      500mya    250mya

# ON THE LAND

**T**he first epoch of the Tertiary Period, the Palaeocene, started with no large land animals. This left many ecological niches available for the animal groups that had survived the end-Cretaceous mass extinction. Non-dinosaurian reptiles, such as crocodiles, lizards, and snakes, flourished in the warm climate and tropical forests. Amphibians also did well in these conditions. However, these groups did not dominate the land as the dinosaurs had done. Instead, mammals and birds evolved to fill the roles of land herbivores and predators.

Mammals entered the Tertiary as mostly nocturnal, rodent-sized animals, and rapidly diversified into many new forms. Marsupials, which had been as common as placental mammals in the Cretaceous Period, were still plentiful during the Early Tertiary. Whereas, in other areas of the world, marsupials gradually lost ground to placentals, Australia's separation from Antarctica left the marsupials there to evolve and flourish in isolation. Large mammalian herbivores appeared only at the very end of the Palaeocene. Carnivorous mammals also appeared at this time, including the hoofed mesonychids. However, these were only small predators. The niche of large carnivores was taken instead by giant, flightless birds such as *Gastornis*.

Through the Eocene and Oligocene, mammals became established as the major lifeform in all the main habitats. Large mammalian carnivores appeared during late Eocene times, and mammals similar to modern forms began to appear in the Oligocene.

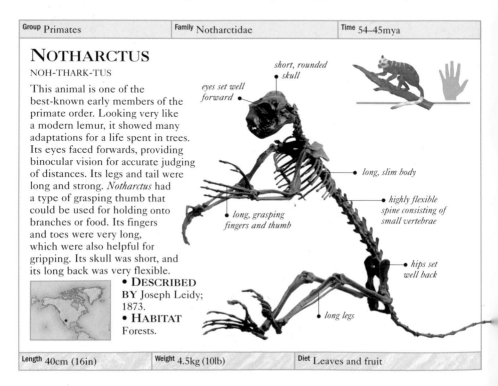

| Group Primates | Family Notharctidae | Time 54–45mya |
|---|---|---|

## NOTHARCTUS

NOH-THARK-TUS

This animal is one of the best-known early members of the primate order. Looking very like a modern lemur, it showed many adaptations for a life spent in trees. Its eyes faced forwards, providing binocular vision for accurate judging of distances. Its legs and tail were long and strong. *Notharctus* had a type of grasping thumb that could be used for holding onto branches or food. Its fingers and toes were very long, which were also helpful for gripping. Its skull was short, and its long back was very flexible.

• **DESCRIBED BY** Joseph Leidy; 1873.
• **HABITAT** Forests.

*short, rounded skull*

*eyes set well forward*

*long, slim body*

*highly flexible spine consisting of small vertebrae*

*long, grasping fingers and thumb*

*hips set well back*

*long legs*

| Length 40cm (16in) | Weight 4.5kg (10lb) | Diet Leaves and fruit |
|---|---|---|

| Group Dinocerata | Family Uintatheriidae | Time 45–35mya |
|---|---|---|

# UINTATHERIUM

YOU-IN-TAH-THEER-EE-UM

*largest horns at back of skull* •

SKULL

At the time when *Uintatherium* ("Uinta beast") existed, it was one of the largest land mammals. The size of a modern rhinoceros, it was heavy limbed, with massive bones. It had three pairs of horns on its face, which varied in size. The largest horns were at the back of the head. All of them seem to have been covered in skin and possibly hair. Males appear to have had larger horns than females. It is possible that the males fought using their horns and tusk-like canine teeth. The barrel-shaped body was carried on column-like legs. *Uintatherium* walked only on its toes, which were very short, as were the other "hand" and "foot" bones. Its elephant-like feet were designed for weight-bearing and walking on dry ground. *Uintatherium* had a very small brain for its skull size compared with modern hoofed mammals.

*tusk-like canine teeth, larger in males* •

• **DESCRIBED BY** Joseph Leidy; 1873.
• **HABITAT** Forests.

*massive, barrel-shaped body* •

*coarse, thick hide* •

*matted hair may have covered rear horns* •

*bony jaw flanges protected tusk-like canines* •

• *pillar-like legs adapted for weight-bearing*

| Length 3.5m (11ft) | Weight 2 tonnes (2 tons) | Diet Leaves, fruit, water plants |
|---|---|---|

| Group Litopterna | Family Didolodontidae | Time 60–50mya |
|---|---|---|

# DIDOLODUS

DIE-DOH-LOH-DUS

The classification of *Didolodus* is still debated by palaeontologists. Some place it with early browsing and rooting ungulates (hoofed animals); others as a primitive litoptern (a now extinct group of hoofed mammals).
Little is known of *Didolodus*. Its teeth were very similar to those of the earliest hoofed mammals, and so it may have resembled them in some respects. It was a browsing animal, with a long tail, and slim legs ending in five-toed feet.
• **DESCRIBED BY** Florentino Ameghino; 1897.
• **HABITAT** Forests.

*long, strong tail*

*long, cylindrical body*

*relatively short, deep head*

*five-toed feet*

| Length 60cm (24in) | Weight 15–20kg (33–44lb) | Diet Leaves |
|---|---|---|

| Group Condylarthra | Family Phenacodontidae | Time 57.8–52mya |
|---|---|---|

# PHENACODUS

FEN-A-COAD-US

*Phenacodus* was one of the earliest ungulate (hoofed) mammals. It was relatively small and lightly built, with limbs ending in five toes. The middle toe was the largest, and the weight of the body was mainly supported on this and the two adjoining toes. These probably had short, blunt hoof-like claws. The head was small, with a proportionately small brain. The jaws held 44 teeth. The back was arched, and the tail was long and powerful. *Phenacodus* probably lived in herds, and it is possible that it was carnivorous or insectivorous as well as herbivorous.
• **DESCRIBED BY** Edward Drinker Cope; 1881.
• **HABITAT** Forests.

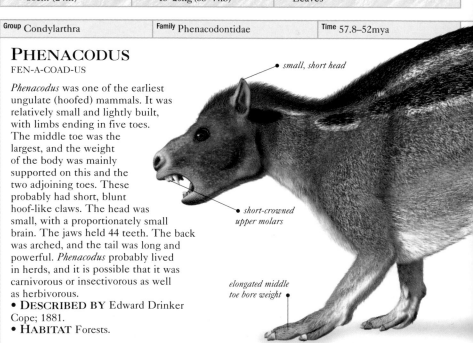

*small, short head*

*short-crowned upper molars*

*elongated middle toe bore weight*

| Length 1.2m (4ft) | Weight 10kg (22lb) | Diet Leaves; possibly tubers and insects |
|---|---|---|

| Group Condylarthra | Family Mesonychidae | Time 45mya |
| --- | --- | --- |

# MESONYX

MEE-ZON-ICKS

This mesonychid carnivore, whose name means "middle claw", had a wolf-like body and agile limbs that ended in five toes with small blunt claws. The long skull had a bony crest to which the large jaw muscles were anchored. This gave a powerful bite. The canine teeth were long and sharp, and the lower molars were thin and blade-like. Palaeontologists have suggested that the mesonychids were the ancestors of modern whales. However, it is now thought that whales are closer to pig-like ancestors.

*wide mouth with powerful bite*

• **DESCRIBED BY** Joseph Leidy; 1894.
• **HABITAT** Scrubland, open woodland.

| Length 1.8m (6ft) | Weight Unknown | Diet Meat, carrion, possibly plants |
| --- | --- | --- |

*arched back*

*molars*

*long, powerfully muscled tail*

*greatly reduced outer toes*

JAW BONE FRAGMENT

| Group Embrithopoda | Family Arsinoitheriidae | Time 38–23mya |
|---|---|---|

# ARSINOTHERIUM

AR-SIN-OH-THEER-EE-UM

*Arsinotherium* is the best-known member of the embrithopods – large, rhino-like animals that were closely related to elephants. Its most notable feature were the two huge, conical horns that jutted out from its snout. These were composed of hollow bone and may have been covered in skin. Adult animals had pointed horns, while they were rounded in juveniles.

• **DESCRIBED BY** Hugh Beadnell; 1906.

• **HABITAT** Forests near rivers.

barrel-like body

44 unspecialized teeth

five-toed feet

| Length 3.5m (11½ft) | Weight Unknown | Diet Tough foliage |
|---|---|---|

| Group Proboscidea | Family Moeritheridae | Time 50–33mya |
|---|---|---|

# MOERITHERIUM

MEE-RI-THEER-EE-UM

This hippo-like animal, which was named after the ancient Greek name for the lake in Egypt where it was found (Moeris), was actually related to elephants. It had a low-slung, long body, with relatively short legs. Its nostrils were at the front of the skull, indicating that it did not have a trunk. The teeth were small, but two of the incisors formed small tusks. It was probably partly aquatic in its lifestyle, as is the modern hippopotamus.

• **DESCRIBED BY** Roy Chapman Andrews; 1923.

• **HABITAT** Rivers and swamps.

ears high on head

elongated, fleshy upper lip

| Length 3m (9¾ft) | Weight 200kg (440lb) | Diet Water plants |
|---|---|---|

| Group Gruiformes | Family Gastornithidae | Time 56–41mya |
|---|---|---|

# GASTORNIS

GAS-TOR-NISS

This giant flightless "Gaston's bird" is now thought by some palaeontologists to be the same species as a similar bird known as *Diatryma*. It was large and heavily built, with tiny wings that were incapable of flight. Its long legs were powerful and armed with clawed feet. Its head was almost the same size as that of a modern horse. There has been great debate over the purpose of *Gastornis*' beak. Some believe that *Gastornis* was a large predator and used its beak to tear at the flesh and crush the bones of its prey. Others contend that *Gastornis* was actually a herbivore that used its beak to shear through vegetation.

- **DESCRIBED BY** Victor Lemoine; 1878.
- **HABITAT** Forests.

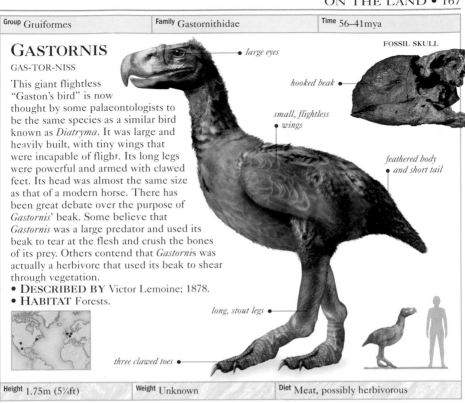

FOSSIL SKULL

large eyes

hooked beak

small, flightless wings

feathered body and short tail

long, stout legs

three clawed toes

| Height 1.75m (5¾ft) | Weight Unknown | Diet Meat, possibly herbivorous |
|---|---|---|

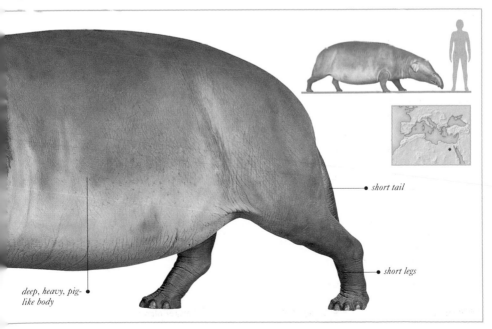

short tail

short legs

deep, heavy, pig-like body

# IN THE WATER

**W**ith the disappearance of the giant marine reptiles of the Mesozoic Period, more modern and recognizable forms of ocean life evolved during the early Tertiary Period. Fish took on more recognizable forms, and new groups of shellfish appeared. The first penguins also evolved at this time, including some giant forms.

At some point in the early Tertiary, mammals moved to fill the ecological niche left open by the absence of large, ocean-dwelling carnivores. The first whale is thought to have been an animal called *Pakicetus*. This mammal seems to have been closely related to the land-dwelling hoofed mammals. Only its skull has been discovered to date, and so little is known of how it actually looked in life. Its claimed

relationship to cetaceans (whales) is due to certain peculiarities in its ear bones which are unique to whales. Its teeth are also ideal for a diet of fish. However, it is clear that this animal, as well as other early whales, had few adaptations for marine life.

The first whales had four walking limbs that could be used for swimming, perhaps with webbed toes. They probably spent most of their time on land, only entering the water to hunt. As they evolved, the front limbs gradually evolved into flippers, a tail fluke appeared, their bodies became more streamlined, and the hind limbs grew smaller. In later whales, the hind limbs are absent altogether. Early whales did not have ears that were capable of detecting ultrasound. They therefore relied on sight for hunting.

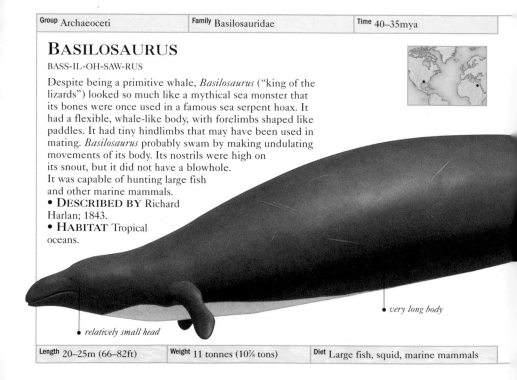

| Group Archaeoceti | Family Basilosauridae | Time 40–35mya |
|---|---|---|

## BASILOSAURUS

BASS-IL-OH-SAW-RUS

Despite being a primitive whale, *Basilosaurus* ("king of the lizards") looked so much like a mythical sea monster that its bones were once used in a famous sea serpent hoax. It had a flexible, whale-like body, with forelimbs shaped like paddles. It had tiny hindlimbs that may have been used in mating. *Basilosaurus* probably swam by making undulating movements of its body. Its nostrils were high on its snout, but it did not have a blowhole. It was capable of hunting large fish and other marine mammals.
• **DESCRIBED BY** Richard Harlan; 1843.
• **HABITAT** Tropical oceans.

*very long body*

*relatively small head*

| Length 20–25m (66–82ft) | Weight 11 tonnes (10⅞ tons) | Diet Large fish, squid, marine mammals |
|---|---|---|

| Group Archaeoceti | Family Protocetidae | Time 50mya |
|---|---|---|

# AMBULOCETUS

AM-BYU-LOH-SEE-TUS

*Ambulocetus* ("walking whale") is thought to be one of the most primitive cetaceans (whales). Its teeth, skull, and ear bones show features unique to this group. As its name suggests, it probably spent most of its time on land, although it may have been rather clumsy. Its feet and hands may have been webbed, and its powerful hindlimbs would have made it a strong swimmer. It is thought to have hunted by ambushing its prey in water as modern crocodiles do.

• **DESCRIBED BY** Hans Thewissen; 1994.

• **HABITAT** Estuaries.

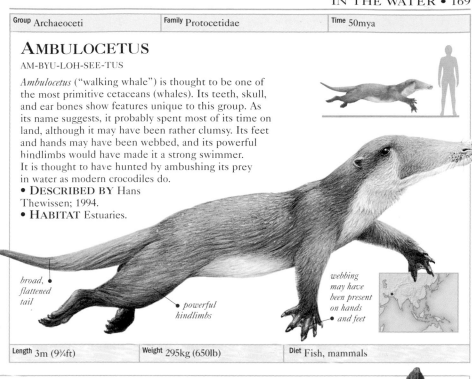

broad, flattened tail

powerful hindlimbs

webbing may have been present on hands and feet

| Length 3m (9¾ft) | Weight 295kg (650lb) | Diet Fish, mammals |
|---|---|---|

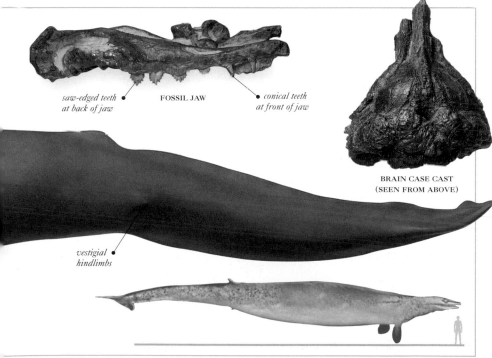

saw-edged teeth at back of jaw    FOSSIL JAW    conical teeth at front of jaw

BRAIN CASE CAST (SEEN FROM ABOVE)

vestigial hindlimbs

# IN THE AIR

T he timing of the first appearance of modern birds is still hotly debated. The standard view of avian evolution states that modern bird forms (Neornithes) first arose in the Palaeocene. A new theory asserts that modern birds were already present at the end of the Cretaceous, and then closely paralleled mammals in an explosive evolution during the Palaeocene and Eocene Epochs of the Early Tertiary.

Whichever view is correct, we know that within ten million years of the start of the Palaeocene all of the major lineages of birds had evolved. All of the major bird orders had appeared by the early Eocene, including primitive herons, swifts, eagles, and owls. It seems likely that all of the bird lineages diverged from a common group fairly soon after the end-Cretaceous extinction.

The Early Tertiary also saw the appearance of the first flying mammals – bats. Some mammal teeth from the Palaeocene found in France show characters of both bats and insectivores (the group including hedgehogs, moles, and shrews). However, it is not known whether these were primitive bats or not. The first undoubted bat fossils date from the Eocene and represent essentially modern-looking forms; by this time bats had evolved all of their characteristic features, perhaps even an early type of echolocation. Their distribution was very different from that seen today, with fruit bats occurring in Europe, rather than in tropical areas, and vampire bats occurring as far north as California.

| Group Chiroptera | Family Uncertain | Time 55–45mya |
|---|---|---|

## ICARONYCTERIS

IK-A-RON-IK-TER-IS

The oldest-known bat, *Icaronycteris* is surprisingly similar to modern forms. Analysis of its skull shows that it may have used a primitive form of echolocation. Its long tail was not joined to the legs by flaps of skin as in modern bats. The arrangement of the many teeth in the mouth indicate an insect diet. This has been confirmed by remains found in the stomach area of fossil remains.
• **DESCRIBED BY** Glen Lowell Jepsen; 1966.
• **HABITAT** Caves.

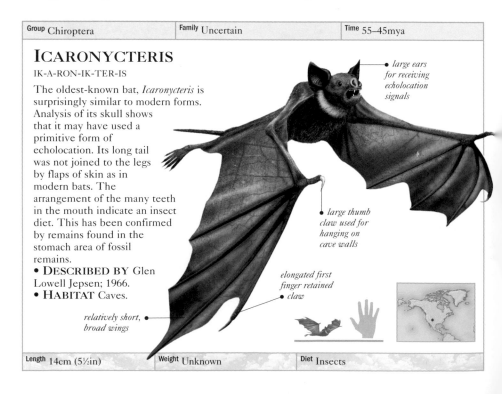

*large ears for receiving echolocation signals*

*large thumb claw used for hanging on cave walls*

*elongated first finger retained claw*

*relatively short, broad wings*

| Length 14cm (5½in) | Weight Unknown | Diet Insects |
|---|---|---|

| Group Anseriformes | Family Presbyornithidae | Time 40–60mya |
|---|---|---|

# PRESBYORNIS

PREZ-BEE-OAR-NIS

This primitive duck was so slenderly built that palaeontologists first thought it was a type of flamingo. Unlike modern ducks, *Presbyornis* had very long legs and presumably was a wader, rather than a swimmer. The relative length of the neck and legs of *Presbyornis* are consistent with a wading, bottom-feeding style. However, the legs were set relatively far back, suggesting that it may also have been a diving bird. Its feet were large and webbed. *Presbyornis* was highly colonial, and seems to have gathered in large flocks to feed by the shores of lakes. Its principal diet was probably based on filter feeding, using the tongue to draw water in like a straw, extracting food by pressing the tongue against the roof of the mouth, and expelling the excess water out of the sides of the bill. Hundreds of *Presbyornis* fossils have been found, representing several species that range from 0.5m (1½ft) to 1.5m (5ft) in height.
• **DESCRIBED BY**
Alexander Wetmore; 1926.
• **HABITAT** Lakeshores.

*salt gland around edge of eye orbit*

*ridge along top of beak*

*long neck*

*long, slim wings*

*slightly built body*

*legs set far back*

*long, slim legs*

*large, webbed feet*

| Height 0.5–1.5m (1½–5ft) | Weight Unknown | Diet Plankton, water plants |
|---|---|---|

# LATE TERTIARY PERIOD

23.5–1.75 MILLION YEARS AGO

The Late Tertiary (the Miocene and Pliocene epochs) saw the continued evolution of mammals. The ice cap that had started to form at the South Pole in the Oligocene continued to expand. By the mid Miocene, it covered the whole of Antarctica, further cooling the world's climate. These temperate conditions led to the development of huge expanses of grassland over Africa, Asia, Europe, and the Americas. The climate continued to cool into the Pliocene, when a large ice cap also formed at the North Pole. Most of the remaining forest areas had disappeared by the end of the Pliocene, but grasslands continued to spread.

## LATE TERTIARY LIFE

The animals of the Miocene and Pliocene were very similar to modern forms. Grasslands were filled with herds of horses, camels, elephants, and antelopes. Large carnivores hunted across the plains, and the first humans evolved from primate ancestors. In the oceans, modern types of fish had appeared, and the primitive forms of whales had given way to more familiar, larger species.

*sharp, hooked beak*

*reduced wings solely for display*

**TERRIBLE BIRDS**
Large carnivorous birds were still some of the world's largest and most terrifying predators. The South American terror bird *Titanis* (left) hunted on open grassy plains. It moved into North America when the Panama Isthmus formed in the Miocene.

| 4,600mya | 4,000mya | 3,000mya |

## LATE TERTIARY LANDMASSES

During the Miocene, Africa collided with Europe, forming the Alps, and India's collision with Asia caused the Himalayas to rise. The Rocky Mountains in North America and the Andes in South America formed. By the Pliocene, a land bridge linked North and South America. Australia continued to drift northwards. By the end of the Pliocene, the continents had almost reached their modern positions.

**BIG CATS**
Many carnivores evolved large stabbing canine teeth. *Thylacosmilus* (right) was a cat-like marsupial found in Miocene and Pliocene South America.

*large canine teeth*

**EARLY ELEPHANTS**
By the beginning of the Miocene, primitive elephant forms, such as the horse-sized *Phiomia* (left) were dying out, and being replaced by more larger forms. These, such as the shovel-tusked *Platybelodon*, would give rise to the mammoths of the Pleistocene and to modern elephant species.

| 2,000mya | 1,000mya | 500mya | 250mya | 0 |

# ON THE LAND

T he grasslands that formed in huge expanses over the world during the Miocene and Pliocene Epochs provided new habitats for mammals to evolve. Exposed to predators on grasslands, animals developed mechanisms for faster running, such as longer, slimmer legs. By the end of the Tertiary, many mammal species closely resembled modern forms.

Hoofed mammals exploited the grassland environments. Camels and antelopes became more diverse, and many horse-like animals appeared during the Miocene. One new type, called *Merychippus*, was far larger than earlier horses and was effectively single-hooved. By the end of the Pliocene, modern horses had evolved.

Also successful were the Deinotheres – a group within the elephant family. These strange-looking creatures had elephant-like bodies and a trunk, but no tusks in the upper jaw. Instead, they possessed a pair of long tusks in the shovel-like lower jaw, which seem to have been used for digging or for scraping bark from trees.

Other elephant groups included the mastodonts, such as *Gomphotherium*, which had large upper and lower tusks. By the start of the Pliocene, a variety of species of modern elephants and mammoths had evolved.

The most impressive carnivores of the Late Tertiary were the sabre-tooth cats. These were larger than modern wild cats, and were armed with long, stabbing canine teeth.

| Group Marsupialia | Family Borhyaenidae | Time 19mya |
|---|---|---|

## CLADOSICTIS

CLAD-OH-SICK-TIS

This carnivorous marsupial species was short lived. Some palaeontologists have suggested that it may have had an otter-like lifestyle – hunting fish in rivers – but it may also have eaten the eggs and young of land-living creatures. *Cladosictis* had a long, lightly built body, short limbs, and a dog-like skull. Its tail was long and thin. The teeth were similar to those of carnivorous placental mammals: there were sharp incisors at the front of the jaw, with pointed canines and shearing molars behind them.
• **DESCRIBED BY** Florentino Ameghino; 1887.
• **HABITAT** Woodland.

*long body and thick neck*

*dog-like snout*

| Length 80cm (2½ft) | Weight Unknown | Diet Small animals, perhaps fish and eggs |
|---|---|---|

| Group Marsupialia | Family Thylacosmilidae | Time 7–5mya |
| --- | --- | --- |

# THYLACOSMILUS

THIGH-LA-CO-SMILE-US

FOSSIL SKULL

*Thylacosmilus* was a large, predatory marsupial. Like the sabre-tooth cats, it sported long, stabbing upper canine teeth. However, in *Thylacosmilus*, these teeth grew continuously throughout life, and there were no incisor teeth in the lower jaw. Bony guards in the lower jaw protected the teeth when the jaws were closed. The neck and shoulders were strong and heavily muscled, allowing the teeth to be driven downwards with great force.
• **DESCRIBED BY** Elmer Riggs; 1933.
• **HABITAT** Plains.

*large, deep skull*

*tooth guards in lower jaw to protect upper canine teeth*

*powerful shoulders*

*stabbing sabre teeth*

*long, powerful hind legs*

*feet with five clawed toes*

| Length 1.2m (4ft) | Weight 115kg (250lb) | Diet Slow-moving, hoofed mammals |
| --- | --- | --- |

| Group Carnivora | Family Amphicyonidae | Time 40–9mya |
|---|---|---|

# AMPHICYON

AM-FIE-SIGH-ON

The amphicyonids were a family of "bear-dogs", of which *Amphicyon* ("ambiguous dog") was a typical member. A powerful predator, it had well-muscled shoulders, a heavily built

*powerful shoulders*

*wolf-like teeth*

body, and strong legs. It may have lived a lifestyle similar to that of modern bears.
• **DESCRIBED BY** H. Schinz; 1825.
• **HABITAT** Plains.

*strong, heavy feet armed with sharp claws*

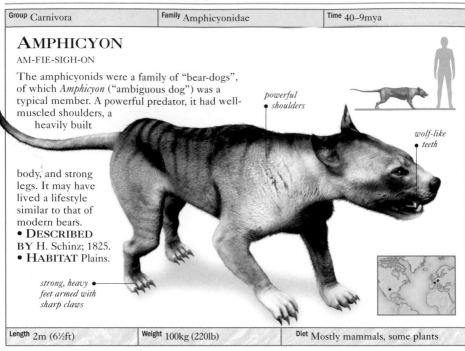

| Length 2m (6½ft) | Weight 100kg (220lb) | Diet Mostly mammals, some plants |
|---|---|---|

| Group Carnivora | Family Felidae | Time 40mya |
|---|---|---|

# EUSMILUS

YOU-SMIL-US

*Eusmilus*, a member of a family of "false sabre-tooth cats", first arose in Europe, and then gradually spread into North America. It was a large and powerful, hunting cat with a long, low body and relatively short legs. Its head and snout were short, with forward-facing eyes that probably allowed binocular vision and therefore accurate judgement of distances – an important attribute for a hunter. Its upper canine teeth were elongated into thick, stabbing "sabre" teeth, just as in the true sabre-teeth cats. These teeth were thick and curved, and extended far below the level of the lower jaw, which was capable of opening to an angle of 90 degrees, enabling it to use these teeth to stab its prey. In comparison, the lower canines were very small. Many of the other teeth normally found in felines are not present – *Eusmilus* had only 26 teeth, compared to about 44 in a modern cat.
• **DESCRIBED BY** Henri Filhol; 1872.
• **HABITAT** Plains.

*short head*

*forward-facing eyes*

*long, curved sabre teeth*

| Length 2.5m (8ft) | Weight Unknown | Diet Mammals |
|---|---|---|

| Group Carnivora | Family Canidae | Time 20–15mya |
|---|---|---|

# CYNODESMUS

SY-NOH-DES-MUS

An early member of the dog family, *Cynodesmus* was a coyote-sized animal with a short snout and a long body. Its legs were similar to those of modern dogs, but were not as efficient for running. The feet had clawed toes, with the claws being partially retractable.

• **DESCRIBED BY** William Berryman Scott; 1893.
• **HABITAT** Plains.

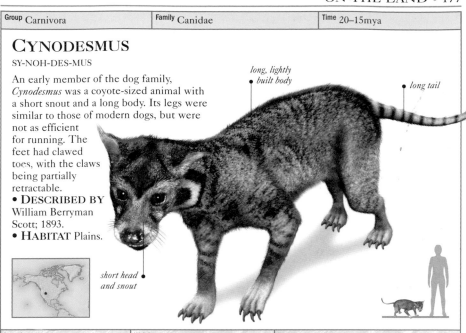

*long, lightly built body*

*long tail*

*short head and snout*

| Length 1m (3½ft) | Weight 70kg (155lb) | Diet Smaller mammals, carrion |
|---|---|---|

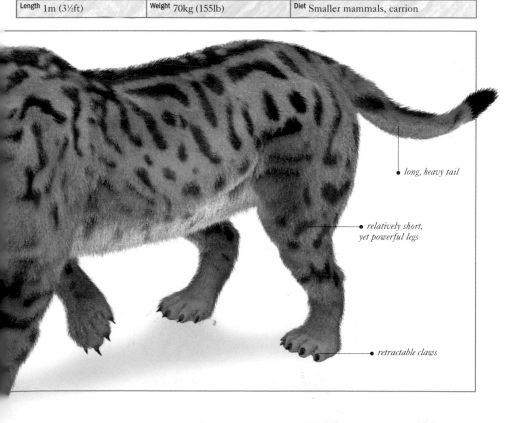

*long, heavy tail*

*relatively short, yet powerful legs*

*retractable claws*

| Group Proboscidea | Family Gomphotheriidae | Time 38mya |
|---|---|---|

# PHIOMIA
FI-OHM-EE-A

This primitive elephant had two pairs of tusks set in very long upper and lower jaws. The tusks on the lower jaw were flattened and formed a shovel-shaped projection that was probably used to collect food or to scrape bark off trees. The tusks in the upper jaw were shorter and were probably used for fighting or for display. The upper lip was likely to have been drawn out into a short trunk. To reduce the weight of the large skull, the bones were filled with air spaces. The rest of *Phiomia*'s body was very similar to that of a modern elephant – with column-like legs and a stocky body.

• **DESCRIBED BY** Henry F. Osborn; 1932.
• **HABITAT** Plains and woodland.

*"shovel tusk"*

*teeth less ridged than in modern elephants*

*cheek teeth*

**LOWER JAW**

*relatively short neck*

*short trunk*

*lower "shovel-tusk" projection*

*hide thought to have been like that of a modern elephant*

*column-shaped legs*

| Length 5m (16ft) | Weight 3 tonnes (3 tons) | Diet Plants |
|---|---|---|

| Group Proboscidea | Family Gomphotheriidae | Time 25–2mya |
|---|---|---|

## GOMPHOTHERIUM

GOM-FO-THEER-EE-UM

Like *Phiomia*, *Gomphotherium* had a pair of upper jaw tusks for fighting and display, and long lower jaws that formed a food "shovel". It had a trunk as long as the lower tusks to help with feeding. Later species had fewer teeth, with more pronounced ridges for grinding.

• **DESCRIBED BY** Baron Georges Cuvier; 1817.
• **HABITAT** Grassland, marsh, and forest.

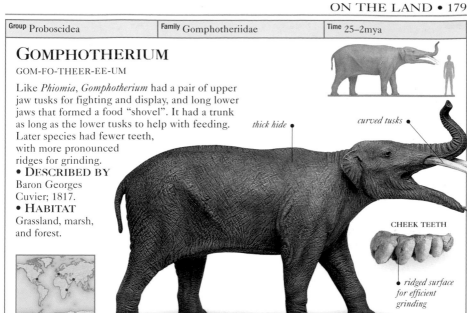

*thick hide* •

*curved tusks* •

CHEEK TEETH

• *ridged surface for efficient grinding*

| Length 5m (16ft) | Weight 4–7 tonnes (3⅞–6⅞ tons) | Diet Plants |
|---|---|---|

| Group Proboscidea | Family Gomphotheriidae | Time 25mya |
|---|---|---|

## PLATYBELODON

PLAT-EE-BEL-OH-DON

The shovel arrangement of the lower tusks in this family of elephants reached extreme proportions in *Platybelodon*. The flattened lower tusks were very broad, with an indentation near the top for the upper pair of tusks to slot into while the mouth was closed. The cheek teeth were flat and there were sharper teeth at the front of the jaw. The trunk was very wide. *Platybelodon* seems to have used its shovel-tusks to scoop up water weeds and other soft plants. The tail was relatively long. As a highly specialized feeder, it was vulnerable to environmental change, and was a short-lived genus.

• **DESCRIBED BY** William Granger; 1930.
• **HABITAT** Wet prairies.

*larger ears than more primitive elephants* •

• *large head*

| Length 6m (20ft) | Weight 4–5 tonnes (3⅞–4⅞ tons) | Diet Soft water plants |
|---|---|---|

| Group Perissodactyla | Family Equidae | Time 25–40mya |
| --- | --- | --- |

# MESOHIPPUS

ME-ZO-HIP-PUS

*Mesohippus* ("middle horse") had features that seem to have been an evolutionary response to more open environments: its legs were longer than those of the earlier "dawn horse" *Eohippus*, and it had lost a toe. Of the three remaining toes, the middle bore most of the animal's weight. These features increased its speed. Its teeth grew larger, increasing their surface area for chewing. The jaw was shallow and the head was quite long and pointed. The eyes were set relatively far apart and far back on the head.

- **DESCRIBED BY** Joseph Leidy; 1870.
- **HABITAT** Open grassland.

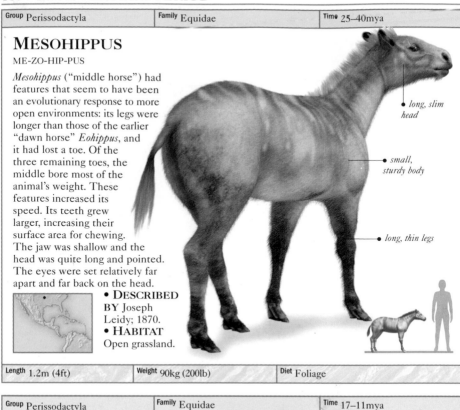

long, slim head

small, sturdy body

long, thin legs

| Length 1.2m (4ft) | Weight 90kg (200lb) | Diet Foliage |
| --- | --- | --- |

| Group Perissodactyla | Family Equidae | Time 17–11mya |
| --- | --- | --- |

# MERYCHIPPUS

MER-EE-CHIP-PUS

*Merychippus* ("ruminant horse") was the first horse to feed exclusively on grass, and the first one to have a head similar to that of modern horses. The muzzle was longer than in earlier horses, the jaw deeper, and the eyes further apart. Its neck was also longer than in earlier horses, as it spent much of the time grazing. The middle toe on each foot had developed into a hoof that did not have a pad on the bottom. In some species the outer two toes only touched the ground when running; in others, they were larger.

- **DESCRIBED BY** Joseph Leidy; 1894.
- **HABITAT** Grassy plains.

long muzzle with high-crowned teeth

body very like those of modern horses

weight supported on central toe

| Length 2m (6.5ft) | Weight 200kg (440lb) | Diet Grass |
| --- | --- | --- |

| Group Perissodactyla | Family Equidae | Time 15–2mya |
|---|---|---|

# HIPPARION

HIP-PAIR-EE-ON

*Hipparion* ("better horse") was one of several groups of grazing three-toed primitive horses that lived in the Miocene. It was a lightly built animal that greatly resembled a modern pony, with a long jaw, and slim legs. The horse's full weight was borne on the enlarged central toe, which had developed a recognizable hoof. The two outer toes were much reduced in size and did not reach the ground. A tendon in the foot increased the springiness of the gait, giving the advantage of greater speeds. The teeth were large and high-crowned for grazing. *Hipparion* was a very successful genus of early horse, spreading over the world in large herds for millions of years.
• **DESCRIBED BY** de Cristol; 1832.
• **HABITAT** Plains.

UPPER JAW BONE

*large premolars*

*high-crowned molars with many cusps*

*large eyes set far back along skull*

*bony pocket (antorbital fossa) larger in males*

*moderately long tail*

*long, squarish muzzle with large nostrils*

BONES OF HIND FOOT

*very slim, light legs*

*elongated foot bone*

*large central toe forming a hoof*

| Length 1.5m (5ft) | Weight 115kg (250lb) | Diet Grass |
|---|---|---|

| Group Ceratomorpha | Family Rhinocerotidae | Time 17 4.5mya |
|---|---|---|

# TELEOCERAS

TELL-EE-OH-SEA-RAS

This mammal was a member of the rhinoceros family. It had a long body and extremely short legs. In fact, the animal's belly must have sometimes dragged along the ground. It had a small, conical nose horn. It is thought to have had a lifestyle like that of a modern hippopotamus, wallowing in water during the day and moving onto land to feed at night.

• **DESCRIBED BY** Othniel C. Marsh; 1877.

• **HABITAT** Rivers.

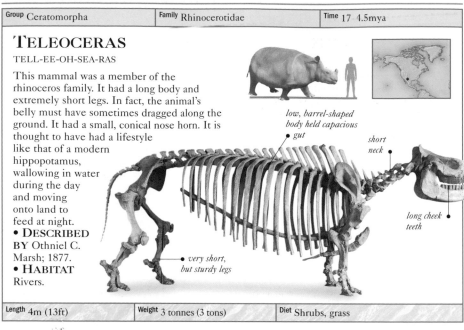

low, barrel-shaped body held capacious gut

short neck

long cheek teeth

very short, but sturdy legs

| Length 4m (13ft) | Weight 3 tonnes (3 tons) | Diet Shrubs, grass |
|---|---|---|

| Group Ceratomorpha | Family Rhinocerotidae | Time 30mya |
|---|---|---|

# PARACERATHERIUM

PAR-A-SER-A-THEER-EE-UM

This early rhinoceros was the largest land mammal known to have lived. Standing 6m (18ft) high at the shoulder, its head alone was over a metre (4ft) long. Hollowed out vertebrae in the back kept the animal's weight down. The powerful legs were long and slim, and there were three toes on each foot. Despite its bulk, *Paraceratherium* was probably a fast runner. It seems to have had a flexible upper lip, allowing it to browse on leaves from trees as modern giraffes do.

• **DESCRIBED BY** Forster Cooper; 1911.

• **HABITAT** Open woodland.

probably long and flexible upper lip

back sloped from neck to hips

long neck allowed animal to browse from tall trees

powerful, heavily muscled legs

| Length 9m (30ft) | Weight 15 tonnes (14¾ tons) | Diet Leaves and twigs |
|---|---|---|

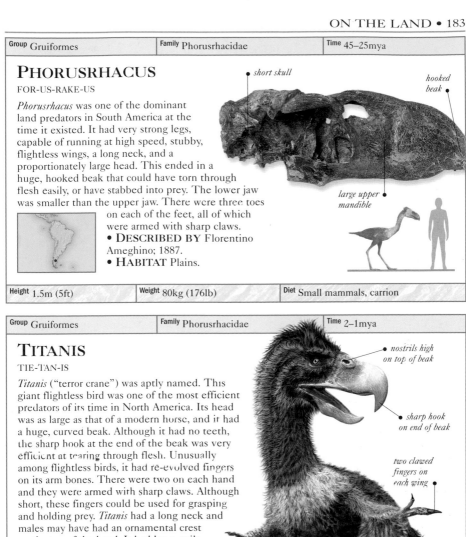

| Group Gruiformes | Family Phorusrhacidae | Time 45–25mya |
|---|---|---|

# PHORUSRHACUS

FOR-US-RAKE-US

*Phorusrhacus* was one of the dominant land predators in South America at the time it existed. It had very strong legs, capable of running at high speed, stubby, flightless wings, a long neck, and a proportionately large head. This ended in a huge, hooked beak that could have torn through flesh easily, or have stabbed into prey. The lower jaw was smaller than the upper jaw. There were three toes on each of the feet, all of which were armed with sharp claws.
• **DESCRIBED BY** Florentino Ameghino; 1887.
• **HABITAT** Plains.

*short skull*

*hooked beak*

*large upper mandible*

| Height 1.5m (5ft) | Weight 80kg (176lb) | Diet Small mammals, carrion |
|---|---|---|

| Group Gruiformes | Family Phorusrhacidae | Time 2–1mya |
|---|---|---|

# TITANIS

TIE-TAN-IS

*Titanis* ("terror crane") was aptly named. This giant flightless bird was one of the most efficient predators of its time in North America. Its head was as large as that of a modern horse, and it had a huge, curved beak. Although it had no teeth, the sharp hook at the end of the beak was very efficient at tearing through flesh. Unusually among flightless birds, it had re-evolved fingers on its arm bones. There were two on each hand and they were armed with sharp claws. Although short, these fingers could be used for grasping and holding prey. *Titanis* had a long neck and males may have had an ornamental crest on the top of the head. It had long, agile legs, and three-toed feet with long talons. It could undoubtedly run at high speeds when hunting. This genus may be the same as *Phorusrhacus*, and there is some discussion about renaming it.
• **DESCRIBED BY** Robert Chandler; 1994.
• **HABITAT** Grassy plains.

*nostrils high on top of beak*

*sharp hook on end of beak*

*two clawed fingers on each wing*

*short wings useless for flight*

*three long-clawed toes*

*powerful, heavily muscled legs*

| Height 2.5m (8ft) | Weight 150kg (330lb) | Diet Mammals |
|---|---|---|

# IN THE WATER

**C**limate change during the Late Tertiary greatly affected marine environments. The polar waters grew colder, and this led to the initiation of ocean currents. The movement of nutrients and marine species caused by these new ocean currents increased the productivity of seas worldwide, and new groups of animals arose to take advantage of these new resources.

Whales diversified from the primitive forms of the Early Tertiary into modern toothed forms. In the late Eocene, the first baleen whales also appeared. These had long sheets of keratin, known as baleen, hanging from their jaws. These enabled them to filter plankton, krill, and small animals and fish from the water. By the Miocene, baleen whales had reached the massive sizes of modern whales.

Other mammals returned to an aquatic lifestyle during the Miocene. Primitive seals, sea lions, walruses, and sea otters are thought to have evolved in the Mid Tertiary in the northern hemisphere. By the Miocene, they had spread south of the equator to dominate coastlines around the world. Current opinion among palaeontologists is that all of these carnivorous groups evolved from an otter-like ancestor.

Whale vertebrae and flipper bones bearing large bite marks are testament to the success of non-mammalian marine animals during the Late Tertiary. The largest fish ever to have existed, the "mega-tooth" shark *Carcharodon* preyed on the large seal and whale populations in the Miocene oceans. This enormous shark was estimated to have been 15m (49ft) long.

| Group Cetacea | Family Squalodontidae | Time 30–20mya |
|---|---|---|

## PROSQUALODON

PRO-SQUAL-OH-DON

*Prosqualodon* ("early saw tooth") may have been an ancestor of later toothed whales. It resembled a dolphin, with a long, streamlined body, a short neck and two flippers. The long, slim snout was filled with pointed teeth. Those at the back of the jaw were triangular, saw-edged, and double-rooted – a primitive feature. The nostrils were positioned on the top of the head between the eye sockets to form a blowhole.
• **DESCRIBED BY** M.R. Dickson; 1964.
• **HABITAT** Oceans.

*blowhole on top of skull*

FOSSIL SKULL AND UPPER JAW

*triangular saw-edged teeth at back of jaw*

*long, narrow snout*

| Length 2.3m (7½ft) | Weight Unknown | Diet Fish |
|---|---|---|

| Group Cetacea | Family Rhabdosteidea | Time 15–5mya |
|---|---|---|

# EURHINODELPHIS

UOU-RHINE-OH-DEL-FIS

*Eurhinodelphis* ("true-nose dolphin") was one of the most common dolphins in the Miocene. Its most distinctive feature was its long snout, which may have been used to strike at its prey. The structure of the ear had become more complex than in earlier toothed whales, indicating that *Eurhinodelphis* had developed some form of echolocation system. The skull was slightly asymmetrical, as in modern toothed whales, with a blowhole at the top of the head.

*asymmetrical skull*

• **DESCRIBED BY**
R. Kellogg; 1925.

*elongated snout*

• **HABITAT**
Oceans.

*hydrofoil-shaped flippers*

*powerful, double-lobed tail*

| Length 3.7m (12ft) | Weight Unknown | Diet Fish |
|---|---|---|

| Group Cetacea | Family Cetotheriidae | Time 15mya |
|---|---|---|

# CETOTHERIUM

SET-OH-THEER-EE-UM

Resembling a small version of the modern rorqual, *Cetotherium* was an early baleen whale, with baleen plates instead of teeth. The inside of the baleen was edged with coarse hairs that filtered krill, plankton, and small fish. *Cetotherium's* baleen plates were probably quite short. It lacked echolocation. Its head was symmetrical and it probably had two blowholes.

*long, streamlined body like modern baleen whales*

• **DESCRIBED BY**
Lyddeker; 1894.

• **HABITAT**
Oceans.

*elongated, wide head*

*short baleen plates*

| Length 4m (13ft) | Weight 2 tonnes (2 tons) | Diet Plankton |
|---|---|---|

# IN THE AIR

**B**y the Miocene, true birds were becoming common. The fossil remains of Late Tertiary birds appear very like birds that are alive now. They all had modern features: horny beaks with no teeth, light limb bones fused together, and a heart with four chambers for greater efficiency in pumping blood. By the end of the Pliocene, all but four of the orders of modern birds had evolved.

Due to the lifestyle and lighter bone structure of birds, bird fossils are less common than those of mammals, and evidence is patchy. Some of the best-known species from the Late Tertiary Period are seabirds, such as petrels, albatrosses, and cormorants. Many of these were far larger, often with a much heavier build than modern forms. Other bird groups that appeared at this time include hawks, storks, herons, parrots, and the modern budgerigars. There are also remains of flamingo-type birds. Birds of prey tended to be larger than their modern counterparts. For example, the massive, vulture-like *Argentavis* was the largest flying bird ever known.

An important step in the evolution of birds occurred during the Pliocene: songbirds appeared for the first time. However, the evolutionary pressures that led to the development of song for territorial and mating display are not yet fully understood.

| Group Neornithes | Family Teratornithidae | Time 6–8mya |
|---|---|---|

## ARGENTAVIS

AR-GEN-TAH-VIS

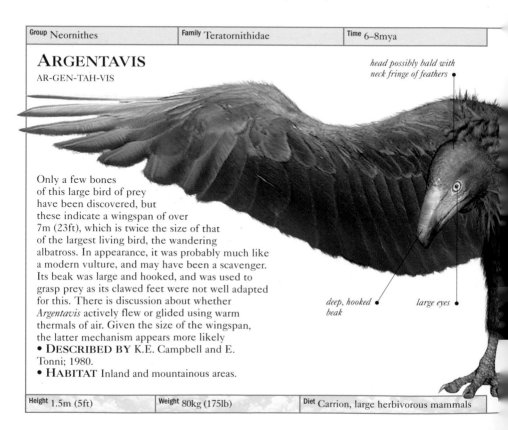

*head possibly bald with neck fringe of feathers*

Only a few bones of this large bird of prey have been discovered, but these indicate a wingspan of over 7m (23ft), which is twice the size of that of the largest living bird, the wandering albatross. In appearance, it was probably much like a modern vulture, and may have been a scavenger. Its beak was large and hooked, and was used to grasp prey as its clawed feet were not well adapted for this. There is discussion about whether *Argentavis* actively flew or glided using warm thermals of air. Given the size of the wingspan, the latter mechanism appears more likely
• **DESCRIBED BY** K.E. Campbell and E. Tonni; 1980.
• **HABITAT** Inland and mountainous areas.

*deep, hooked beak*

*large eyes*

| Height 1.5m (5ft) | Weight 80kg (175lb) | Diet Carrion, large herbivorous mammals |
|---|---|---|

| Group Osteodontornithidea | Family Pelagornithidae | Time 30–28mya |
|---|---|---|

# OSTEODONTORNIS

OS-TEE-OH-DON-TOR-NIS

One of the largest birds ever to have flown, *Osteodontornis* was a bony-toothed seabird. It had a large, heavy body, and long, narrow wings designed for gliding long distances. The neck had a natural S-shaped curve, meaning that rhe head was held over the shoulders in flight. The beak was stout and rounded, with tooth-like bony projections edging each jawbone.

- **DESCRIBED BY** Hildegarde Howard; 1962.
- **HABITAT** Seashores.

*pelican-like head*

*large wingspan of up to 6m (20ft)*

*rounded bill with small hook at end*

| Length 1.2m (4ft) | Weight Unknown | Diet Fish |
|---|---|---|

*wing feathers up to 1.5m (5ft) long*

*long wings compared to body size*

*large feet with three forward-facing clawed toes*

# QUATERNARY PERIOD

1.75 MILLION YEARS AGO – PRESENT

The Quaternary Period includes the Pleistocene and Holocene Epochs. The Pleistocene was a time when the world was in the grip of the Great Ice Age, with enormous ice sheets covering most of the northern hemisphere. Glaciers also formed in the high mountain regions of the world, including the Andes and the Himalayas. Over the next one and a half million years the Earth passed through at least four ice ages. Between ice ages, the climate was warmer. The most recent ice age ended about 10,000 years ago at the beginning of the Holocene, and saw mass extinctions of mammal species.

## QUATERNARY LIFE

Animals responded to the colder conditions of the Pleistocene by migrating towards equatorial regions (for example, lizards) or evolving furry coats (for example, mammoths and the woolly rhino, *Coelodonta*). Truly modern humans, *Homo sapiens*, evolved during the Pleistocene, along with other, less successful human species, such as *Homo neanderthalensis*.

• *large canine teeth*

• *powerful hindlimbs*

## CANINE CARNIVORES

Many species of dog lived during the Pleistocene. *Canis dirus* (left), was very like a modern wolf, but heavier. It survived into the Holocene. Fossil remains show that dire wolves and sabre-tooth cats often fought over territory and food.

| 4,600mya | 4,000mya | 3,000mya |
|----------|----------|----------|
|          |          |          |

## QUATERNARY LANDMASSES

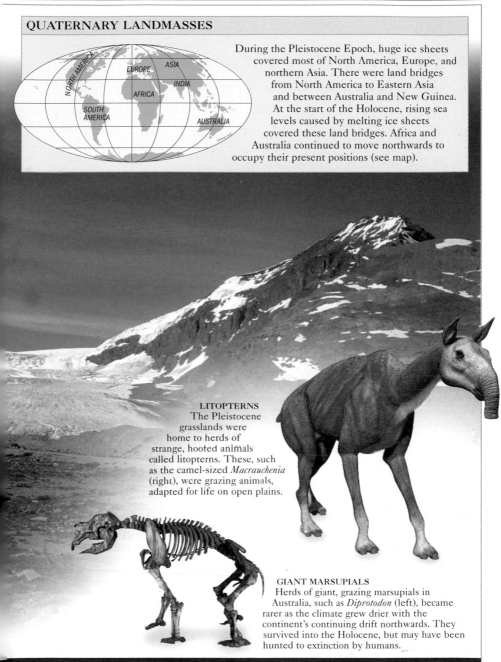

During the Pleistocene Epoch, huge ice sheets covered most of North America, Europe, and northern Asia. There were land bridges from North America to Eastern Asia and between Australia and New Guinea. At the start of the Holocene, rising sea levels caused by melting ice sheets covered these land bridges. Africa and Australia continued to move northwards to occupy their present positions (see map).

**LITOPTERNS**
The Pleistocene grasslands were home to herds of strange, hoofed animals called litopterns. These, such as the camel-sized *Macrauchenia* (right), were grazing animals, adapted for life on open plains.

**GIANT MARSUPIALS**
Herds of giant, grazing marsupials in Australia, such as *Diprotodon* (left), became rarer as the climate grew drier with the continent's continuing drift northwards. They survived into the Holocene, but may have been hunted to extinction by humans.

2,000mya        1,000mya    500mya    250mya    0

# ON THE LAND

**A** t the start of the Pleistocene, the first epoch of the Quaternary Period, land animals exhibited far greater diversity than those of today. The northern grasslands were filled with many different species of deer, antelope, horse, and cattle. Camels ranged all over North America, and had spread into South America and Asia across the Panama and Bering land bridges respectively. Large cats were found worldwide, most of them armed with long canine teeth. Foxes and dogs continued to evolve and spread, and bears lived throughout Europe, Africa, and North America.

The Pleistocene saw two major evolutionary changes. There were at least four ice ages during the epoch, during each of which most of Europe, northern Asia, and North America became covered in ice sheets. Many mammals adapted to the freezing conditions by growing to larger sizes and evolving thick fur.

Another major evolutionary advance was the appearance of new human species. *Homo erectus* appeared about 1.6 million years ago, and *Homo sapiens neanderthalensis* about 100,000 years ago, at about the same time as true modern man, *Homo sapiens sapiens*. Neanderthals died out about 35,000 years ago.

The last ice age ended about 10,000 years ago, at the start of the Holocene. This coincided with mass extinctions of many mammal species, especially in the Americas and Australia. These extinctions may have been due to a combination of rapid climate change and the activities of the expanding human population.

| Group Carnivora | Family Canidae | Time 9,000ya |
|---|---|---|

## CANIS DIRUS

KAN-ISS DIE-RUS

This extinct member of the dog family, whose name means "dire wolf", was a larger and heavier version of the modern wolf. It had a wider head, stronger jaws, and longer teeth than modern members of the dog family. It had long, powerful legs, and its toes had blunt claws that could not be retracted. It was probably both a scavenger and an active hunter.
• **DESCRIBED BY** Joseph Leidy; 1858.
• **HABITAT** Grassland and woodland.

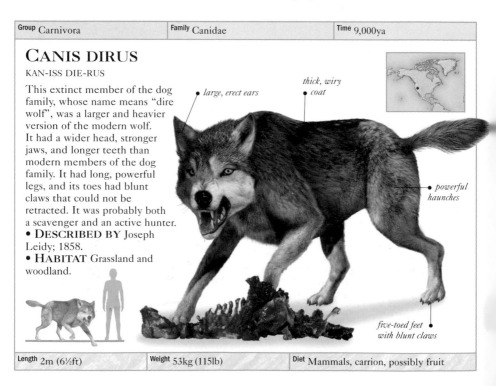

*large, erect ears*

*thick, wiry coat*

*powerful haunches*

*five-toed feet with blunt claws*

| Length 2m (6½ft) | Weight 53kg (115lb) | Diet Mammals, carrion, possibly fruit |
|---|---|---|

| Group Carnivora | Family Felidae | Time 5–1.5mya |
|---|---|---|

# DINOFELIS

DIE-NOH-FEEL-IS

*Dinofelis* ("terrible cat") was a panther-sized cat. It had flattened canine teeth that were intermediate in length between those of the sabre-tooth cats and those of biting cats, such as lions. It was probably an agile climber with long, strong legs, and sharp, retractable claws. Its tail was long and flexible and could be used to aid balance. The skull of *Dinofelis* was short and its eyes were forward-facing and positioned for binocular vision – essential for judging distances accurately when hunting or leaping. Its coat was likely to have a similar pattern of camouflage to those of modern forest-dwelling cats.

• **DESCRIBED BY** Otto Zdansky; 1924.
• **HABITAT** Dense forest.

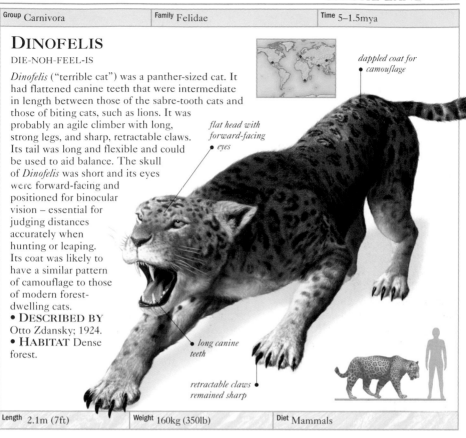

*dappled coat for camouflage*

*flat head with forward-facing eyes*

*long canine teeth*

*retractable claws remained sharp*

| Length 2.1m (7ft) | Weight 160kg (350lb) | Diet Mammals |
|---|---|---|

| Group Carnivora | Family Felidae | Time 1mya–4,000ya |
|---|---|---|

# PANTHERA

PAN-THAIR-A

There were several subspecies of lion (*Panthera leo*) that are now extinct. *Panthera leo spelaea*, the European cave lion, was the largest cat ever to have lived. It is often seen in cave paintings. *Panthera leo atrox* lived in North America. Both subspecies killed prey by biting the neck with their canine teeth, and had sharp claws that could be retracted under a flap of skin.

• **DESCRIBED BY** Goldfuss; 1810.
• **HABITAT** Grassland.

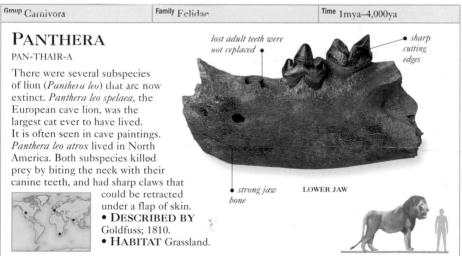

*lost adult teeth were not replaced*

*sharp cutting edges*

*strong jaw bone*    LOWER JAW

| Length 3.5m (11ft) | Weight 235kg (520lb) | Diet Meat |
|---|---|---|

| Group Carnivora | Family Felidae | Time 2.5mya–10,000ya |
|---|---|---|

# SMILODON

SMILE-OH-DON

*Smilodon* was the cat popularly thought of as a sabre-tooth tiger. Its sharp canine teeth were huge, and were serrated along their rear edges to increase their cutting ability. They were also oval in cross-section. This meant that they were strong while presenting minimum resistance when biting. Such long teeth meant that the cat's jaw had to open to an angle of more than 120 degrees to allow the teeth to be driven into its prey. However, it seems the teeth may have broken easily if they came into contact with bone. *Smilodon* therefore probably hunted by biting through an animal's neck. *Smilodon*'s arms and shoulders were very powerful, in order to produce a strong downwards motion of the head. *Smilodon* appears to have hunted in packs, probably preying on large, slow, thick-skinned animals. Males may have had a mane similar to that of modern lions.

- **DESCRIBED BY** Plieninger; 1846.
- **HABITAT** Grassy plains.

## FOSSIL SKULL

*Smilodon* is very well known. Over 2,000 individuals have been excavated from the Rancho La Brea tar pits, a famous prehistoric predator trap, in Los Angeles, California.

• *jaw capable of opening 120 degrees*

• *short, sharp molars*

• *serrated rear edge of "sabre" teeth*

| Length 1.5–2.5m (5–8¼ft) | Weight 320kg (710lb) | Diet Large mammals |
|---|---|---|

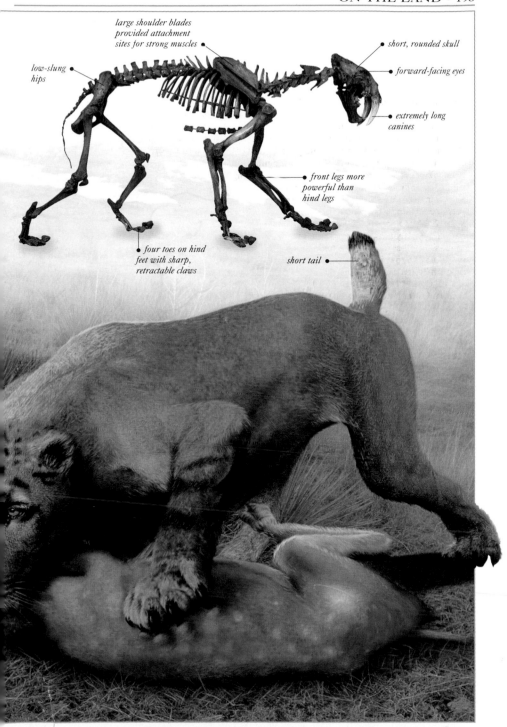

large shoulder blades
provided attachment
sites for strong muscles

short, rounded skull

low-slung
hips

forward-facing eyes

extremely long
canines

front legs more
powerful than
hind legs

four toes on hind
feet with sharp,
retractable claws

short tail

| Group Litopterna | Family Macraucheniidae | Time 7mya – 20,000ya |
|---|---|---|

# MACRAUCHENIA

MAK-RAW-CHEN-EE-A

This curious animal (whose name means "great llama") had a number of camel-like features, such as its size, its small head, and long neck. However, its three-toed feet were more like those of a rhinoceros. The unusual position of the nostrils, high on the skull between the eyes, suggests that this animal had a moderately long trunk. The legs were long and slim, but *Macrauchenia* was probably not a fast runner. The flexibility and strength of the ankles, however, suggest it was a relatively agile animal. The high-crowned cheek teeth, along with the presence of a trunk, indicate that *Macrauchenia* may have been a browser and a grazing animal.

- **DESCRIBED BY** Richard Owen; 1840.
- **HABITAT** Woodland.

camel-like body shape

possible flexible trunk

long toe bone

RIGHT FOREFOOT BONES

| Length 3m (10ft) | Weight 700kg (1,540lb) | Diet Plants |
|---|---|---|

| Group Rhinoceratoidea | Family Rhinocerotidae | Time 1.8mya – 10,000ya |
|---|---|---|

# COELODONTA

SEEL-OH-DON-TA

The woolly rhinoceros, *Coelodonta* ("hollow tooth"), evolved to withstand cold conditions. Its fur was thick and shaggy, its body was massive with short legs, and its ears were small. It had a huge pair of horns on its snout, the front one of which grew to over 1m (3¼ft) in length in older ms.

- **DESCRIBED BY** J.F. Blumenbach 1799.
- **HABITAT** Tundra.

thick, shaggy, grey-brown fur

small ears to reduce heat loss

long horn made of matted hair

| Length 3.5m (11ft) | Weight 3–4 tonnes (3–4 tons) | Diet Plants |
|---|---|---|

| Group Proboscidea | Family Elephantidae | Time 1.8mya – 9,000ya |

# MAMMUTHUS IMPERATOR

MAM-UT-US IM-PER-A-TOR

The largest of all mammoth species, the imperial mammoth was probably the largest animal alive during the last ice age. Unlike the woolly mammoth, this mammoth was well-adapted to the warmer climates it lived in and did not have such thick fur. Besides its immense size, its most distinguishing feature was its tusks. These curled backwards evenly and were up to 4.8m (15ft) long. They could weigh up to 84kg (185lb). Some palaeontologists have suggested that the imperial mammoth is the same species as the Columbian mammoth, which was identical except for twisted tusks.
• **DESCRIBED BY** Joseph Leidy; 1870.
• **HABITAT** Plains.

*fatty hump behind head*

*back sloping down from shoulders to hips*

*short hair over the whole body*

*long, thick tusks*

*flexible trunk*

*elephantine legs*

| Height 4.5m (15ft) | Weight 8–10 tonnes (8–10 tons) | Diet Grass, leaves, flowering plants |

| Group Proboscidea | Family Elephantidae | Time 120,000–6,000ya |
|---|---|---|

# MAMMUTHUS PRIMIGENIUS

MAM-UT-US PRIM-EE-GEN-EE-US

*Mammuthus primigenius*, the woolly mammoth, was relatively small for a mammoth. It was adapted to living in the cold climates of northern tundras, with a thick coat of long dark hair overlying a downy undercoat. A thick layer of fat under the skin helped in insulation, and there was also a fatty hump behind the head used for food storage. Its ears were smaller than those of modern elephants, helping to reduce heat loss. The long, curved tusks appear to have been used to scrape away ice from the ground when feeding, as well as for protection and in dominance rituals. The woolly mammoth survived until relatively recent times, and palaeontologists are therefore very familiar with its anatomy and appearance. Several well-preserved specimens have been found frozen in the permafrost of Siberia and Alaska, and cave paintings by early humans depict it clearly.

• **DESCRIBED BY** J.F. Blumenbach; 1799.
• **HABITAT** Frozen tundra.

*small, rounded ears*

*short tail*

**FROZEN REMAINS OF A
YOUNG MAMMOTH**

*long, curved tusks*

| Length 3.5m (11½ft) | Weight 2.75 tonnes (3 tons) | Diet Low-lying tundra vegetation |
|---|---|---|

ridges for grinding
tough plant material

red hair colour
due to chemical
reaction after
death

UPPER CHEEK TOOTH

PRESERVED HAIR

fatty hump used as
energy store

tall, domed head

hair up to 90cm
(3ft) long

| Group Ratites | Family Dinornithidae | Time 2mya–AD1600 |
|---|---|---|

# AEPYORNIS TITAN
APE-EE-OAR-NIS TIE-TAN

*Aepyornis titan*, commonly called the "elephant bird of Madagascar" was the heaviest bird species known to have existed. It was a wingless bird, with long, thick legs and feet ending in three widely spread toes. The thickness of the thigh bone indicates that *Aepyornis* was generally a slow-moving bird and could probably not run at high speeds. The small head had a toothless beak, and the only protection against predators was the bird's size and strength. Several eggs have been found fossilized in the mud of swampy areas near rivers.

• **DESCRIBED BY**
Isidore Geoffroy-Saint-Hilaire; 1851.
• **HABITAT**
Forests.

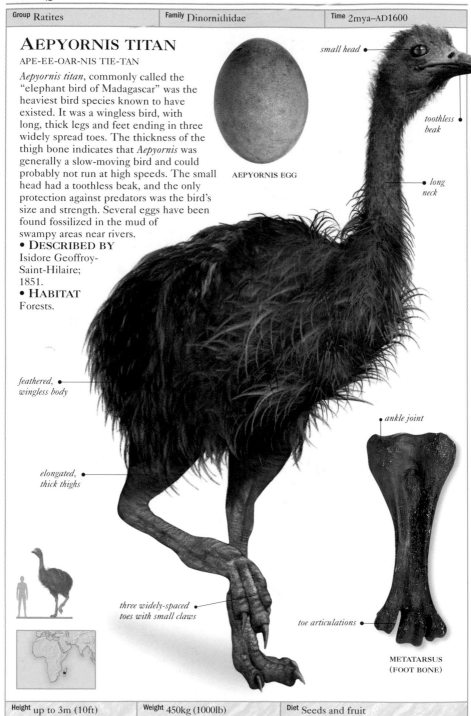

small head

toothless beak

long neck

AEPYORNIS EGG

feathered, wingless body

elongated, thick thighs

ankle joint

three widely-spaced toes with small claws

toe articulations

METATARSUS (FOOT BONE)

| Height up to 3m (10ft) | Weight 450kg (1000lb) | Diet Seeds and fruit |
|---|---|---|

| Group Ratites | Family Dinornithidae | Time 2mya–AD1800 |
|---|---|---|

# DINORNIS MAXIMUS
DIE-NOR-NIS MAX-EE-MUS

This was the tallest flightless bird ever to have existed, and was one of a dozen types of moa that survived in New Zealand until modern times. It was a slow-moving bird, with a bulky body, long, heavily-built legs, and a long neck. Preserved feathers show that its plumage was mostly grey and fluffy. Its beak was short and sharp-edged, and was used to shear at vegetation. Gizzard stones were used to help digest plant material. The numbers of *Dinornis* declined rapidly after the arrival of humans in New Zealand about 10,000 years ago, and they were hunted to extinction by about 200 years ago.
• **DESCRIBED BY** Richard Owen; 1843.
• **HABITAT** River areas, bushland

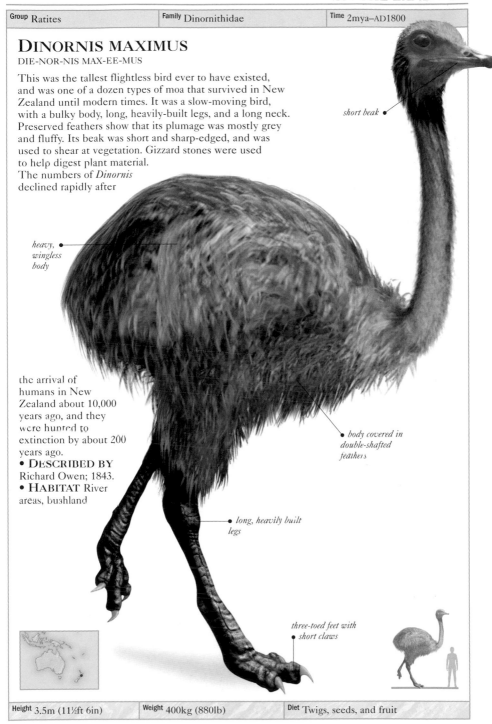

*short beak*

*heavy, wingless body*

*body covered in double-shafted feathers*

*long, heavily built legs*

*three-toed feet with short claws*

| Height 3.5m (11½ft 6in) | Weight 400kg (880lb) | Diet Twigs, seeds, and fruit |
|---|---|---|

# ADDITIONAL DINOSAURS

This section consists of a brief description of over 300 dinosaurs, not included in the main body of the book. The entries are arranged alphabetically and each includes, wherever possible, its geological period and the country in which the principal fossil finds were made.

***Abrictosaurus*** A small, early ornithopod dinosaur. May be a female *Heterodontosaurus*. Jurassic. South Africa.

***Achelousaurus*** A ceratopsian that appears to be an intermediate form between *Einiosaurus* and *Pachyrhinosaurus*. Late Cretaceous. USA.

***Acrocanthosaurus*** An *Allosaurus*-like theropod with spines on the back supporting a sail or ridge. Early Cretaceous. USA.

***Adasaurus*** A lightly built dromaeosaur with long, sickle-shaped claws on each hind foot. Late Cretaceous. Mongolia.

***Aegyptosaurus*** A sauropod known only from isolated bones. Late Cretaceous. North Africa.

***Aeolosaurus*** A large sauropod. Late Cretaceous. Argentina.

***Afrovenator*** A theropod. Cretaceous. Africa.

***Agilisaurus*** A lightly built, herbivorous dinosaur. Possibly a hypsilophodontid. Mid Jurassic. China.

***Alamosaurus*** The last known sauropod and North America's only known titanosaur. Late Cretaceous. USA.

***Albertosaurus*** A *Tyrannosaurus*-like theropod. Late Cretaceous. North America.

***Alectrosaurus*** A large theropod. Late Cretaceous. China and Mongolia.

***Algoasaurus*** A small sauropod. Early Cretaceous. South Africa.

***Alioramus*** A tyrannosaurid theropod with unusual crests running down the snout. Late Cretaceous. Mongolia.

***Aliwalia*** An early theropod known only from a thigh bone. Late Triassic. South Africa.

***Alocodon*** A small, ornithopod dinosaur known only from teeth. Late Jurassic. Portugal.

***Altirhinus*** An iguanodontid with a beak on its snout and a spiked thumb on each hand. Early Cretaceous. Mongolia.

***Alvarezsaurus*** A small, lightly built, theropod with an extremely long, thin, flat tail. Late Cretaceous. Argentina.

***Alwalkeria*** A primitive theropod. Late Triassic. India.

***Alxasaurus*** A large, primitive therizinosaur. Cretaceous. Mongolia.

***Amargasaurus*** A sauropod with unusually long spines running along its back. Early Cretaceous. Argentina.

***Ammosaurus*** A sauropod with large hands and thumb claws. Early Jurassic. USA.

***Ampelosaurus*** A large, titanosaurid sauropod dinosaur. Late Cretaceous. France.

***Amtosaurus*** Possibly an ankylosaur, but identity and classification are doubtful. Late Cretaceous. Mongolia.

***Amurosaurus*** A hadrosaur similar to *Lambeosaurus*. Not yet formally described. Cretaceous. Russia.

***Amygdalon*** A large sauropod. Late Jurassic. Southern Argentina.

***Anasazisaurus*** A hadrosaur known only from a skull. Late Cretaceous. USA.

***Anatosaurus*** Former name of *Edmontosaurus* and *Anatotitan*.

***Anatotitan*** A hadrosaur. Late Cretaceous. USA.

**Anchiceratops** A long-frilled ceratopsian. Late Cretaceous. Canada.

**Andesaurus** An enormous titanosaurid sauropod. Cretaceous. Argentina.

**Angaturama** A *Spinosaurus*-like theropod. Early Cretaceous. Brazil.

**Anserimimus** An *Ornithomimus*-like dinosaur. Late Cretaceous. Mongolia.

**Antarctosaurus** A very large, heavily built sauropod. Late Cretaceous. South America, India, and Russia.

**Aragosaurus** A huge sauropod. Early Cretaceous. Spain.

**Aralosaurus** A hadrosaur ornithopod known only from a skull. Late Cretaceous. Kazakhstan.

**Araucanoraptor** A theropod with a sickle claw on each foot. Late Cretaceous. Argentina.

**Archaeornithoides** A theropod with unserrated teeth. Late Cretaceous. Mongolia.

**Archaeornithomimus** An *Ornithomimus*-like dinosaur with primitive clawed fingers. Late Cretaceous. North America and China.

**Achillobator** A large deinonychosaur with a sickle-shaped claw on each foot. Late Cretaceous. Mongolia.

**Argyrosaurus** A large sauropod. Late Cretaceous. South America.

**Arkansaurus** A theropod, perhaps an ornithomimid. Late Cretaceous. USA.

**Arrhinoceratops** A horned ceratopsian with a short nose horn. Late Cretaceous. Canada.

**Arstanosaurus** A hadrosaur with a flat head. Late Cretaceous. Kazakhstan.

**Asiaceratops** Primitive ceratopsian. Fragmentary remains only. Late Cretaceous. Russia.

**Astrodon** A brachiosaurid sauropod mainly known from teeth. Early Cretaceous. USA.

**Atlantosaurus** A *Diplodocus*-like sauropod. Late Jurassic. USA.

**Atlascopcosaurus** A *Hypsilophodon*-like dinosaur. Early Cretaceous. Australia.

**Aublysodon** Small *Tyrannosaurus*-like theropod with smooth teeth. Late Cretaceous. North America.

**Austrosaurus** A primitive sauropod dinosaur. Cretaceous. Australia.

**Avaceratops** A small ceratopsian dinosaur, possibly a juvenile. Late Cretaceous. USA.

**Avimimus** An *Oviraptor*-like theropod. The most bird-like dinosaur known. May have had feathered wings. Late Cretaceous. Mongolia and China.

**Avipes** A small theropod or *Lagosuchus*-like dinosaur with bird-like feet. Triassic. Germany.

**Azendohsaurus** A primitive prosauropod. One of the earliest dinosaurs known. Fossil remains comprise teeth and part of jaw. Late Triassic. Morocco.

**Bactrosaurus** A duck-billed ornithopod with a flat head and high-spined vertebrae. Late Cretaceous. China and Uzbekstan.

**Bagaceratops** A very small ceratopsian. Late Cretaceous. Mongolia.

**Bagaraatan** A primitive theropod. Late Cretaceous. Mongolia.

**Bahariasaurus** A tetanuran theropod. Full classification uncertain. Late Cretaceous. Egypt and Niger.

**Bambiraptor** A juvenile theropod with a sickle-shaped claw on the second toe. Originally thought to be a juvenile *Velociraptor* or *Saurornitholestes*. Late Cretaceous. USA.

**Barsboldia** A large duck-billed ornithopod. Late Cretaceous. Mongolia.

**Becklespinax** A theropod with long spines along its back. Early Cretaceous. England.

**Beipiaosaurus** A herbivorous theropod with primitive feathers. Cretaceous. China.

**Bellusaurus** A small sauropod. May be young of another genus. Jurassic. China.

**Bienosaurus** An early thyreophoran. Cretaceous. China.

**Bihariosaurus** An *Iguanodon*-like ornithopod known only from fossil teeth and bone fragments. Late Cretaceous. Romania.

**Blikanosaurus** Bulky sauropodomorph. Late Triassic. South Africa and Lesotho.

**Borogovia** A *Troodon*-like theropod with a sickle-shaped claw on each foot. Late Cretaceous. Mongolia.

**Brachyceratops** A ceratopsian with nose horn and two brow horns. Late Cretaceous. USA.

**Brachylophosaurus** Primitive hadrosaurid ornithopod with a flat crest on the top of its head. Late Cretaceous. North America.

**Breviceratops** A ceratopsian. Late Cretaceous. Mongolia.

**Brontosaurus** Former name of *Apatosaurus*.

**Bugenasaura** An ornithopod. Late Cretaceous. USA.

**Byronosaurus** A *Troodon*-like theropod. The first of its family with unserrated teeth. Late Cretaceous. Mongolia.

**Caenagnathus** A lightly built tetanuran theropod, originally thought to be a bird. Late Cretaceous. North America.

**Callovosaurus** An ornithopod. Mid Jurassic. England.

**Camelotia** A large prosauropod. Late Triassic. England.

**Campylodoniscus** A long-necked titanosaur sauropod known from scanty remains. Late Cretaceous. Argentina.

**Carcharodontosaurus** A large carnosaur. Cretaceous. Africa.

**Cathetosaurus** A sauropod known only from scanty fossils. May be the same as *Camarasaurus*. Late Jurassic. USA.

**Cedarosaurus** A *Brachiosaurus*-like sauropod. Late Cretaceous. USA.

**Ceratops** A ceratopsian known from two horn cores and a single skull bone. Late Cretaceous. USA.

**Cetiosauriscus** A diplodocid sauropod. Jurassic. England.

**Changdusaurus** A stegosaurid ornithischian. Jurassic. China

**Chaoyoungosaurus** A small, bipedal ornithischian, probably a pachycephalosaur. Late Jurassic. China.

**Craspedodon** An ornithischian known from teeth. Late Cretaceous. Belgium.

**Chassternbergia** A large nodosaur. May be the same genus as *Edmontonia*. Late Cretaceous. North America.

**Chialingosaurus** A stegosaur with two rows of small plates down its back. Mid Jurassic. China.

**Chilantaisaurus** A large *Allosaurus*-like carnosaur. Late Cretaceous. China and Russia.

**Chindesaurus** A lightly built theropod. One of the earliest known dinosaurs. Late Triassic. North America.

**Chirostenotes** An oviraptorid theropod with a parrot-like head and toothless beak. Late Cretaceous. Canada.

**Chubutisaurus** An unusual sauropod with heavily hollowed vertebrae. Late Cretaceous. Argentina.

**Chungkingosaurus** A stegosaurid. Late Jurassic. China.

**Claosaurus** A primitive hadrosaur. Late Cretaceous. USA.

**Coloradisaurus** A plateosaurid sauropod. Late Triassic. Argentina.

**Conchoraptor** A small oviraptorid theropod. Late Cretaceous. Mongolia.

**Cryolophosaurus**. A theropod. Early Jurassic. Antarctica.

**Dacenturus** An early stegosaurid with two rows of asymmetrical plates along its back and large spines along its tail. Late Jurassic. England, France, Portugal, and Spain.

**Duspletosaurus** A heavily built tyrannosaurid theropod with brow horns. Late Cretaceous. Canada.

**Datousaurus** A *Cetiosaurus*-like sauropod with a long neck and a very solid skull. Mid Jurassic. China.

**Deltadromeus** A long-limbed and fast-running tetanuran theropod. Late Cretaceous. Morocco.

**Diceratops** A large, two-horned ceratopsian. Late Cretaceous. USA.

**Dicraeosaurus** A diplodocid sauropod with a long neck and a whip-like tail. Jurassic. Tanzania.

**Dinotyrannus** A large tyrannosaurid. Late Cretaceous. North America.

**Draconyx** An *Iguanodon*-like dinosaur. Late Jurassic. Portugal.

**Dracopelta** A nodosaur. Late Jurassic. Portugal.

**Dromiceiomimus** An *Ornithmimus*-like dinosaur. Cretaceous. Canada.

**Dryptosauroides** A large theropod known from only a few vertebrae. Late Cretaceous. India.

**Dryptosaurus** The first theropod to be discovered in North America. Late Cretaceous. USA.

**Dystylosaurus** A large either brachiosaurid or diplodocid sauropod. Late Jurassic. USA.

**Echinodon** A small, early ornithischian. Late Jurassic. England.

**Edmarka** A large theropod known only from a few bones. May be the same as *Torvosaurus*. Late Jurassic. USA.

**Einiosaurus** A ceratopsian. Late Cretaceous. USA.

**Elaphrosaurus** A lightly built theropod. Previously classed as an ornithomimid, nowadays usually considered a ceratosaur. Cretaceous. Tanzania.

**Elmisaurus** A theropod known from hands and feet. Late Cretaceous. Mongolia.

**Elvisaurus** Informal name for *Cryolophosaurus*.

**Emausaurus** An ornithischian with skin covered with cone-shaped and flat armour plates. Jurassic. Germany.

**Enigmosaurus** A large therizinosaur. Cretaceous. Mongolia.

**Eobrontosaurus** A diplodocid sauropod. Jurassic. USA.

**Eoceratops** A primitive ceratopsian with a short frill and three short facial horns. Late Cretaceous. North America.

**Eolambia** An early hadrosaur-like ornithopod. Cretaceous. USA.

**Eotyrannus** A theropod. Cretaceous. England.

**Epachthosaurus** A very large armoured sauropod. Cretaceous. Argentina.

**Epanterias** A huge *Allosaurus*-like theropod known from fragmentary remains. Late Jurassic. USA.

**Erectopus** A therizinosaur. Cretaceous. France and Egypt.

**Erlikosaurus** A large theropod. Late Cretaceous. Mongolia.

**Eucoelophysis** A theropod. Triassic. USA.

**Euhelopus** A large sauropod with a very long neck and bulky body. Jurassic. China.

*Euronychodon* A tetanuran theropod. Cretaceous. Portugal and Uzbekistan.

*Euskelosaurus* A large prosauropod. Early Jurassic. Lesotho, South Africa, and Zimbabwe.

*Eustreptospondylus* A large tetanuran theropod with a primitive hip structure. Jurassic. England.

*Fabrosaurus* An ornithiscian, that may be the same genus as *Lesothosaurus*. Early Jurassic. Lesotho and South Africa.

*Frenguellisaurus* A primitive carnivorous dinosaur that may be the same as *Herrerasaurus*. Triassic. Argentina.

*Fulgurotherium* An ornithopod. Very fragmentary remains. Cretaceous. Australia.

*Futabasaurus* A tyrannosaurid theropod. Cretaceous. Japan.

*Garudimimus* An *Ornithomimus*-like dinosaur. A small crest near its eyes distinguishes it from other similar dinosaurs. Cretaceous. Mongolia.

*Gasparinisaura* A very small ornithopod, probably a juvenile. Cretaceous. Argentina.

*Genyodectes* A large theropod. Cretaceous. Argentina.

*Geranosaurus* An ornithischian with fangs and a beak. Jurassic. South Africa.

*Gilmoreosaurus* A primitive ornithischian hadrosaur. Cretaceous. China.

*Giraffatitan* An enormous, lightly built, *Brachiosaurus*-like sauropod. Jurassic. Tanzania.

*Gojirasaurus* A large theropod. Late Triassic. USA.

*Gongbusaurus* An ornithischian. Jurassic. China.

*Gorgosaurus* A tyrannosaurid, once thought to be *Albertosaurus*. Cretaceous. North America.

*Goyocephale* A pachycephalosaur with a thick-skull, flat-head, knobs and spikes on the skull, and large teeth. Cretaceous. Mongolia.

*Gryposaurus* A hadrosaurid. Cretaceous. Canada.

*Haplocanthosaurus* A sauropod. Late Jurassic. USA.

*Harpymimus* A primitive *Ornithomimus*-like tetanuran. Early Cretaceous. Mongolia.

*Hesperosaurus* A primitive stegosaurid with a single row of rounded plates along its back. Originally called *Hesperisaurus*. Jurassic. USA.

*Histriasaurus* A large sauropod that may have had a sail along the back. Early Cretaceous. Croatia.

*Homalocephale* A pachycephalosaur with a flat skull bordered by bony knobs. Late Cretaceous. Mongolia.

*Hoplitosaurus* An ankylosaur. Early Cretaceous. USA.

*Hulsanpes* A small theropod known only from foot bones. Late Cretaceous. Mongolia

*Hypacrosaurus* A large hadrosaur with a small fin along its back. Cretaceous. North America.

*Hypselosaurus* A small titanosaurid sauropod, whose eggs were the first dinosaur eggs discovered. Late Cretaceous. France and Spain.

*Kritosaurus* A hadrosaurid. Late Cretaceous. Argentina.

*Labocania* A tetanuran theropod. Late Cretaceous. Mexico.

*Laosaurus* An ornithischian known only from fragmentary fossils. Jurassic. North America.

*Laplatasaurus* An armoured sauropod that had a very long neck with grooved vertebrae. Late Cretaceous. Argentina and Uruguay.

*Leaellynasaura* A small hypsilophodontid with large eyes. Early Cretaceous. Australia.

**Leptoceratops** A primitive ceratopsian from Cretaceous. North America.

**Lexovisaurus** A *Stegosaur*-like dinosaur with thin plates along its back and two long shoulder spikes. Jurassic. England and France.

**Lophorhothon** A hadrosaurid. Cretaceous. USA.

**Loricosaurus** A sauropod known only from bony plates embedded in its skin. Cretaceous. Argentina.

**Losillasaurus** An enormous diplodocid sauropod. Jurassic and Cretaceous. Spain.

**Lycorhinus** An early ornithopod. Jurassic. South Africa.

**Magyarosaurus** A small titanosaurid sauropod. Late Cretaceous. Romania.

**Majungatholus** A large theropod with a small horn over the eyes. Late Cretaceous. Madagascar.

**Malawisaurus** A sauropod. Early Cretaceous. Malawi.

**Maleevus** An ankylosaur known only from partial skull remains. Late Cretaceous. Mongolia.

**Marshosaurus** A large theropod. Late Jurassic. USA.

**Masiakasaurus** A theropod. Cretaceous. Madagascar.

**Megaraptor** A theropod known from an incomplete skeleton (including a sickle-shaped claw, metatarsal, ulna, and finger bone). Cretaceous. Argentina.

**Melanorosaurus** A large sauropod. Late Triassic and Early Jurassic. Lesotho and South Africa.

**Metriacanthosaurus** A theropod with high dorsal spines. Cretaceous. England.

**Microceratops** A small ceratopsian similar to *Protoceratops*. Late Cretaceous. China and Mongolia.

**Micropachycephalosaurus** A tiny pachycephalosaur – one of the smallest dinosaurs known. Late Cretaceous. China.

**Microraptor** A bird-like theropod whose feet were adapted for climbing. The arms and legs were covered with feathers. Cretaceous. China.

**Microvenator** A bipedal herbivorous or carnivorous oviraptorid dinosaur. Early Cretaceous. China and USA.

**Mussaurus** A *Plateosaurus*-like prosauropod known only from remains of hatchlings – the smallest dinosaur skeletons yet discovered. Triassic. Argentina.

**Muttaburrasaurus** An *Iguanodon*-like ornithopod. Early Cretaceous. Australia.

**Mymoorapelta** An ankylosaurid. Cretaceous. Australia.

**Naashoibitosaurus** A hadrosaur known only from a skull. May be a species of *Kritosaurus*. Cretaceous. USA.

**Nanosaurus** A small ornithischian. Jurassic. North America.

**Nanotyrannus** A theropod known only from a small skull. Many palaeontologists think *Nanatyrannus* is a juvenile *Tyrannosaurus*. Cretaceous. USA.

**Nanyangosaurus** An ornithopod dinosaur. Cretaceous. China.

**Nedcolbertia** A small theropod known from three partial skeletons. Early Cretaceous. USA.

**Nemegtosaurus** A sauropod known only from a skull. Late Cretaceous. Mongolia and China.

**Neovenator** An *Allosaurus*-like theropod, with a "puffin-like" skull profile. Early Cretaceous. England.

**Ngexisaurus** A lightly built theropod. Mid Jurassic. China.

**Nigersaurus** A primitive diplodocid sauropod. Early Cretaceous. Niger.

*Nipponosaurus* A small hadrosaur with a bony head crest. Cretaceous. Russia.

*Noasaurus* A small theropod with a sickle-shaped claw on each foot, which was similar to that of dromaeosaurs, but had a unique retractor tendon. Cretaceous. Argentina.

*Nothronychus* The first therizinosaur found outside Asia. It may have been feathered. Cretaceous. USA.

*Notoceratops* A ceratopsian known only from a jaw bone. Cretaceous. Argentina.

*Nqwebasaurus* A theropod with a very large claw on the first finger. Cretaceous. South Africa.

*Nyasasaurus* A very early prosauropod of uncertain classification. Triassic. East Africa.

*Ohmdenosaurus* A sauropod known from one complete shin bone. Early Jurassic. Germany.

*Omeisaurus* A large *Cetiosaurus*-like sauropod with a very long neck. Jurassic. China.

*Opisthocoelicaudia* A large, short-tailed *Camarasaurus*-like sauropod. Cretaceous. Mongolia.

*Orcomimus* An *Ornithomimus*-like theropod. Cretaceous. USA.

*Ornatotholus* A pachycephalosaur once thought to be female *Stegoceras*. Cretaceous. North America.

*Orodromeus* An ornithopod found with unhatched eggs and young. Its young are thought to have been able to fend for themselves after hatching. Late Cretaceous. USA.

*Orthomerus* A hadrosaur named for its straight thigh bone. Cretaceous. Netherlands.

*Oshanosaurus* An early sauropod. Early Jurassic. China.

*Othnielia* Small ornithopod with very long legs, five-fingered hands, long tail, and horny beak. Jurassic. USA.

*Ozraptor* A tetanuran theropod with three-fingered hands and a stiff tail. Jurassic. Australia.

*Pachyrhinosaurus* A short-frilled ceratopsian that may have had a snout horn. Cretaceous. North America.

*Panoplosaurus* A nodosaurid ankylosaur with no tail club. Cretaceous. North America.

*Paranthodon* A stegosaur known from a jaw bone with teeth. Cretaceous. South Africa.

*Parksosaurus* An ornithopod. Cretaceous. North America.

*Patagonykus* A dromaeosaur or a primitive bird, with long legs and tail and short arms. Late Cretaceous. Argentina.

*Patagosaurus* A primitive *Cetiosaurus*-like sauropod. Mid Jurassic. Argentina.

*Pawpawsaurus* A large nodosaur with armour over most of its body but no tail club. Cretaceous. USA.

*Pelecanimimus* The first ornithomimosaur discovered in Europe. It had about 220 teeth, more than any other known theropod, and fossil remains show evidence of feathers. Cretaceous. Spain.

*Pelorosaurus* A sauropod known from incomplete skeletons and fossilized skin impressions. Early Cretaceous. England and France.

*Phyllodon* A small *Hypsilophodon*-like dinosaur. Jurassic. Portugal.

*Pinacosaurus* An ankylosaur. Cretaceous. Mongolia.

*Pisanosaurus* A small, possibly ornithopod, early ornithischian known only from fragmentary fossils. Late Triassic. Argentina.

*Piveteausaurus* A theropod of indeterminate size known from scanty remains. Jurassic. France.

*Planicoxa* Recently discovered ornithopod. Cretaceous. USA.

**Pleurocoelus** A small *Brachiosaurus*-like sauropod, whose vertebrae had deep hollows. Cretaceous. USA.

**Poekilopleuron** A *Megalosaurus*-like theropod. Jurassic. France.

**Polacanthus** A primitive ankylosaur with spines. Cretaceous. England.

**Prenocephale** A *Stegoceras*-like pachycephalosaur. Cretaceous. Mongolia and North America.

**Probactrosaurus** An *Iguanodon*-like ornithopod dinosaur. Early Cretaceous. China.

**Proceratosaurus** A crested theropod. Jurassic. England.

**Prosaurolophus** A hadrosaur. Late Cretaceous. North America.

**Protarchaeopteryx** A bird-like, non-flying, theropod with feathers on the arms, most of the body, and on the short tail. Early Cretaceous. China.

**Protoavis** A primitive bird or theropod dinosaur. Its partly toothless jaw and breastbone were bird-like. Late Triassic. USA.

**Protohadros** The oldest-known hadrosaur. Late Cretaceous. USA.

**Pyroraptor** A *Deinonychus*-like dinosaur. May be the same as *Variraptor*. Cretaceous. France.

**Qantassaurus** A kangaroo-sized ornithopod. Cretaceous. Australia.

**Quaesitosaurus** Large, diplodocid sauropod known only from a partial skull. Cretaceous. Mongolia.

**Quilmesaurus** A medium-sized theropod. Late Cretaceous. Argentina.

**Rahonavis** A dinosaur or primitive bird with sickle-shaped toe claws and a long, bony tail. Late Cretaceous. Madagascar.

**Rapetosaurus** A recently discovered *Titanosaurus*-like sauropod. Late Cretaceous. Madagascar.

**Rebbachisaurus** A diplodocid sauropod dinosaur that may have had a sail on its back. Cretaceous. Morocco and Niger.

**Revueltosaurus** A poorly known ornithischian. Late Triassic, USA.

**Rhabdodon** An *Iguanodon*-like ornithopod. Late Cretaceous. Austria, France, Romania, and Spain.

**Rhoetosaurus** A *Cetiosaurus*-like sauropod. Mid Jurassic. Australia.

**Ricardoestesia** A small theropod. Cretaceous. North America.

**Rioarribasaurus** A small theropod. Late Triassic. USA.

**Riojasaurus** A heavily built prosauropod. Late Triassic and Early Jurassic. Argentina.

**Ruehleia** A recently discovered primitive *Plateosaurus*-like prosauropod. Triassic. Germany.

**Saichania** An ankylosaur with a clubbed-tail, and bony spikes and knobs running along its sides. Both body armour and belly armour have been found. Cretaceous. Mongolia.

**Saltopus** A tiny, primitive theropod. Late Triassic. Scotland.

**Santanaraptor** A theropod known from partial skeleton and skin impressions. Early Cretaceous. Brazil.

**Sarcolestes** An early nodosaur or ankylosaur known only from a partial lower jaw. Jurassic. England.

**Saurophaganax** A large carnosaur. May be *Allosaurus*. Jurassic. USA.

**Sauroposeidon** A *Brachiosaurus*-like sauropod. Cretaceous. USA.

**Saurornitholestes** A *Velociraptor*-like theropod. Cretaceous. Canada.

**Scipionyx** A theropod, perhaps a maniraptor, known from a single hatchling that includes soft tissues. Cretaceous. USA.

**Secernosaurus** A hadrosaur – the first to be found in South America. Cretaceous. Argentina.

**Segisaurus** A goose-sized, bird-like theropod whose collar bone was similar in structure to that of true birds. Jurassic. USA.

**Segnosaurus** A strange theropod of uncertain size. May have been a plant eater. Cretaceous. Mongolia.

**Sellosaurus** A lightly built prosauropod that some palaeontologists judge to be the same genus as *Efraasia*. Late Triassic. Germany.

**Shamosaurus** An ankylosaur. Cretaceous. Mongolia.

**Shanshanosaurus** A lightly built theropod. Cretaceous. China.

**Shantungosaurus** The largest-known hadrosaur. Late Cretaceous. China.

**Shanxia** An ankylosaur. Late Cretaceous. China.

**Siamosaurus** A large, sail-backed, *Spinosaurus*-like theropod. Cretaceous. Thailand.

**Siamotyrannus** A tyrannosaurid theropod. Cretaceous.Thailand.

**Silvisaurus** A nodosaur with a relatively long neck, and spines jutting out from the back, and perhaps the tail. Cretaceous. USA.

**Sinornithosaurus** A recently found dromaeosaurid. The fossil had traces of downy fibres on its skin. Jurassic. China.

**Sinosauropteryx** A feathered theropod. Jurassic. China.

**Sinraptor** A large theropod. Late Jurassic. China.

**Sonorasaurus** A *Brachiosaurus*-like sauropod. Cretaceous. USA.

**Stenopelix** A ceratopsian, perhaps similar to *Psittacosaurus*, known from hip and leg bones. Early Cretaceous. Germany.

**Stokesosaurus** A theropod that may have been the earliest tyrannosaurid. Jurassic. USA.

**Struthiosaurus** An ankylosaur. Late Cretaceous. Europe.

**Stygimoloch** A pachycephalosaur with strange spikes and bumps on the skull. Cretaceous. USA.

**Stygivenator** A tyrannosaurid theropod. Cretaceous. USA.

**Supersaurus** A diplodocid sauropod. One of the longest dinosaurs yet discovered. Late Jurassic. USA.

**Syntarsus** A lightly built theropod with fused foot bones. Triassic. South Africa, USA, and Zimbabwe.

**Szechuanosaurus** An *Allosaurus*-like theropod. Jurassic. China.

**Tangvayosaurus** A titanosaurid sauropod. Cretaceous. Asia.

**Talarurus** An ankylosaur. Cretaceous. Mongolia.

**Tarchia** An ankylosaur with a very large tail club and large braincase. Cretaceous. Mongolia.

**Telmatosaurus** A hadrosaur. Cretaceous. France, Romania, and Spain.

**Tendaguria** A recently discovered sauropod. Jurassic. Tanzania.

**Tenontosaurus** A large ornithopod with relatively long arms. Cretaceous. North America.

**Texasetes** An ankylosaur. Cretaceous. USA.

**Teyuwasu** A recently discovered theropod. Known from leg bones. Triassic. Brazil.

**Thescelosaurus** An ornithopod dinosaur, whose fossilized four-chambered heart was found. Cretaceous. North America.

**Timimus** A theropod known from leg bones. Cretaceous. Australia.

*Torvosaurus* A large theropod. Late Jurassic. USA.

*Tsintaosaurus* A poorly known hadrosaur that may have had a bony crest on the head. Cretaceous. China.

*Tylocephale* A small pachycephalosaur known only from incomplete skull. Cretaceous. Mongolia.

*Ultrasaurus* A sauropod. Cretaceous. South Korea.

*Unenlagia* A bird-like theropod. Cretaceous. Argentina.

*Utahraptor* A large dromaeosaurid. Cretaceous. USA.

*Valdoraptor* A tetanuran theropod known from footbones. Early Cretaceous. England.

*Variraptor* A recently discovered dromaeosaurid theropod. Late Cretaceous. France.

*Venenosaurus* A titanosaurid sauropod. Cretaceous. USA.

*Walkeria* A primitive theropod. Late Triassic. India.

*Wannanosaurus* A tiny, primitive pachycephalosaur. Cretaceous. China.

*Wuerhosaurus* A stegosaur with smaller plates than *Stegosaurus*. Early Cretaceous. Mongolia.

*Xenotarsosaurus* A theropod known from a few vertebrae and hind-leg bones. Cretaceous. Argentina.

*Xiaosaurus* A small ornithischian. Jurassic. China.

*Xuanhanosaurus* A tetanuran theropod. Mid Jurassic. China.

*Xuanhuasaurus* An ornithischian. Cretaceous. China.

*Yandusaurus* Ornithopod ornithischian. Jurassic. China.

*Yaverlandia* An early pachycephalosaur. Cretaceous. England.

*Yunnanosaurus* A large prosauropod – the only prosauropod known with self-sharpening, chisel-shaped teeth. Jurassic. China.

*Zephyrosaurus* A *Hypsilophodon*-like dinosaur known from a partial skull and vertebrae. Cretaceous. USA.

*Zigongosaurus* Probably the same dinosaur as *Omeisaurus*. Jurassic. China.

*Zizhongosaurus* A primitive sauropod. Jurassic. China.

*Zuniceratops* An early ceratopsian with brow horns. Cretaceous. USA.

# GLOSSARY

This glossary is an easy-reference guide to the technical terms that are used in this book. It focuses mainly on the terms used to describe different groups of dinosaurs and other forms of prehistoric life. It also includes scientific names used to describe anatomical features. If you cannot find the term you are looking for here, check the general index as the information you require may be found elsewhere in the book. Words in bold type within the entries have their own glossary entry.

• **ACANTHODIANS**
The earliest jawed vertebrates. Primitive fish, also known as spiny sharks, that lived from the Ordovician to the Carboniferous.

• **ACETABULUM**
The hip socket.

• **AEROFOIL**
The curved surface of a wing that aids flight by creating an upward force.

• **AËTOSAURS**
A group of early **thecodonts** that superficially resembled crocodiles, with bulky bodies and leaf-shaped teeth.

• **AGNATHANS**
"Jawless fish" – primitive vertebrates that flourished in Early Palaeozoic times.

• **ALGAE**
Primitive plants and plant-like organisms.

• **ALLOSAURS**
Large, fairly primitive **tetanuran** (stiff-tailed) **theropods.**

• **AMMONITES**
Extinct, predatory, marine invertebrates (**cephalopods**). These animals had a shell (usually spiral-coiled) containing air filled chambers; the animal lived only in the outer chamber.

• **AMNIOTES**
Animals whose eggs contain an amnion, a membrane that surrounds the embryo. Mammals, birds, and reptiles are amniotes.

• **AMPHIBIANS**
Vertebrates whose young live in the water (breathing through gills), but usually live on land as adults (breathing with lungs). Living amphibians include newts, salamanders, frogs, and toads.

• **ANAPSIDS**
Primitive reptiles with no hole in the skull behind the eye. Anapsids include the turtles and their extinct kin.

• **ANCHIASAURIDS**
A group of small, lightly built early **sauropodomorphs** of the Late Triassic Period.

• **ANGIOSPERMS**
Flowering plants, which produce seeds enclosed in fruit (an ovary).

• **ANKYLOSAURS**
A family of heavily armoured, plant-eating, **quadrupedal ornithischian** dinosaurs that lived from the Mid Jurassic to the Late Cretaceous Periods.

• **ARBOREAL**
An organism that spends most of its life in trees, off the ground.

• **ARCHAEOCYTES**
Primitive whales that lived during the Eocene Epoch. Some had hind limbs.

• **ARCHOSAURS**
A major group of reptiles that includes the **crocodilians**, **pterosaurs**, **dinosaurs**, and **aves** (birds).

• **ARTHROPODS**
A group of invertebrates with **exoskeletons** made of chitin, segmented bodies, and jointed limbs. Insects, spiders and scorpions, **trilobites**, and **crustaceans** are members of this group.

• **ARTIODACTYLS**
**Ungulates** (hoofed mammals) with an even number of toes. Pigs, camels, deer, giraffes and cattle are modern animals in this group.

• **AVES**
The scientific name for birds.

• **BALTICA**
An ancient continent of the Palaeozoic Era.

• **BIPEDAL**
Walking on the hindlimbs rather than on all-four legs. See also **Quadrupedal.**

• **BIVALVES**
Aquatic molluscs enclosed by a two-part, hinged shell.

• **BRACHIOPODS**
Marine invertebrates with two joined valved shells.

• **BRACHIOSAURIDS**
A group of huge **sauropods** with spoon-shaped teeth and long forelimbs. They lived in the Late Jurassic and Early Cretaceous Periods.

• **BRAINCASE**
The bones of the skull that contain and protect the brain.

• **BRONTOTHERES**
Also known as titanotheres. An extinct family of large, rhinoceros-like mammals.

• **BROWSER**
An animal that eats tall foliage (leaves, trees, or shrubs).

• **CAMARASAURIDS**
A group of relatively short-necked **sauropods** of the Jurassic and Cretaceous Periods.

• **CARINATES**
A group of birds with deep-keeled breastbones.

- **CARNIVORA**
A group of sharp-toothed, meat-eating mammals, including cats and dogs.
- **CARNOSAUR**
A group of large theropods that lived during the Jurassic and Cretaceous Periods.
- **CENTROSAURINES**
A group of rhinoceros-like **ceratopsian** dinosaurs – most had long horns on the snout and a short neck frill.
- **CEPHALOPODS**
Molluscs with tentacles surrounding a large head. These soft-bodied invertebrates include squid, octopuses, cuttlefish, and **ammonites**.
- **CERAPODS**
A group of **ornithischian** dinosaurs that included the **ornithopods** and the **marginocephalians**.
- **CERATOPSIANS**
A group of plant eating **ornithischian** dinosaurs with beaks and bony head frills along the back of the skull.
- **CERATOSAURS**
A major group of **theropod** dinosaurs – those in which the three hip bones (**ilium, ischium,** and **pubis**) are fused.
- **CETACEANS**
Marine mammals with a streamlined body and flippers for limbs. The group includes whales and dolphins.
- **CETIOSAURIDS**
A group of early **sauropods** of the Jurassic Period.
- **CHORISTODERES**
A group of crocodile-like **diapsid** reptiles, also known as champsosaurs.
- **CLADE**
A grouping of animals (or other organisms) that share anatomical features derived from the same ancestor.
- **COELUROSAURS**
A group of **tetanuran**

theropods that includes the **maniraptorans, ornithomimids,** and **tyrannosaurids**
- **COLD BLOODED**
See **ectotherms**.
- **CONDYLARTHS**
A group of herbivorous mammals that arose in the Early Tertiary. Some had clawed feet, others had blunt hooves.
- **CONFUCIORNITHIDS**
A family of early birds similar to *Confuciornis*.
- **CREODONTS**
A group of meat-eating mammals with clawed feet, a small brain, large jaws, and many sharp teeth that were the dominant carnivorous mammals during the Tertiary Period.
- **CROCODILIANS**
A group of **archosaurs** that includes alligators, crocodiles, and gavials. They evolved during the Late Triassic Period.
- **CRINOIDS**
Plant shaped echinoderms (sea lilies).
- **CRUSTACEANS**
A class of invertebrates with a hard exoskeleton, jointed legs, and a bilaterally symmetrical segmented body.
- **CYCADS**
Primitive seed plants that dominated Jurassic habitats. They are palm-like trees, with separate male and female plants.
- **CYNODONTS**
A group of herbivorous and carnivorous **synapsids** that appeared late in the Permian Period and were the ancestors of mammals.
- **DEINONYCHOSAURS**
A group of advanced **theropod** dinosaurs with a long, sharp, sickle-shaped claw on the second toe of each hind foot.

- **DIAPSIDS**
A **clade** of animals, distinguished by two temporal **fenestrae**, that includes **archosaurs** and **lepidosaurs**.
- **DICYNODONTS**
Pig-like, herbivorous **therapsids** with two large tusks in the upper jaw.
- **DIMORPHISM**
Having two forms, for example, sexual dimorphism between males and females of the same species.
- **DINOCEPHALIANS**
Late Permian **therapsids**. Some were meat-eating, others were plant-eating or omnivores.
- **DINOSAURS**
A **clade** of reptiles, partly distinguished by a largely to fully open **acetabulum** and erect limbs. They were wholly terrestrial. Only one major group of dinosaurs, **aves** (birds), survived after the end of the Cretaceous.
- **DIPLODOCIDS**
A family of huge sauropods characterized by a small head with peg-like teeth and nostrils opening at the top of the head.
- **DOCODONTS**
A group of primitive mammals.
- **DROMAEOSAURIDS**
A family of small, fast **theropods**, with large, retractable, sickle-shaped toe claws and large eyes.
- **ECHINODERMS**
Salt-water invertebrates whose living members have five arms or divisions of the body (or multiples of five).
- **ECTOTHERMS**
Animals, often called "cold blooded", whose internal temperature changes with the surrounding environment.
- **ELASMOSAURS**
A family of long-necked **plesiosaurs**.

- **ENANTIORNITHES**
A group of toothless birds that lived during the Cretaceous. Their shoulder blade (scapula) and coracoid (a small bone connected to the scapula) are oriented in the opposite way to that of modern birds.
- **ENDOTHERMS**
Animals, often called "warm blooded", that maintain a relatively constant internal temperature by generating their own body heat.
- **EUORNITHES**
Modern "true" birds.
- **EOSUCHIANS**
A now-redundant term used to describe lizard-like **diapsids** that probably gave rise to lizards and snakes.
- **EURASIA**
The continent formed by the combined land masses of Europe and Asia.
- **EURYAPSIDS**
A group of extinct marine reptiles with a single opening in the skull behind the eye socket. They included **plesiosaurs, nothosaurs, placodonts,** and **ichthyosaurs.**
- **EVOLUTION**
The theoretical process by which the gene pool of a population changes in response to environmental pressures, natural selection, and genetic mutations.
- **EXOSKELETON**
A tough, outer body covering made of chitin (a type of protein) or calcium carbonate.
- **FAMILY**
A group of related or similar organisms. A family contains one or more **genera.**
- **FEMUR**
The thigh bone.
- **FENESTRA (pl. fenestrae)**
A natural, window-like hole or opening in a bone. The skull has many fenestrae.

- **FIBULA**
The smaller of the two bones of the lower leg.
- **FOSSIL**
Mineralized skeletons or casts of ancient plants and animals (or their traces, such as footprints).
- **FURCULA**
The "wishbone" in birds.
- **GASTRALIA**
Thin ribs in the belly area not attached to the backbone.
- **GASTROPODS**
A class of **molluscs** with a sucker-like foot and often a spiral shell.
- **GENUS (pl. genera)**
A group of related or similar organisms. A genus contains one or more **species.** A group of similar genera comprise a **family.**
- **GONDWANA**
The southern supercontinent formed after the break-up of the supercontinent **Pangaea.** It included present-day South America, Africa, India, Australia, and Antarctica.
- **GRACILE**
Small and slender. Some species have both gracile and **robust** forms, possibly representing differences between males and females.
- **GRAPTOLITE**
Extinct, tiny marine colonial animals, with a soft body and a hard outer covering.
- **GRAZER**
An animal that eats low-lying vegetation, such as grasses.
- **GYMNOSPERMS**
Seed-bearing plants that do not produce flowers.
- **HADROSAURS**
A group of "duck-billed" Cretaceous **quadrupedal ornithopods.**
- **HERBIVORE**
An animal that eats plants.
- **HESPERORNITHIFORMS**
A family of early birds similar to *Hesperornis.*

- **HOMEOTHERMIC**
An animal that keeps a fairly constant body temperature.
- **HORSETAIL**
A primitive, spore-bearing plant with rhizomes that was common during the Palaeozoic and Mesozoic Eras.
- **HYPSILPHODONTIDS**
A group of small, herbivorous **ornithopod ornithischians** that were widespread in the Jurassic and Cretaceous Periods.
- **IAPETUS OCEAN**
The precursor of the Atlantic Ocean, between the ancient continents of **Laurentia** and **Baltica.**
- **ICHTHYORNITHIFORMS**
A family of early birds similar to *Ichthyornis.*
- **IGUANODONTIDS**
A group of herbivorous **ornithopod ornithischians** that were widespread in the Cretaceous Period.
- **ILIUM**
One of the three (paired) bones of the pelvis.
- **INSECTIVORE**
An organism (animal or plant) that eats insects.
- **INVERTEBRATES**
Animals without a backbone.
- **ISCHIUM**
One of the three (paired) bones of the pelvis.
- **JUVENILE**
A young or immature individual.
- **K-T EXTINCTION**
The mass extinction that occurred at the boundary of the Cretaceous and Tertiary Periods.
- **LAGOMORPHS**
A group of mammals that became widespread in the Tertiary Period and includes modern rabbits and hares.
- **LAGOSUCHIANS**
A group of early **archosaurs** that were probably ancestors of the **dinosaurs.**

- **LAURASIA**
The northern supercontinent formed after the break up of **Pangaea.**
- **LAURENTIA**
An ancient continent of the Palaeozoic Era.
- **LEPIDOSAURS**
The group of reptiles that includes snakes and lizards.
- **LEPOSPONDYLS**
Small, extinct **amphibians** that resembled salamanders or snakes. They lived through the Carboniferous and Permian Periods.
- **LITOPTERNS**
A group of extinct hoofed mammals that resembled camels and horses.
- **LOBE-FINNED FISH**
A group of fish whose fins are supported on fleshy lobes. Lobe-finned fish appeared during the Silurian Period.
- **LYCOPODS**
A group of **lycopsid** plants, also known as club mosses. They were at their peak in the Carboniferous Period.
- **LYCOPSIDS**
Primitive **vascular** plants that evolved during the Devonian Period.
- **MANIRAPTORANS**
A group of advanced **theropods** with bird-like characteristics. It included **dromaeosaurs, oviraptorids, troodontids, therizinosaurs,** and **aves.**
- **MARGINOCEPHALIANS**
A group of **ornithischian** dinosaurs with a bony frill or shelf on the back of the skull. This group includes the **ceratopsians** and **pachycephalosaurs.**
- **MARSUPIALS**
Mammals, including modern-day kangaroos, that give birth to small, undeveloped young that grow and mature in a pouch on the mother's abdomen.

- **MASTODONS**
An extinct group of mammals closely related to elephants.
- **MEGALOSAURS**
A group of large **theropods,** less advanced than **allosaurs.**
- **MESOSAURS**
Extinct, lizard-like aquatic reptiles.
- **MOLLUSCS**
A group of invertebrates including **gastropods** and **cephalopods.**
- **MONOTREMES**
Primitive egg-laying mammals. The platypus and echidnas are the only living representatives of this group.
- **MOSASAURS**
Large marine reptiles that lived during the Cretaceous Period.
- **MULTITUBERCULATES**
Rodent-like mammals of the Late Jurassic to Early Tertiary Periods. All were very small.
- **MYRIAPODS**
A group of many-legged **arthropods** that includes centipedes and millipedes.
- **NAUTILOIDS**
Primitive **cephalopods** with thick shells. Only a single genus survives.
- **NEOGNATHAE**
A group of birds that evolved during the Late Cretaceous. They include most flying birds plus swimming and diving birds such as modern penguins.
- **NEORNITHES**
The **clade** of modern birds that have feathers, a beak covered in horn, and a four-chambered heart.
- **NODOSAURS**
A group of **quadrupedal ornithiscian** armoured dinosaurs.
- **NOTHOSAURS**
Extinct marine reptiles with four paddle-like limbs that lived during the Triassic Period.

- **ODONTORNITHES**
A group of Cretaceous birds with conical teeth in both jaws.
- **ORBIT**
The eye socket.
- **ORNITHISCHIANS**
"Bird-hipped" dinosaurs – one of the two main dinosaur groups. They were **herbivores** and had hoof-like claws. See also **Saurischians.**
- **ORNITHODIRANS**
The **archosaur clade** that includes **dinosaurs,** their early ancestors the **lagosuchians,** and **pterosaurs.**
- **ORNITHOMIMIDS**
A group of **theropod** dinosaurs whose name means "bird-mimic". They outwardly resembled flightless birds.
- **ORNITHOPODS**
A group of **ornithischian dinosaurs** that have no hole in the outer, lower jaw and a long pubis that extends farther forwards than the **ilium.** They were beaked, mostly **bipedal herbivores.**
- **ORNITHOTHORACES**
A clade of birds that had evolved the alula – a feather that directs air over the upper surface of the wing.
- **OVIPAROUS**
A term used to describe animals that hatch from eggs.
- **OVIRAPTORIDS**
A family of toothless **maniraptoran theropods.**
- **PACHYCEPHALOSAURS**
A group of **bipedal ornithischian** dinosaurs with immensely thick skulls.
- **PALAEONTOLOGY**
The branch of biology that studies the forms of life that existed in former geologic periods.
- **PALAEONTOLOGIST**
A scientist who studies **palaeontology.**

- **PANGAEA**
A supercontinent consisting of all of Earth's landmasses that formed at the end of the Palaeozoic Era.
- **PAREIASAURS**
A group of early **anapsid** reptiles with massive, heavy bodies and stout limbs. Close relatives of turtles.
- **PELYCOSAURS**
The earliest **synapsids**, pelycosaurs evolved during the Carboniferous and became extinct during the Permian Period.
- **PERMINERALIZATION**
The process in which minerals are deposited within the fabric of a bony fossil.
- **PERISSODACTYLS**
A group of hoofed mammals that includes horses, rhinoceroses, and tapirs.
- **PETRIFICATION**
The process by which organic tissue turns to stone.
- **PHYTOSAURS**
A group of extinct semi-aquatic **archosaurs** superficially resembling crocodiles.
- **PLACENTALS**
Mammals whose unborn young are nourished by an organ called a placenta.
- **PLACODERMS**
A class of jawed fish protected by armour plates.
- **PLACODONTS**
Aquatic reptiles that lived in shallow seas during the Triassic, becoming extinct at the end of the period. Many had turtle-like shells.
- **PLESIOSAURS**
Large marine reptiles of the Mesozoic Era with pairs of flipper-shaped limbs.
- **PLIOSAURS**
Large, short-necked **plesiosaurs**.
- **PREDATOR**
An animal that preys on other animals for food.

- **PREHENSILE**
Able to grasp something by wrapping around it. An animal with a prehensile tail is able to grasp branches with it, for example.
- **PRIMITIVE**
Having characteristics similar to those of earlier forms.
- **PROBOSCIDEANS**
A group of mammals with trunks that includes modern elephants as well as the now-extinct mammoths.
- **PROCOLOPHONIDS**
A group of early herbivorous **Anapsids** of the Triassic Period.
- **PROSAUROPODS**
A group of early sauropodomorph dinosaurs that lived in the Late Triassic and Early Jurassic Periods.
- **PROTOZOANS**
General term for single-celled animals.
- **PSITTACOSAURS**
A group of **bipedal**, herbivorous **ceratopsians** with a parrot-like beak.
- **PTERODACTYLOIDS**
Short-tailed **pterosaurs** that replaced earlier long-tailed forms.
- **PTEROSAURS**
Flying **archosaurs** closely related to the dinosaurs.
- **PUBIS**
A bone that is part of the pelvic girdle. It points downwards and slightly towards the front in **saurischians** and downwards and towards the tail in **ornithischians**.
- **PYGOSTYLE**
The short tailbone of a bird, formed from fused tail **vertebrae**.
- **QUADRUPEDAL**
Walking on four legs. See also **Bipedal**.
- **RADIUS**
One of the two lower arm bones.

- **RATITES**
Flightless birds.
- **REPTILES**
The common name for a group of animals characterized by having scales (or modified scales), being cold-blooded, and laying eggs with shells.
- **RHYNCHOSAURS**
Herbivorous, land-dwelling **diapsid** reptiles from the Late Triassic Period.
- **ROBUST**
Large form of a species. See also **Gracile**.
- **SACRUM**
The **vertebrae** of the lower back fused to the pelvis.
- **SARCOPTERYGIANS**
A group of bony fish with fleshy fins, including lungfish, coelacanths, and many extinct forms.
- **SAURISCHIANS**
"Lizard-hipped" dinosaurs – one of the two main dinosaur groups. Saurischians are divided into the **theropods** and **sauropodomorphs**. See also **Ornithischians**.
- **SAUROPODOMORPHS**
Large, four-legged, long-necked herbivorous **saurischian** dinosaurs. They are commonly divided into the **prosauropods** and the **sauropods**.
- **SAUROPODS**
Huge, **quadrupedal**, herbivorous dinosaurs with long necks, small heads, and long tails.
- **SAUROPTERYGIANS**
An group of extinct aquatic reptiles from the Mesozoic Era. They include **plesiosaurs**, **nothosaurs**, and **placodonts**.
- **SCLEROTIC RING**
A ring of bones that supports the structure of the eye.
- **SCUTE**
A bony plate with a horny outer covering embedded in the skin.

• **SEED FERNS**
Primitive seed plants
(Pteridosperms) that grew in
swampy areas through the
Palaeozoic and Mesozoic Eras.

• **SIRENIANS**
A group of mammals that
includes modern sea cows
(manatees).

• **SPECIES**
In Linnaean classification, the
level below a **genus**. Only
individuals within the same
species can breed and
produce viable, fertile young.

• **STEGOSAURS**
Four-legged **ornithischian**
dinosaurs with bony plates
and/or spikes down the neck,
back, and tail.

• **STERNUM**
The breastbone.

• **SYNAPSIDS**
A group of **tetrapod
vertebrates** distinguished by
having a skull with a low
opening behind the eyes.
Synapsids include the
**mammals, pelycosaurs**, and
many other Permian and
Triassic forms.

• **TARSAL**
Ankle bone.

• **TELEOSTS**
A group of advanced bony
fish.

• **TEMNOSPONDYLS**
A group of early **tetrapods**.

• **TETANURANS**
One of the major groups of
**theropod** dinosaurs. The rear
part of the tails of tetanurans
were stiffened by interlocking
bony ligaments on the
**vertebrae**.

• **TETHYS SEA**
A shallow sea that existed
during the early Mesozoic
Era, separating the northern
landmass of **Laurasia** from
**Gondwana** in the south.

• **TETRAPODS**
Four-legged **vertebrates** and
the vertebrates descended
from them.

• **THALATTOSAURS**
Large, lizard-like marine
reptiles that lived in the
Triassic Period.

• **THECODONTS**
A group of socket-toothed
**archosaurs** that lived during
the Triassic Period.

• **THERAPSIDS**
A general term used to
describe **synapsids** in the
Permian and Triassic Periods.

• **THERIZINOSAURS**
A group of strange **theropod**
dinosaurs that had a toothless
beak and four toes on each
foot.

• **THEROPODS**
A suborder of **saurischian**
dinosaurs. They were **bipedal
carnivores**.

• **THYREOPHORANS**
Armoured, plated, and/or
spiked **ornithischian**
dinosaurs. They included the
**ankylosaurs, nodosaurs,**
and **stegosaurs**.

• **TIBIA**
The shin bone.

• **TRICONODONTS**
An extinct group of small,
early mammals that lived from
the Triassic until the
Cretaceous Period.

• **TRILOBITES**
Early **arthropods** with
external skeletons divided
into three lobes.

• **TROODONTIDS**
A group of small, lightly built,
long-legged **tetanuran
theropods** with unusually
large **braincases**.

• **TYRANNOSAURIDS**
A family of very large
**tetanuran theropods** with
two-fingered hands, small
arms, a large head, sharp
teeth, and powerful hind legs.

• **ULNA**
One of the two bones of the
lower arm.

• **UNGULATES**
Hoofed mammals such as
horses.

• **VASCULAR PLANTS**
Land-living plants with a
specialized system of tubes
that carry water and nutrients.

• **VERTEBRAE (sing.
vertebra)**
The linked bones that form
the backbone in **vertebrates**.

• **VERTEBRATES**
Animals with a backbone and
a skull made of bone or
cartilage.

• **WARM BLOODED**
See **Endotherms**.

# INDEX

# ACKNOWLEDGMENTS

Dorling Kindersley would like to thank Alison Woodhouse for
proofreading the text and Jane Parker for compiling the index.

The publisher would like to thank the following for their kind permission
to reproduce their photographs:
(Abbreviations key: b=bottom, c=centre, l=left, r=right, t=top,
b/g=background)

10: Queensland Museum; 11br, cr: Royal Tyrrell Museum, Canada;
13tr: Corbis; 20/21b/g: Corbis/Roger Ressmeyer; 22/23: Corbis /ML
Sinibaldi; 24/25b/g: Corbis/Yann Arthus-Bertrand; 26/27b/g:
Corbis/David Muench 27cl: Natural History Museum; 28/29b/g:
Corbis /Geoffrey L. Rotman; 30/31b/g: Corbis/Michael & Patricia
Fogden; 30cl: Natural History Museum; 32/33b/g: Getty
Images/William J. Hebert; 34/35b, c: Corbis/Michael & Patricia
Fogden; 34/35t Getty Images/Harvey Lloyd; 36/37b/g: Getty
Images/Harvey Lloyd; 37br: Natural History Museum, London; 38br:
Corbis; 38tc: Natural History Museum; 44b: State Museum of Nature;
45tr: Carnegie Museum of Art, Pittsburgh; 48t: American Museum of
Natural History; 49b:Yorkshire Museum; 51b: Natural History
Museum, London; 58/59b/g: Corbis:/Michael & Patricia Fogden; 63tr:
Science Photo Library; 65tc: State Museum of Nature; 65tr:
Smithsonian Institution; 66/67: Royal Tyrrell Museum, Canada; 67br:
Carnegie Museum of Art, Pittsburgh; 68/69b/g: Corbis; 74cr: Natural
History Museum; 75tr: Carnegie Museum Of Art, Pittsburgh; 75cr: The
Institute of Archaeology, Beijing; 76b: American Museum of Natural
History; 78/79b/g: Corbis; 80tc: Natural History Museum, London;
82c: Royal Tyrrell Museum, Canada; 82/83b/g: Getty Images; 83t:
Senekenberg Nature Museum; 84b: Leicester Museum; 86b: Royal
Tyrrell Museum, Canada; 89b: Natural History Museum, London;
94/95b/g: Natural History Museum, London; 96: Hunterian Museum;
97: Natural History Museum, London; 99bl: Natural History Museum,
London; 101b: Natural History Museum, London; 102/103b/g: Corbis;
104/105b/g: Corbis; 111c: Natural History Museum, London; 112b:
Getty Images; 114tr: American Museum of Natural History; 115b:
American Museum of Natural History; 116: Senekenberg Nature
Museum; 118: American Museum of Natural History; 123tr: Science
Photo Library; 124t: Museo Argentino de Cirendas Naturales, Buenos
Aires; 127c: Natural History Museum, London; 129tr: American
Museum of Natural History; 130t: Natural History Museum, London;
130/131b/g: Getty Images; 131br: Royal Tyrrell Museum, Canada;
133t: Queensland Museum; 134cl: Natural History Museum, London;
135tr: Witmer Laboratories; 135cr: Natural History Museum, London;
136b: Auscape; 136tr, cl: Royal Tyrrell Museum, Canada; 137b:
Natural History Museum, London; 137tr: Science Photo Library;
138/139b/g: Corbis; 139tc, cr: Natural History Museum, London.
140cl: Ligabue Study and Research Centre, Italy; 140c: Royal Tyrrell
Museum, Canada; 143cr: Smithsonian Institution; 144b: Natural
History Museum, London; 144t: Royal Tyrrell Museum, Canada; 145c:
Royal Tyrrell Museum, Canada; 146t: Natural History Museum,
London; 152/153b/g: Getty Images; 155b: Aero Vironment Inc; 155c:
Science Photo Library; 158/159b/g: Corbis; 160/161b/g: Corbis; 162b:
American Museum of Natural History. 163tr: Natural History Museum,
London; 165b: Natural History Museum, London; 166t: Natural
History Museum, London; 167tr: Natural History Museum, London;
172/173b/g: Corbis; 179b: Corbis; 182t: American Museum of Natural
History; 183b: Natural History Museum, London; 188/189b/g: Corbis;
192/193b/g: Corbis; 197tl, tr: Natural History Museum, London; 198b:
Natural History Museum, London.

All other images © Dorling Kindersley. For further information, see
www.dkimages.com